On Being a Scholar-Practitioner

Practical Wisdom in Action

Maria Piantanida
Patricia L. McMahon
Marilyn Llewellyn

Wisdom of Practice Series

Learning Moments Press
Pittsburgh, PA

On Being a Scholar-Practitioner:
Practical Wisdom in Action
Published by Learning Moments Press
Pittsburgh, PA 15235
learningmomentspress.com

ISBN-13: 978-0-9976488-8-1

BISAC Subject:
Education/Research (EDU037000);
Education/Philosophy, Theory & Social Aspects (EDU 04000)

Onix audience Code: 06 Professional & Scholarly

Book Layout:
Mike Murray, pearhouse.com

We dedicate this book with gratitude to

Noreen B. Garman

Our Teacher, Mentor, Colleague, Friend

TABLE OF CONTENTS

SECTION 1

Introduction

A Call for Learning
A Call for Scholarly Practice

Another common and mistaken idea hidden in the word "learning" is that learning and doing are different kinds of acts. Thus, not many years ago I began to play the cello. I love the instrument, spend many hours a day playing it, work hard at it, and mean someday to play it well. Most people would say that what I am doing is "learning to play" the cello. Our language gives us no other words to say it. But these words carry into our minds the strange idea that there exist two very different processes: (1) learning to play the cello; and (2) playing the cello. They imply that I will do the first until I have completed it, at which point I will stop the first process and begin the second; in short, that I will go on "learning to play" until I have "learned to play" and that then I will begin "to play."

Of course, this is nonsense. There are not two processes, but one. We learn to do something by doing it. There is no other way.

– JOHN HOLT, 1976

1

Introduction

PURPOSE OF THE BOOK

The purpose of this book is to explicate the concepts of "Scholar-Practitioner" and "practical wisdom" in relation to those engaged in educational endeavors. For many, the pairing of scholar with practitioner may seem odd, even contradictory. Often "educational practitioner" is associated with the role of teacher, principal, and superintendent in K-12 settings. "Scholar" is associated with the role of professor or researcher in colleges and universities. Rather than defining "practitioner" and "scholar" in terms of role and setting, others define it as a stage of professional development. With this framing, novices begin as practitioners and, by earning advanced academic degrees, become scholars.

The title, *On Being a Scholar-Practitioner*, suggests an alternative to the view of "scholar" as a role distinct from "practitioner." We posit, instead, that "Scholar-Practitioner" is a way of being, the embodiment of a mindset that one brings to one's professional work. Regardless of institutional setting or role, one can, from the very beginning of one's professional life, cultivate a mindset in which action informs understanding and understanding informs action. The recursive interplay of acting and knowing is the essence of what Aristotle described as *praxis* which

> ...depended on our ability to *perceive* the situation,
> to have the appropriate *feelings* or desires about it,
> to *deliberate* about what was appropriate in these
> circumstances and to *act*...It was about performing a

particular social practice well...and that meant figuring out the right way to do the right thing in a particular circumstance, with a particular person, at a particular time.[1]

The subtitle of this book, *Practical Wisdom in Action*, underscores the point that the Scholar-Practitioner mindset is not a lofty set of ideas with little practical relevance. Rather, practical wisdom guides our decisions and actions as we work, day in and day out, to fulfill our responsibilities as educators. Because our decisions and actions affect the lives of others—particularly students—practical wisdom is crucial for ethical practice. In exploring the concept of practical wisdom, we draw from the work of Barry Schwartz, a professor of social theory and social action, and Kenneth Sharpe, a professor of political science, who explain:

> Practical wisdom is akin to the kind of skill that a craftsman needs to build a boat or a house, or that a jazz musician needs to improvise. Except that practical wisdom is not a technical or artistic skill. It is a moral skill—a skill that enables us to discern how to treat people in our everyday social activities.[2]

To be clear, "moral skill" does not mean moralizing, teaching religious dogma, or imposing particular moral beliefs on others. In the world of education, in the arena of schools, moral skill requires a commitment to the educative purpose of our relationships with others, an extensive repertoire of pedagogical understanding, and a capacity to discern the nuances of specific contexts. Taken together commitment, understanding, and discernment allow Scholar-Practitioners to act wisely.

Wisdom cannot be acquired simply by reading or classroom activities. Nor can it be gained through experience alone. Practical wisdom, we contend, entails cultivation of six intertwining qualities embodied by Scholar-Practitioners. These are:

- Pedagogical Wisdom,
- Theoretical Understanding,

- Contextual Literacy,
- Ethical Stewardship,
- Metacognitive Reflection, and
- Aesthetic Imagination.

The aim of the book is to offer a conception of educators that goes beyond mastery of specific techniques, methods or skills to the cultivation of a Scholar-Practitioner mindset conducive to practical wisdom.

RATIONALE FOR THE BOOK

The impetus to write this book arose from three concerns: (1) a persistent narrative about our failing schools; (2) the rate of teacher flight from the profession; and (3) the privileging of rules over professional judgment. To begin, Maria recounts the following experience, illustrative of the failing schools narrative:

> In the spring of 2009, I was sitting in a room with my fellow jurors. Our mid-morning break was running past its allotted 15 minutes, presumably because the judge and attorneys were conferring on esoteric points of law. Out of boredom, we were munching our way through boxes of muffins, bagels, and sweet rolls. Listlessly, one juror began to peruse the local paper. "They're talking about exit exams from high school again," she announced. "Well, it's probably a good idea," chimed in another. "Something has to be done to make sure kids are learning."
>
> "That's for sure. I know in my district they're talking about extending the school year to 12 months. What do you think about that?"
>
> "My district's talking about that, too. And maybe making the school day longer. I'm for that. Teachers have too much time off for what they're paid."

"You can say that again. Ours were threatening to strike again—over salary and benefits. What else is new?"

"Yeah. I wouldn't mind having my summers off. But that kind of break isn't good for the kids. They forget too much. There needs to be more accountability. Those exit exams would help with that."

"It's good that they're finally checking to see if schools are helping kids meet the standards. Can you imagine graduating kids who can't read? It's a shame, but it happens all the time."

Mercifully, the judge's assistant called us back into the courtroom at this juncture. Yet, I couldn't help but think about how this brief exchange captured so many of the assumptions that drive public narratives about our "failing public schools."

If this were an isolated anecdote, it would be of no consequence. Unfortunately, it seems that the jurors' jaundiced view is emblematic of a wider mistrust, not only of education, but of social institutions in general. As Schwartz and Sharpe observe:

> We Americans are growing increasingly disenchanted with the institutions on which we depend. We can't trust them. They disappoint us. They fail to give us what we need. This is true of schools that are not serving our kids as well as we think they should.[3]

A number of philanthropic foundations (including The Gates Foundation), federal and state governments, and The Carnegie Foundation apparently share the jurors' sentiments as they have invested millions of dollars to improve the quality of education in the United States. Despite these efforts, the narrative of failing schools persists. As president of The Carnegie Foundation for the Advancement of Teaching, Anthony Bryk was invited to give a distinguished scholar lecture at the 2014 annual meeting of the American Educational Research Association. Included in his remarks was this rather disheartening account of school improvement initiatives:

For more than two decades, educators—practitioners, policy makers, researchers, and community leaders— have been actively pursuing reform. These efforts were manifest in a myriad of ways, including efforts to restructure the governance of public schooling, transform teacher education, develop comprehensive school reform models, and set more ambitious educational goals and accountability. Though these reforms were helping some schools improve, the problem was that our aspirations for schooling in America were increasing at a much faster rate. A chasm was growing between what we sought and what we could routinely achieve, and the chasm was greatest for our most disadvantaged students and communities.[4]

Bryk goes on to mention a number of reform initiatives intended to address high dropout rates, weak student engagement, weak in-service programs, and inadequate school and instructional leadership. Such reform efforts yielded little change and in some instances, like high stakes testing, actually had negative consequences. These repeated attempts at school improvement take a toll on those working in "failing schools."

As Schwartz and Sharpe point out:

If it were only…students who were dissatisfied, it would be easy to affix the blame on… teachers for not caring or for lacking the expertise to help. But the disenchantment we experience as recipients of services is often matched by the dissatisfaction of those who provide them…Most teachers want to teach kids the basics and at the same time excite them with the prospects of educating themselves. But teachers feel helpless faced with the challenge of reconciling these goals with mandates to meet targets on standardized tests, to adopt specific teaching techniques, and to keep up with ever-increasing paperwork. No one is satisfied—not the professionals and not their clients.[5]

Over the course of our teaching careers, we have met many talented teachers who are feeling demoralized. For many, teaching is a calling emanating from a desire to make a difference in the lives of others and a passion to share their love of a subject. Thus, many enter teaching with high hopes, good intentions, and idealism. Individuals bring with them images of how they will enact the role of teacher. These images are shaped by a lifetime in school, by mythic figures in movies and television, by cultural metaphors, by their personality, and by their style of relating to the world. When teachers enter practice settings where they can fulfill their role in a way that is consistent with their image of "being teacher," they probably experience a great deal of satisfaction. When they enter settings in which their imagined identity as teacher is thwarted, the idealism that drew them to teaching erodes, and many choose to flee the profession. University of Pennsylvania Professor Richard Ingersoll has been studying the issue of teacher turnover for a number of years and in a 2015 NPR interview, he commented:

> Every year, thousands of fresh-faced teachers are handed the keys to a new classroom, given a pat on the back and told, "Good luck!"
>
> Over the next five years, though, nearly half of those teachers will transfer to a new school or leave the profession altogether—only to be replaced with similarly fresh-faced teachers.[6]

Ingersoll offers a number of reasons that contribute to this alarming state of affairs which costs schools billions of dollars per year. While salary is one factor, of greater importance is

> ...the issue of voice, and having a say, and being able to have input into the key decisions in the building that affect a teacher's job. This is something that is a hallmark of professions. It's something that teachers usually have very little of, but it does vary across schools and it's very highly correlated with the decision whether to stay or leave.

Some might say that lack of control contributes to teacher burnout. But teacher educator, Doris Santoro makes an important distinction between "burnout" and "demoralization."

> Burnout is only one possible manifestation of dissatisfaction, and it is one that lays the problem squarely at the feet of teachers. When we say a teacher has "burned out," we suggest that there is something wrong with the individual, and we imply that teachers come to the profession with a finite amount of personal and professional resources. The logic of burnout suggests that if these resources were not in sufficient abundance or were not properly conserved, then they will dry up...

> In contrast...demoralization characterizes the problem as a value conflict experienced as a result of policies, mandates, and school practices. The individual teacher has not failed. In demoralization, experienced educators understand that they are facing a conflict between their vision of good work and their teaching context...The values that teachers bring to the work (serving students and their communities, upholding the dignity of the profession) are still worthwhile, but are being thwarted by the conditions in which they work.[7]

Considering the twofold problem of teacher flight and narratives of school/teacher failure brings us to our third concern, a deep-seated belief that imposing scientifically established rules will improve the situation. We take the liberty of quoting Schwartz and Sharpe at length on the fallacy of this rule-bound mentality.

> Most experienced practitioners know that rules only take them so far. Rules can't tell practitioners how to do the constant interpretation and balancing that is part of their everyday work...[T]eachers attempting to teach *and* inspire...are not puzzling over a choice between the "right" thing and the "wrong" thing. The common

quandaries they face are choices among right things that clash, or between better and best, or sometimes between bad and worse…

These sorts of quandaries don't have pat, one-size-fits-all answers. Good rules might be useful as guides as we try to manage these multiple aims, but they will never be subtle enough and nuanced enough to apply in every situation. Aristotle recognized that balancing acts like these beg for wisdom, and that abstract or ethereal wisdom would not do. Wisdom has to be practical, because the issues we face are embedded in our everyday work. They are not hypotheticals being raised in college ethics courses. They are quandaries that any practitioner must resolve in order to do her work well. Practical wisdom is not musing about how someone else in a hypothetical situation ought to act. It's about "What am I to do?"—right here and right now, with this person. A practically wise person doesn't merely speculate about what's proper; she does it.

Acting wisely demands that we be guided by the proper aims or goals of a particular activity. Aristotle's word for the purpose or aim of a practice was *telos*. The telos of teaching is to educate students…Every profession… has a telos, and those who excel are those who are able to locate and pursue it. So a good practitioner is motivated to aim at the telos of her practice. But it takes wisdom—practical wisdom—to translate the very general aims of a practice into concrete action.[8]

If rules are necessary, but not sufficient, to achieve the purpose of education, then it is crucial to recognize the importance of practical wisdom. Some might contend that it is impossible to <u>teach</u> wisdom. In a sense this may be true. But it is possible to create conditions in which professionals are able to cultivate wisdom for themselves. By embracing the stance of Scholar-Practitioner, educators can embark on a journey to cultivate practical wisdom. This is not necessarily an easy journey, but it can be a very fulfilling one.

ORGANIZATION OF THE BOOK

Overall the book is organized into seven sections. Each section is set off with a cover page highlighting key concepts that are addressed in the following chapters. *Section I: A Call for Learning—A Call for Scholarly Practice* comprises two chapters. After this introductory chapter, we explore, in Chapter 2, the nature of learning consistent with the cultivation of practical wisdom. Taking the position that learning is the process of making meaning of experience and that narrative is a fundamental way in which we humans make meaning, we conclude Chapter 2 with the recommendation that readers construct an evolving narrative of their journey as a Scholar-Practitioner.

Section II: The Quality of Pedagogical Wisdom begins in Chapter 3 with scholar Max van Manen's[9] concept of pedagogical moments as the site of educational practice and suggests that Scholar-Practitioners draw upon a reservoir of *Pedagogical Wisdom* when responding to the dilemmas embedded in such moments. As noted above, making such choices often calls for more than the straightforward application of techniques and best practices. It calls for the wisdom to know which technique, which practice, fits the specific situation. In Chapter 4: Balancing with Pedagogical Wisdom, we consider a number of pressure points which challenge educators to respond wisely.

Section III: The Quality of Theoretical Understanding begins in Chapter 5 with a distinction between knowledge and understanding. Typically, discussions of teacher competence stress the importance of content or disciplinary knowledge. For Scholar-Practitioners such knowledge is necessary, but not sufficient. The concept of *knowledge* connotes public repositories of codified information. The concept of *understanding* connotes an integration of knowledge into an individual's conceptual schema. Understanding, then, allows for more sophisticated and nuanced use of knowledge; it is essential for responding with wisdom in pedagogical moments. In this chapter we highlight several bodies of theory that wise practitioners are able to draw upon. Chapter 6 offers a theoretical framework for thinking about curriculum structures and how they promote the cultivation of practical wisdom. Chapter 7 looks at touchstones for navigating the complex terrain of theoretical discourses.

For teachers, the classroom is their predominant context of practice. One of the joys of teaching used to be the opportunity to enter one's classroom, shut the door, and focus on the lesson at hand. Today, however, larger forces at the school, district, state and national levels are intruding into the classroom and shaping (even controlling) what happens as teachers strive to enact their pedagogy. Scholar-Practitioners understand that they no longer have the luxury of ignoring these external forces. *Section IV: The Quality of Contextual Literacy* begins in Chapter 8 by discussing the scope of contexts in which educational practice is nested—the micro, mezzo, and macro. Chapter 9: Cultivating Contextual Literacy suggests that we always "read" contexts through our own autobiographical lenses, and therefore, it is incumbent upon Scholar-Practitioners to gain insight into the stories that shape their interpretations of experience.

Section V: The Quality of Ethical Stewardship stresses a twofold commitment of Scholar-Practitioners. Chapter 10 addresses the power differential within teacher-learner relationships and administrator-teacher relationships. Being mindful of the potential for misuse and abuse of their role-inscribed power, Scholar-Practitioners are committed to ethical practice. Chapter 11 shifts focus to the broader responsibilities of Scholar-Practitioners to preserve the best of the profession and to advance it through scholarship and advocacy.

Section VI: The Quality of Metacognitive Reflection looks at capacities that support theorizing from the situational details of experience. As educational philosopher John Dewey reminds us, the educational nature of experience does not lie in the details of the experience per se, but in the meaning we draw from it.[10] Thus, *Metacognitive Reflection* encompasses capacities for immersion in experience, careful observation, discernment, analysis, interpretation, and conceptual representation of insights into the significance of experience. Chapter 12 looks at three facets of reflection—recollective, introspective, conceptual—that come into play as Scholar-Practitioners make meaning of their experiences. Chapter 13 shifts attention to the crafting of scholarly narratives that allow Scholar-Practitioners to share personal and private learning in broader, public arenas.

Section VII: The Quality of Aesthetic Imagination begins in Chapter 14 with a continuum of aesthetic sensibilities that underpin the representation and generation of understanding. The book concludes with a call for Releasing Imagination in Chapter 15.

We resonate with John Holt's view that we learn by doing. In the case of scholarly practice, our actions inform our thinking and our thinking informs our actions. This is a recursive process of reflecting on experience and making meaning of it. For this reason, we end each chapter with a series of Reflective Prompts which invite readers to record the meanings they have made from the experience of encountering ideas in the book. This is cultivating the mindset of Scholar-Practitioner by engaging in it.

AUDIENCE FOR THE BOOK

Before considering who might find this book of interest, we want to acknowledge the professional contexts which have shaped our thinking about Scholar-Practitioners and the qualities associated with that mindset. Among us, we have extensive experience working in a variety of contexts and capacities, but our primary context has been our teaching of undergraduate and graduate students in teacher education programs. As a result, we write most frequently in terms of teaching and learning, teachers and students, and classroom settings. We recognize, however, that many other professionals work in schools including administrators, curriculum and instructional specialists and school counselors. Beyond the confines of formal educational institutions, many other community-based organizations include education as a component of their mission. Many museums, libraries, churches, and not-for-profit agencies in the health and human services arena offer both formal and informal educational programs. The common thread connecting individuals in such diverse roles and settings is a deep-seated belief that learning can enhance one's quality of life. Therefore, we hope that anyone with a passion for education will resonate with the ideas explored in this book.

From pre-service to experienced education professionals, we hope that the book might be used to catalyze discussions in a variety of contexts. At the undergraduate and graduate levels, the book might serve as a course text in schools of education. Of particular relevance in higher education are new initiatives to make the Doctorate of Education more directly focused on scholarly practice.[11] In pre-K through 12 schools and other organizations with an educational mission, the book might be used in in-service workshops, continuing education programs, and institutional orientations. In higher education, where Ernest Boyer[12] flagged scholarship of teaching as one of four priorities of the professoriate, the book might be useful in faculty development efforts. Although many faculty identify most strongly with their discipline, there are also faculty (many in the health professions) who are committed to improving their own teaching practice as well as reforming the nature of education in their programs.

As we move deeper into the 21st century, the challenges to our educational institutions will continue to increase placing new demands on those working at all levels of education. It is our belief that the wisdom of Scholar-Practitioners can—indeed must—play a central role in how education is re-imagined.

ABOUT THE AUTHORS

In writing this book, we join the chorus of those calling for radical transformation of education in the United States. Given the plethora of current reform movements, a few words of clarification are in order. We are not among those who are striving to dismantle public schooling to benefit for-profit corporations. Nor are we aligned with those who, in the name of accountability, impose rigid teaching scripts and draconian testing policies in our nation's classrooms. Rather, we situate ourselves conceptually at the confluence of multiple theoretical and philosophical traditions including progressive education, critical pedagogy, feminist pedagogy, and reconceptualist curriculum.

REFLECTIVE PROMPTS

What thoughts, feelings, and questions are evoked by the ideas in this chapter? *p.8 Ingersoll "issue of voice..." p.9 Santoro "demoralization."*

In what ways do my responses to the ideas in this chapter contribute to my understanding of being a Scholar-Practitioner?

As I reflect on teachers (and others) I have encountered in my life, who stands out because they seemed especially wise? What qualities made them seem wise; what did I learn from them?

NOTES

1 Barry Schwartz and Kenneth Sharpe, *Practical Wisdom: The Right Way to Do the Right Thing* (New York: Riverhead Books, 2010), 5-6.

2 Schwartz and Sharpe, 8.

3 Schwartz and Sharpe, 1.

4 Anthony S. Bryk, "2014 AERA Distinguished Lecture. Accelerating How We Learn to Improve," *Educational Researcher* 44, no 9 (2015): 467.

5 Schwartz and Sharpe, 1-2.

6 Richard Ingersoll, interviewed by Owen Phillips for NPR, March 30, 2015, "Revolving Door of Teachers Costs Schools Billions Every Year."

7 Doris A. Santoro, "Fighting Educator Burnout. Is It Burnout? Or Demoralization?" *Educational Leadership* 75 (on-line journal), (June 2018): 10.

8 Schwartz and Sharpe, 6-7.

9 Max van Manen, *The Tact of Teaching: The Meaning of Pedagogical Thoughtfulness* (Albany NY: SUNY Press, 1991).

10 John Dewey, *Experience and Education* (New York: Collier Books, 1938).

11 See Jill Alexa Perry, ed. *The EdD and the Scholarly Practitioner: The CPED Path* (Charlotte, NC: Information Age Publishing, 2016) and Jill Alexa Perry and David Lee Carlson, eds, *In Their Own Words: A Journey to the Stewardship of the Practice in Education* (Charlotte, NC: Information Age Publishing, 2013.)

12 Ernest L. Boyer, *Scholarship Reconsidered: Priorities of the Professoriate* (New York: The Carnegie Foundation for the Advancement of Teaching, 1990).

2

The Scholar-Practitioner Journey

NATURE OF SCHOLAR-PRACTITIONER LEARNING

C urriculum theorist, Dwayne Huebner posits that education is a way to tend to the journey of the self or soul.[1] The journey of self as a Scholar-Practitioner can take many twists and turns, and this has been the case for us. When we first became teachers, we did not think of ourselves as scholars. It was not until we were immersed in the doctoral dissertation process that we began to grapple with this identity, often with great resistance. Scholars were those whose books we read. Scholars were those who presented papers and gave keynote speeches at national conferences. Scholars were those who had major government or foundation funding to conduct research. Scholars were others, not us.

We cannot pinpoint any particular moment when we realized that we, too, could claim the identity of "scholar." In hindsight, however, we came to see that publications, presentations, funding, and recognition were the external manifestations of something deeper—a way of being in and relating to the world. Scholarship emanates from curiosity, a love of learning, an appreciation of complexity, a tolerance for ambiguity, and a relentless need to make sense of one's experience. We now understand that when we entered the field of education, we brought these sensibilities to our work. But they existed in nascent form waiting to be developed. Development occurred almost imperceptibly as we took university courses, read books and journals, joined professional associations, attended conferences, and eventually, albeit timidly, gave conference presentations, submitted articles for publication, and wrote books. Through these efforts we entered into Communities of Practice and engaged in conversations with others who shared our passion for education. As members of these communities, we learned that those we had seen as SCHOLARS were struggling as we were to understand the complexities of education. We also learned that "being a scholar" is not a fixed role but a process of always becoming as nascent sensibilities blossom into more robust and nuanced capabilities.

Coming to accept "Scholar-Practitioner" as our way of being has not been straightforward. There have been missteps along the way; some minor; some quite painful. But these have propelled us on a path of learning whose nature we have come to value deeply. We characterize this form of learning as:

FIGURE 2.1 - SCHOLAR-PRACTITIONER LEARNING

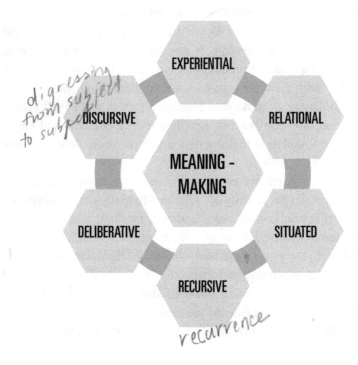

digressing
from subject
to subject

recurrence

Skinner —
learn = observable behavior

Learning is Making Meaning: Two contrasting views of learning have been evolving since the early 20th century. The behavioral view, grounded in the work of psychologists B.F. Skinner and John B. Watson, defines learning as an observable change in behavior. This view draws upon scientific traditions in which variables can be controlled to produce desired outcomes. Over the decades, a great deal of time and effort has been expended in the search for specific instructional variables that will result in desired learning outcomes. The language of behaviorism has morphed over the decades from behavioral objectives, to competency statements, to skills sets, to best practices. Underlying these variations in terminology is a shared belief that by exercising control over the right external variables specific learning outcomes can be predicted, observed, and measured.

In contrast to this view is a tradition grounded in existential philosophy that defines learning as making meaning of experience. This view holds that individuals are not passive recipients of instruction but are active agents. As such, they interpret all experience (including schooling) in light of their personal goals, needs, desires, capabilities, biases, and world view. In the behavioral view, learning is seen as motivated by external rewards (or punishments). In the existential view, learning is seen as intrinsically motivated by the individual's need to make sense of life experiences. As will be apparent in the following chapters, our view of learning is situated in the meaning-making view of learning, and this applies to professionals engaged in their own learning and professionals as they support the learning of others.

existential

Learning is Experiential: As indicated by the preceding comments, we espouse the experiential nature of learning in which we make sense of the events of our lives. It is not unusual to hear students contrast "real world experience" to "academic experience." The events occurring within formal educational settings are seen as separate from the events occurring elsewhere in their lives. Sadly, "separate from" all too often is a code word for less relevant or less compelling. When students ask, "Why do I need to know this? When will I ever have to use (_____fill in the blank_____)?" they are signaling a disconnection between the experience of instruction and the meaning of that instruction in the course of their lives. The ramifications of this disconnection permeate the world of Scholar-Practitioners as they struggle to connect academic learning to their daily practice and as they struggle to help their students connect with the subject being taught.

One troubling, but not uncommon, manifestation of this struggle occurs when pre-service teachers leave the college environment and enter "the real world" of practice where they may face a painful dilemma. On one hand they are prepared through university programs to understand current thinking and practices in their field of study. On the other hand, they enter school environments where this knowledge may not be incorporated into practice and may be dismissed as ivory tower idealism. Thus, beginning teachers may experience conflicted loyalty to faculty whom they respect and experienced teachers whose respect they want to earn. They may frame these conflicted feelings as an either-or choice between one form of experience and another. We find this bifurcated view of experience to be counterproductive. Wherever we are, whatever is happening at any given time is our experience. For good or ill, we can use that experience to deepen our understanding of ourselves, our practice, and our world. This more expansive view of experiential learning informs the journey of Scholar-Practitioners.

Learning is Relational: Learning is relational in the sense that we learn with, from and through our interactions with others. From the time we are born, we begin to learn through our connections with ever-expanding circles of individuals and groups. Learner-Teacher relationships are shaped by special circumstances. Often it is our relationships with teachers—both good and bad—that we remember long after we have forgotten the content that the teacher was presenting. Recently, Maria went to a reunion of those who attended grades K-9 at the same community school. One guest of honor was a gentleman who had taught geography and later served as principal. As Maria listened to others reminisce fondly about the teacher/principal's actions, she was struck by the fact that she remembered only two interactions with him. In the first, he accused her of having her more artistically talented sister color in a map of Australia, a task to which she had lovingly devoted a great deal of time and effort. In the second, he predicted that if she skipped a grade and graduated a year early as she desperately wanted to do, she would be a social misfit for the rest of her life. Fortunately, neither interaction resulted in a failure to achieve a satisfying adulthood. But sadly, for many young persons, non-nurturing relationships with teachers and principals do have damaging and lasting effects. For this reason, we see Scholar-Practitioners as those who are continually cultivating their capacity for engaging in relationships that respect the dignity and worth of each individual.

Learning is Situated: Experience does not happen in a vacuum. Each experience is situated within the individual's on-going life journey. Past experiences and the anticipation of future experiences influence how we respond to current experiences. Beyond this highly personal context, experiences are situated within organizational, social, cultural, historical, and political contexts. These contexts are fluid and dynamic. The rate at which knowledge is generated and our world is changing seems to increase every year. In part, evolving technology has placed us in a digital environment where we are constantly bombarded with information from around the globe. Dealing with this ever-changing landscape is essential for Scholar-Practitioners.

Learning is Recursive: Learning is recursive in the sense that ideas are continually revisited from different vantage points. Education is fraught with many challenging issues, dilemmas, problems, and questions. Any of these might be studied for an entire professional life. Just when we think we finally understand an issue, something new occurs and calls our understanding into question. When we remain receptive to new ideas, experiences, information, points of view, etc. we may need to dismantle the conceptual frameworks we have already constructed and rework them to incorporate new understandings.

This recursive view of learning takes us back to the distinction between a behavioral approach to education and an existential approach. Learning outcomes stated as "terminal objectives" or mastery of particular competencies/skills convey the impression that learning comes to an end point. Although this may be characteristic within the artificial time constraints of an academic calendar, learning for Scholar-Practitioners continues far beyond the end of a particular course, semester, or academic program. For this reason, we prefer to structure learning in terms of generative themes that can serve as broad umbrellas for an endless array of more specific learning goals. In

Chapter 1, we introduced six qualities of Scholar-Practitioners, which when stated as generative themes can guide a lifetime of professional learning:

- Responding with Pedagogical Wisdom
- Deepening Theoretical Understanding
- Developing Contextual Literacy
- Serving as an Ethical Steward of education
- Embodying Metacognitive Reflection
- Exercising Aesthetic Imagination

Some might criticize these themes as being too general or vague to be useful, but that misses the crux of the matter. It is Scholar-Practitioners, as they engage with the dilemmas of practice, who provide the specificity in terms of what most intrigues them or most frustrates them or most excites them. This is internally motivated learning that is self-perpetuating. Understanding spawns new questions in an ever broadening and deepening spiral.

Learning is Discursive: A key way in which ideas are advanced is by sharing them with others—orally and in writing. Discursive learning entails a willingness and capacity to exchange ideas, hear responses to those ideas, and take those responses into account. This is highly charged discourse in which different beliefs and values about education are put forward, challenged, modified, defended, etc. Discursive learning requires a willingness to be vulnerable, to make one's often preliminary thinking public. This is one reason that the relational nature of learning is so important. Without trusting, respectful relationships, discursive learning is likely to shut down.

Learning is Deliberative: In the fast-paced world of practice where educators are bombarded by never-ending demands on their time and attention, rapid decision-making and fast action are valued. Opportunities for quiet deliberation do not come easily. Yet, Scholar-Practitioners understand that important issues require careful thought. Probing deeply into ideas helps to forestall ill-conceived, superficial responses to complex dilemmas. Thus, carving out time for deliberation becomes an essential aspect of Scholar-Practitioner learning.

Learning is Reflective: Reflective learning entails a capacity to step back from the details of an experience and reflect on its meaning.

While reflection begins with a recollection of situational details—who, what, when, where—it does not stop there. It entails interpreting situational details to make sense of them; to figure out how we felt about a situation and what contributed to those feelings; to use concepts to put the situational details into perspective. This reflective process brings us full-circle to the view of learning as making meaning of experience and to a fundamental quality of Scholar-Practitioners—i.e., Metacognitive Reflection.

We began this discussion of learning with Dwayne Huebner's view of education as a way to tend to the journey of the self. In the next section, we suggest that Scholar-Practitioners write an evolving autobiographical narrative, not simply to document their journey, but to construct its meaning.

SCHOLAR-PRACTITIONER NARRATIVE

One of the ways that humans make meaning of their lives is to create stories and, in so doing, shape their sense of identity. Identity, of course, is not singular or fixed. It evolves as new experiences are encountered and new learning occurs. Often our role influences the ways in which we respond to experiences and the meanings we make of them. Because we spend so many years in the role of student, that often dominates our reactions within formal education programs. For example, successful students are skillful in understanding teacher expectations, completing assignments, and taking tests. Ideally, these are congruent with what an individual wants to learn. In such cases, the self as student and the self as learner merge. However, when individuals encounter educational experiences at odds with their personal goals, needs, interests, etc., the role of self as student may overshadow the self as learner. Similarly, at times the immediacy of action may bring the self as practitioner to the foreground and only in later moments can the self as scholar reassert its contemplation of the action-oriented events.

The following diagram illustrates the multi-faceted identity of Scholar-Practitioner. Looking at the ideas presented throughout the book through these different facets can reveal different insights and meanings. What makes sense to the student-self may not make sense to the learner-self or vice versa. The same applies to the practitioner-self and the scholar-self. The important point is to remain flexible and open. Just as the facets of a prism refract light in different ways, each Scholar-Practitioner facet can reveal different nuances of experiences and ideas.

FIGURE 2.2 - MULTIFACETED IDENTITY AS SCHOLAR PRACTITIONER

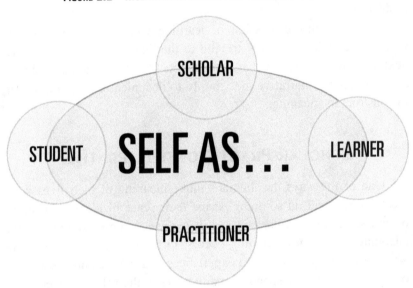

To encourage looking at ideas from multiple perspectives, we conclude each chapter with Reflective Prompts. Reflection occurs through a variety of modalities—writing, doodling, meditating, drawing, dancing, music, and many more. One aspect of being a Scholar-Practitioner is embracing one's way of reflecting on experience, in this case the experience of reading. We hope that readers will experiment with various modalities as they reflect on the prompts.

It is unlikely that all of the prompts will be equally evocative for all readers. We hope that readers will choose to respond to the prompts that speak most strongly to them. Perhaps ideas in later chapters of the book or some life situation will draw readers back to prompts that they skipped earlier. Given the recursive nature of learning, resonating with different prompts at different stages of one's journey is entirely understandable.

reoccurring

Because learning as a Scholar-Practitioner is discursive and deliberative, we encourage readers to organize their reflections into an evolving Scholar-Practitioner *Narrative* that can be shared with others. By engaging in such writing and by sharing their narrative with others, Scholar-Practitioners can begin to form a Community of Practice in which to nurture their growth and development.

REFLECTIVE PROMPTS

What thoughts and feelings are evoked by the ideas in this chapter?

In what ways do my responses to the ideas in this chapter contribute to my understanding of being a Scholar-Practitioner?

What questions are evoked by the ideas in this chapter? Where do those questions fit within my plan for continued learning?

Where am I on my life's journey; what has brought me to this place on my journey?

What professional interests, hopes and concerns am I bringing to my journey as a Scholar-Practitioner?

What do I see as my professional purpose; what do I hope to accomplish?

What people and events have been important in shaping who I am as a student, learner, practitioner, and scholar?

How would I describe my capacity for the nature of learning described in this chapter?

When I think about the four facets of self (Figure 2.2), through which one(s) do I filter information and experiences? Am I able to shift comfortably and effectively among the different perspectives?

NOTES

1 Dwayne Huebner, "Education and Spirituality," *Journal of Curriculum Theorizing* 11, no. 2 (1995): 13-34.

teacher + learner

experiences shapes us

input + output

narrative + vulnerability

ever evolving and learning

SECTION II

The Quality of Pedagogical Wisdom

Pedagogical wisdom entails the capacity to respond wisely in pedagogical moments.

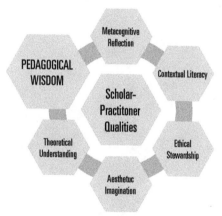

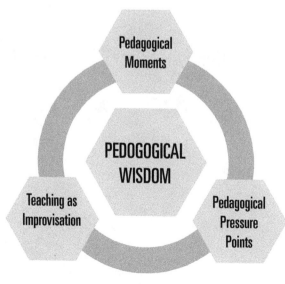

3

Pedagogigal Wisdom

TEACHING AS IMPROVISATION

On the first night of a course on methods for teaching secondary English, Patricia (Pat) invited students to introduce themselves and describe what they hoped to learn. When it was Jenny's[1] turn to comment, she said, "I want to know what to do all the time no matter what happens so I never make a mistake in the classroom." Longing for such certainty has driven decades of research into best teaching practices, precise instructional methods, effective techniques, and "teacher-proof" materials. Despite all of the effort and money that have gone into such educational research, hard and fast rules for practice have remained elusive. In the now classic work on reflective practice, Donald Schon observed:

> In the varied topography of professional practice, there is a high, hard ground where practitioners can make effective use of research-based theory and technique, and there is a swampy lowland where situations are confusing "messes" incapable of technical solution.[1]

Underlying Jenny's desire for certainty is an unrealistic desire for predictability and control. It assumes one can enter into the swampy lowlands with a predetermined script and, as in formal theater, everyone will play their assigned role. Understandably, inexperienced teachers like Jenny may seek reassurance in detailing exactly what they will

---

1 We have used pseudonyms throughout the book when we are recounting anecdotes like this. When full names are given we are either citing the individual's published work or have been granted permission to quote them.

do. The fallacy of this thinking is simply that human beings and social interactions are far more complex. Individuals bring to educational encounters endless variations in intellectual, emotional, social, psychological, spiritual, and physical needs and desires. Scholar-Practitioners understand that these human dynamics are as much a part of educational life as formal instructional plans. Scholar-Practitioners do not equate presentation of well-scripted information with learning. Authentic learning is mediated through the human capacity to make meaning of experience.

Consider, for example, students who successfully complete math courses but hate math. Or students who sit in the back of a lecture hall and send text messages while a professor presents information that is far less compelling than where their friends will meet for coffee. Perhaps during a lesson on sharing, a preschool child sees little point in giving up a favorite toy. During student teaching, pre-service teachers may reject what they've learned in college as unworkable in the "real world." Noted physician and author, Atul Gawande recounts his missing the significance of studying Tolstoy's *Death of Ivan Ilyich* in a course on medical ethics:

> What worried us [medical students] was knowledge.
> While we knew how to sympathize, we weren't at all
> certain we would know how to properly diagnose and
> treat. We paid our medical tuition to learn about the
> inner process of the body, the intricate mechanisms of
> its pathologies, and the vast trove of discoveries and
> technologies that have accumulated to stop them. We
> didn't imagine we needed to think about much else. So
> we put Ivan Ilyich out of our heads.[2]

In *Being Mortal*, Gawande goes on to explain how he came to understand the importance of empathy in the wise, ethical and humane practice of medicine. The same can be said for empathy in the wise, ethical, humane practice of education.

Simply put, the most well-planned and well-presented pedagogical "script" will be marginally effective if individuals are not fully engaged.

From the youngest child in preschool to students in graduate school to professionals in practice—being an active participant in educational encounters increases the likelihood of engagement and, in turn, more authentic learning. With this view, improvisation is a more apt metaphor for teaching than formal theater.

In improvisational theater, a group of actors creates a performance without using a detailed script. Some groups specialize in short skits only a few minutes long, and others specialize in fully improvised one- or two-act plays of an hour or more. These performances emerge from limited prompts and evolve unpredictably through unscripted dialogue, on stage and in front of an audience. In a similar way, an effective classroom "performance" emerges from classroom discourse, and is not scripted by the lesson plan or by the teacher's predetermined agenda. In a study of improvised theater dialogues, R. Keith Sawyer referred to this type of discourse as collaborative emergence.[3] Both classroom discussion and theater improvisation are *emergent* because the outcome cannot be predicted in advance, and they are *collaborative* because no single participant can control what emerges; the outcome is collectively determined by all the participants.

The generative quality of improvisational conversation is stressed by actor Alan Alda. After playing Hawkeye Pierce on the television series *M*A*S*H*, Alda went on to host a show called *Scientific American Frontiers* in which he interviewed famous scientists engaged in cutting edge research. His aim was to make science accessible and exciting to the general public. In his memoir, *If I Understood You, Would I Have This Look on My Face?* Alda recounts how he drew upon his training in improvisation to engage the scientists in warm, humorous, and insightful conversations. Improvisation—engaged conversation—at its best is relational and, Alda contends, requires open listening.

> ...I was supposedly in conversation with the solar panel scientist, and I wasn't relating to him. Slowly, it was beginning to dawn on me: It's not just in acting that genuine relating has to take place—real conversation can't happen if listening is just my waiting for you to finish talking.

> I so loved this idea—that on the stage the other
> actor has to be able to affect you if a scene is to take
> place—that I came to the conclusion that, even in life,
> unless I'm responding with my whole self—unless,
> in fact, I'm willing to be changed by you—I'm
> probably not really listening. But if I do listen—
> openly, naively, and innocently—there's a chance,
> possibly the only chance that true dialogue and real
> communication will take place between us.[4]

We call special attention to Alda's point that open listening and genuine relating create the potential for change, not only in the other, but in oneself as well. Scholar-Practitioners value this mutuality of learning within improvisational, pedagogical moments. Max van Manen describes pedagogical moments as situations fraught with heightened meaning because:

> ...an action is required even if that action may be
> non-action. That active encounter is the pedagogical
> moment. In other words, a pedagogical situation is
> the site of everyday pedagogical action, everyday
> pedagogical practice. The pedagogical moment is
> located at the center of that praxis."[5]

Improvising in Pedagogical Moments

It would be a mistake to think that improvisational acting with its potential for spontaneity, surprise, and serendipity is unstructured. Similarly, teaching without a rigid script is not unstructured. In both contexts, successful improvisation depends upon actors following deep principles. As Alan Alda emphasizes, open listening is one of those principles. Another is the principle to "always say 'yes and'." If an actor in an improvisational scene rejects an idea put forward by another actor, the scene falls flat. Interestingly, when our colleague Noreen Garman attended a seminar with noted French critical theorist, Jacques Derrida, he commented that the response to student questions "must always first be yes" The "yes" does not mean "you are right" or "I agree" or "I approve." Rather, it invites continued engagement. It welcomes the speaker into a conversational space rich with potential meaning. It affirms that the speaker is worthy of attention.

Beyond the "yes" lie choices, and knowing which choice to make means "figuring out the right way to do the right thing in a particular circumstance, with a particular person, at a particular time."[6] This is where the scripted performance of teaching fails. It is impossible to predict when a pedagogical moment will arise. It is impossible to predict what spoken and unspoken needs infuse a moment with heightened meaning. It is impossible to predict what the right action at that particular moment will be. The only predictable certainty is that pedagogical moments will arise and, in all likelihood, no pre-rehearsed script will be suitable for response. Given this, what guides the Scholar-Practitioner's response in a pedagogical moment?

The starting point is to recognize that choosing any course of action is, at heart, an ethical choice because our actions have consequences, not just for ourselves but for others. In the swampy lowlands, ethical choices are guided, not by technical rules, but by a practical wisdom "...that enables us to discern how to treat people in our everyday social activities."[7] In this regard, educational philosopher John Dewey offers a principle akin to the medical profession's fundamental ethical principle, "First, do no harm." In *Experience and Education*,[8] Dewey contends that some experiences are mis-educative in that they undermine an individual's desire and capacity for further learning. In contrast, educative experiences engender both the desire and capacity to continue learning. This is the *telos*—the purpose—of education. Thus, in the heat of pedagogical moments, Scholar-Practitioners draw upon the quality of Pedagogical Wisdom to respond in ways that welcome, invite and affirm the desire and capacity for learning. This, of course, is easier said than done. As Schon reminds us:

> In real-world practice, problems do not present themselves to the practitioner as givens. They must be constructed from the materials of problematic situations which are puzzling, troubling, and uncertain. In order to convert a problematic situation to a problem,

a practitioner must do a certain kind of work. He [sic] must make sense of an uncertain situation that initially makes no sense.[9]

The Pedagogical Wisdom necessary for making sense of nebulous, complex and confusing "messes of practice" entails a capacity to be present in the moment, to discern what is significant, and to respond in an educative manner. Again, Alan Alda helps to clarify what it means "to be present in the moment."

> It's being so aware of the other person that, even if you have your back to them, you're observing them. It's letting everything about them affect you; not just their words, but also their tone of voice, their body language, even subtle things like where they're standing in the room or how they occupy a chair. Relating is letting all that seep into you and have an effect on how you respond to the other person.[10]

In her book, *Spirituality and Pedagogy: Being and Learning in Sacred Spaces*, Marilyn recounts a pedagogical moment that exemplifies this type of intense, relational awareness. On the first day of school, John's first grade teacher welcomed her young students to the classroom, but for John these overtures were not enough.

> The young boy timidly made his way to a self-selected space beneath the teacher's tan metal desk where he remained for the entire day. The following morning, John...once again made his way to the spot beneath the teacher's desk. Day after day, John returned to that place...One day the teacher brought a blanket, a pillow and a flashlight and handed them to John. He took the blanket and laid it out carefully under the desk. John then propped the pillow against the inside of the desk and leaned against it as he explored a children's book by the light of the flashlight.[11]

This situation continued for nearly a month until John slowly began to emerge from his safe haven and, over the course of a few days, cautiously moved across the classroom until he claimed his assigned desk.

To us this is a remarkable example of openness in which the teacher discerned John's fear and responded in a way that respected his need to feel safe. As the pedagogical moment stretched from days to weeks, John's teacher undoubtedly worried about the effect of his behavior on the other students as well as on her reputation as a classroom manager. Being open to the pedagogical moment meant being keenly aware of her young student's needs as well as her own feelings. By discerning his fears and trusting her intuitive response to those fears, she maintained a safe space in which John could acclimate to school as he was ready. The teacher embodied and acted upon the ethical principle, "first and foremost nurture the desire and capacity for further learning."

Pedagogical moments take many different forms. John's behavior's spoke so loudly that the moment was impossible to miss. Others are more subtle. Our colleague Marjorie Logsdon, in her study of pedagogical authority, recounts a moment in her classroom which caught her off-guard:

> "Where is all of this going? Gina asked.
>
> "Where is all of this going?" I repeated to myself. "What does she mean?"
>
> I felt caught. Thrown. I tried to gather myself even though panic made my throat dry. She had challenged the way I was allowing the discussion to unfold, I thought, and this is a mere two weeks into the school year.

Gina was a bright, competent, high achieving student in a well-regarded Catholic girls' high school. When Marjorie changed the classroom norms from lecturing about a literary text to a discussion of students' responses to the text, Gina was disoriented by the new ground rules for being successful. As Marjorie admits, she felt threatened by Gina's question, shut down, and the next day retreated behind the podium where she felt more in control. The improvisational nature of the teaching and learning was short-circuited; an educative opportunity was missed.[12]

As the anecdotes of John's teacher and Marjorie illustrate, pedagogical moments challenge Scholar-Practitioners to remain open and to discern—consciously and intuitively—the significant features of the moment. Often the first signal that one is caught in a pedagogical moment is an internal pressure to DO or SAY SOMETHING. Practice would not be so messy if there were time to discern what "the something" should be. It would be nice if the precipitating cause of a pedagogical moment were sufficiently clear that the appropriate response would be obvious. It would also be nice if the consequences of one's choice of action were equally clear. Unfortunately, this is seldom the case, so, as Schon suggests, an interpretation of the mess precedes action. The interpretation, in turn, shapes the response and sets in motion a cascade of consequences.

John's teacher, for example, could have framed the pedagogical moment as a behavioral problem and offered tokens in exchange for school appropriate behavior. Or she might have interpreted it as a disciplinary problem and responded by reprimanding John, keeping him inside during recess, or sending him to the principal's office. Or she might have interpreted the moment in terms of psycho-social-emotional problems and referred him for a psychological evaluation of his "learning disability." Implicit in these interpretations is an assumption that some flaw in John needs to be fixed. John's teacher, however, interpreted the "mess" as age-related anxiety in a strange situation. Rather than exacerbating the anxiety and risk the consequence of a full-blown school phobia, the teacher's empathy, compassion and creativity gave John, literally and figuratively, the space he needed to gain a sense of comfort and belonging.

When Marjorie later reflected on her pedagogical moment with Gina, she realized that she had interpreted Gina's question as a challenge to her competence and pedagogical authority. Instinctively, she responded in a self-protective mode, retreating behind the podium and resorting to a dazzling lecture on various schools of literary interpretation. Once she came to that realization, she was able to resume her efforts to change the nature of her pedagogical practice. In writing about these and other experiences that had shaped her ingrained beliefs about authority, Marjorie used the metaphor of the alchemist's efforts to transmute baser metals into gold. In their laboratories, alchemists used crucibles to burn off impurities. For Marjorie and for teachers throughout the ages, the classroom has been the laboratory, and pedagogical moments are the crucibles through which Pedagogical Wisdom is tempered.

Cultivating a Capacity for Pedagogical Wisdom

Parker Palmer begins *The Courage to Teach* with the assertion "we teach who we are" and eloquently expresses this existential truth:

> After three decades of trying to learn my craft, every class comes down to this: my students and I, face to face, engaged in an ancient and exacting exchange called education. The techniques I have mastered do not disappear, but neither do they suffice. Face to face with my students, only one resource is at my immediate command: my identity, my selfhood, my sense of this "I" who teaches—without which I have no sense of the "Thou" who learns.[13]

Understanding this "I who teaches" is the wellspring from which Pedagogical Wisdom emanates and cultivating this quality entails understanding (and often challenging) one's values, assumptions, biases, and beliefs. Lack of such self-understanding can lead to what we call "dangerous pedagogies" in which the emotional and psychological needs of teachers supersede the needs of their students. Robin Williams' character in *The Dead Poets Society* offers a stunning example of the unintended tragic consequences set in motion when a charismatic teacher's ego, rather than sensitivity to a student's needs, dominates the pedagogical moment.

Probing "the I who teaches" is not for the faint of heart. It requires a willingness to be vulnerable, to admit mistakes, to question taken-for-granted assumptions, to feel foolish, to look honestly at oneself. It requires doubt and humility. Jenny's desire for mistake-free practice creates a rigid and brittle shell. Even fairly mild pedagogical moments can pierce this shell resulting in a sense of incompetence and failure. Jenny will be far better able to develop as a Scholar-Practitioner if she is able to accept her own fallibility and to embrace a stance of learner.

As hard as it may be, pedagogical moments that have gone awry are often the best clues to the learning we need to pursue. In our own work, we have met many teachers who have entered graduate school because some long ago pedagogical moment continued to haunt them. They are driven to learn more so the next time they will be able to respond in a more educative fashion. For example, Brianne, a bright, enthusiastic, and dedicated pre-school teacher, enrolled in a Master of Arts in Teaching program we had created. When asked to describe a pedagogical moment, Brianne recounted a meeting in which the mother of a student angrily complained, "All you have them do is play. You've already written my son off as someone who can't learn. You're cheating him out of the knowledge he needs to succeed." Several years after the fact, Brianne was still struggling with this pedagogical moment—not with a student but with a parent whom Brianne needed to engage in an educative conversation about the role of play in childhood learning.

Discerning the significance of pedagogical moments contributes to the cultivation of Pedagogical Wisdom, because they are rich with potential learning. In Brianne's case, the moment gives rise to several questions:

- How can I respond more effectively the next time a parent challenges the role of play in early childhood education?
- How confident am I in my understanding the role of play in children's learning?
- What does this moment tell me about my vulnerability to being challenged?
- Would I have responded differently if it had been the student's father or my principal?
- How can I respond when my competence or instructional intentions are challenged?

By posing questions that move beyond the specifics of one pedagogical moment, Scholar-Practitioners can develop a broader and deeper repertoire of responses. Brianne may never again encounter a parent who specifically challenges the pedagogical use of play, but by probing that moment, Brianne can be better prepared to respond in analogous moments.

Remaining open allows Scholar-Practitioners to discern the complexity inherent in pedagogical moments. Rather than minimizing or ignoring the complexity as less experienced Scholar-Practitioners might do, more seasoned Scholar-Practitioners begin to tease apart the dynamics of moments to see what they might yield:

- Does the difficulty stem from a student's confusion about the subject matter at hand?
- Is there a mismatch between my instructional method and the student's mode of learning?
- Has some misunderstanding jeopardized trust and respect between the student and me?
- Are disruptive student behaviors interfering with classroom conversation?
- Are personal troubles preoccupying a student's attention?
- Am I preoccupied with personal problems?
- Does something about this student evoke negative reactions?
- Have I been caught off guard because I don't know the answer to the student's question?

Posing such questions allows the Scholar-Practitioner to interpret and re-interpret the "mess of the moment" in a variety of ways. Different interpretations can suggest alternative responses that can be tried when similar situations arise in the future. When a response to a pedagogical moment misses the mark, there are opportunities to examine the resulting consequences, to think "it might have been more educative if I had said this or done that." Through openness, discernment, questioning, trial and error, patterns begin to emerge. In this way, as Scholar-Practitioners mature, they accumulate an ever-growing repertoire of responses upon which they can draw in the improvisational heat of pedagogical moments.

Cultivating a Repertoire of Pedagogical Wisdom

Alan Alda talked about his goal of creating humor early in his improvisational career. When he began to work on the *Scientific American Frontiers*, he had a different purpose—educating the public about science. To accomplish this educative purpose, he assumed the stance of uninformed but curious learner. By conveying his genuine desire to understand, he was able to call forth explanations that were free of technical jargon and the stiffness of scholarly presentations. Scholar-Practitioners, however, cannot enter educational encounters without knowledge of the content they are teaching. As Valerie, a student teacher, learned, it is risky to have a superficial understanding of her content area and to think of improvisational teaching as "winging it." Valerie tended to approach her work in a cavalier fashion, assuming she knew more about math than her 11th grade students. One day, as she stood at the chalk board, writing out the solution to a complicated equation, a student interrupted, saying, "That's wrong." He proceeded to explicate the error in Valerie's approach to the problem and soon his classmates were turning to him for the lesson and ignoring Valerie. Scholar-Practitioners have an obligation to bring a reservoir of content knowledge to their practice. At the same time, they must maintain a sense of wonder, passion and curiosity about their students' educational needs as well as their content area. As their reservoir of content knowledge expands, Scholar-Practitioners have more material to draw upon in order to give more nuanced answers to students' questions, to convey complicated ideas, and to clarify misconceptions.

In addition to cultivating a robust fund of content knowledge, Scholar-Practitioners need to cultivate a repertoire of pedagogically sound methods, techniques, and materials—not in an abstract, decontextualized way, but wedded to their pedagogical aims. Robert Sternberg and Joseph Horvath describe this blending of content and method as pedagogical-content knowledge which includes:

> Knowledge of how to explicate particular concepts…
> how to demonstrate and rationalize procedures and
> methods…and how to correct students' naive theories
> and misconceptions about subject matter…[14]

One professor in a school of pharmacy expressed this form of knowledge when he commented, "I have a story of medicinal chemistry that works. Students understand it." He had honed this story over years of teaching and had worked out the nuances of helping students to grasp complex ideas. As Scholar-Practitioners mature, they add more and more nuanced stories to their repertoire, thereby wedding knowledge with technique to convey ideas to students whose readiness to learn can vary dramatically. Like master artisans who deftly use the "tools of their trade" to achieve specific effects, Scholar-Practitioners are able to draw from an array of instructional approaches to support learning.

Assessment may be the thorniest constituent in a Scholar-Practitioner's repertoire of knowledge and skills. At its best, assessment is wedded to the Scholar-Practitioner's capacity to discern what is happening within the context of a learning environment. Are students engaged? Does each student understand the material being presented? Do important questions need to be addressed? Does an instructional technique need to be adjusted? Just as the medical profession uses multiple indicators of a patient's health, Scholar-Practitioners rely on multiple indicators of learning. These indicators are used to fine-tune the educative value of pedagogical moments. Unfortunately, this appropriate and ethical use of assessment was swept aside by the exclusive emphasis on standardized test scores spawned by the No Child Left Behind legislation. It remains to be seen whether the most recent iteration of school accountability, the Every Student Succeeds Act (ESSA), will ameliorate the devastating effects of standardized testing mania. For now, however, we emphasize the point that Scholar-Practitioners use a range of assessment methods to better understand and address the learning needs of students.

Classroom management techniques, often seen as a major constituent of the Scholar-Practitioner's repertoire, require careful attention. When classroom management is used as a euphemism for authoritarian-style discipline, the result may be teacher-imposed order. One assumption is that teachers must be "in charge" or "in command" in order for pedagogy to be effective. Just as a theater performance would be ruined if the audience members were talking or randomly walking about or eating or letting their cell phones ring, a scripted pedagogical performance could be ruined by "off-task" behaviors. Improvisational pedagogy, however, calls for active participation and this can look quite messy. Mikki, one of our graduate students, talked with great anxiety about an afternoon when she had organized group learning projects in the school library. She was feeling quite pleased with the level of energy and excitement in the room as second graders read, talked, and drew with great animation. In the midst of all this activity, Mikki caught a glimpse of the principal walking past the library door and frowning. She was convinced that the principal judged the situation as out of control and her as incompetent. Neither Mikki nor we know what the principal was actually thinking, but we do know that active engagement is crucial for authentic learning. So, Scholar-Practitioners are challenged to create welcoming spaces where learners feel safe and respected, where a sense of community, belonging and self-worth can flourish.

We say "challenged" because destructive forces can encroach upon the sites of pedagogical practice. At the most basic level, elementary, secondary and post-secondary schools can no longer be considered safe sanctuaries. After the tragedies at Columbine, Sandy Hook, Virginia Tech, and Parkland, schools, communities, and law enforcement agencies have struggled with the best approaches to assure safety. Installing metal screening devices, hiring security guards, and arming teachers are among the measures that have been adopted by some school districts. We are not oblivious to the potential for violence and the need for safeguards. However, we are troubled by the image of schools as battle zones where fear dominates and the threat of retaliatory violence is used as a deterrent. Such conditions complicate efforts to create environments that nurture learning.

At a less catastrophic level, the Scholar-Practitioner's repertoire must include strategies for dealing with moments fraught with disciplinary issues. We are reminded of the moment described by our student Lauren who teaches special education classes at a middle school. She was several months pregnant when an angry student threw a chair at her. What constitutes a pedagogically wise response in a moment fraught with fear for one's unborn child, fear for other students' safety, concern for an out-of-control-student? Brad, who teaches in a school district where dozens of students have been killed by peers, struggles to find a wise response when school resumes after the latest fatality. Bullying—both in school and in cyberspace—erode the sense of belonging and community necessary for authentic learning.

There are no easy answers to these dilemmas. And that, perhaps, is the most important point for Scholar-Practitioners. The forces giving rise to disciplinary moments cannot be addressed by glib slogans, simplistic techniques, or authoritarian dictates. Boundaries are necessary, but they need not be restrictive or oppressive. When established with fairness and respect, they circumscribe a space where individuals can come together, fully engaged in the excitement of learning.

Pedagogical Wisdom and the *Telos* of Education

When adults are asked what they remember from their years of formal schooling, they often respond with memories of teachers—the special ones who encouraged or inspired or the really awful ones who were mean and disparaging. A 70 year old friend of Maria's still talks with bitterness about a high school teacher who told her point blank that she was too stupid to go to college. Now a nursing administrator with a Master's degree, this friend prevailed in spite of, not because of a teacher's words. It is an understatement to say this teacher lacked Pedagogical Wisdom. Yet how often do individuals receive subtle and not so subtle messages that corrode their self-worth and self-confidence? How often, in a cascade of criticism, do legislators tell school districts they aren't good enough; school boards tell superintendents they aren't good enough; superintendents tell principals they aren't good enough; principals tell teachers they aren't good enough; teachers tell students they aren't good enough? Carrots and sticks are brought to bear in order to motivate, to evoke greater effort, to fuel improvement, to assure accountability. In the process, the invitation of "yes, tell me more" is lost and like young John, we are tempted to crawl under a sheltering desk. All of us (students, teachers, administrators, society at large) need Scholar-Practitioners who hold true to the *telos* of education—to bring forth, to lead toward the fullest realization of each individual's potential.

REFLECTIVE PROMPTS

What thoughts and feelings are evoked by the ideas in this chapter?

In what ways do my responses to the ideas in this chapter contribute to my understanding of being a Scholar-Practitioner?

What questions are evoked by the ideas in this chapter? Where do those questions fit within my plan for continued learning?

What ideas do I want to incorporate into my evolving Scholar-Practitioner Narrative?

As I reflect on my experiences as student/learner/teacher, what Pedagogical Moments come to mind? What circumstances gave rise to the moment(s)? What was my role? What was the significance of the moment(s)? What resulted from the moment(s)? What insights have I gained through these reflections?

How do I characterize the pedagogical repertoire upon which I can draw during pedagogical moments?

In what ways do I continually strive to broaden and deepen my pedagogical repertoire?

NOTES

1 Donald A. Schon, *The Reflective Practitioner: How Professionals Think in Action* (New York: Basic Books, 1983), 42.

2 Atul Gawande, *Being Mortal: Medicine and What Matters in the End* (New York: Metropolitan Books, 2014), 3.

3 For additional information about emergence, improvisation and creativity see references for R. Keith Sawyer in the bibliography.

4 Alan Alda, *If I Understood You, Would I Have This Look on My Face?* (New York: Random House, 2017), 18-19.

5 Max van Manen, *The Tact of Teaching: The Meaning of Pedagogical Thoughtfulness* (Albany NY: SUNY Press, 1991), 41. In *The Tact of Teaching* and in two subsequent books, van Manen makes it clear that pedagogical moments arise between young persons and adults in a variety of roles including parents, counselors and others who are responsible for nurturing growth and learning. *Researching Lived Experience: Human Science for an Action Sensitive Pedagogy* addresses a mode of inquiry that promotes deeper understanding not only in education but in related fields like nursing and psychology. *Phenomenology of Practice: Meaning-Giving Methods in Phenomenological Research and Writing* delves more deeply into the philosophical underpinnings of inquiry in practice. See Bibliography for full references.

6 Barry Schwartz and Kenneth Sharpe, *Practical Wisdom: The Right Way to Do the Right Thing* (New York: Riverhead Books, 2010), 5-6.

7 Schwartz and Sharpe, 5.

8 John Dewey, *Experience and Education* (New York: Collier Books, 1938).

9 Schon, 40.

10 Alda, 10.

11 Marilyn Llewellyn, *Spirituality and Pedagogy: Being and Learning in Sacred Spaces* (Pittsburgh: Learning Moments Press, 2017), 53. For a theoretic explication of spiritual language and pedagogy see Marilyn Llewellyn, "Reclaiming a Spiritual Language and Embracing a Spirituality of Liberation," *Journal of Curriculum and Pedagogy* 2, no 2 (Winter 2005): 70-77.

12 Marjorie Barrett Logsdon, *A Pedagogy of Authority* (Pittsburgh: Learning Moments Press, 2017).

13 Parker Palmer, *The Courage to Teach* (San Francisco: Jossey-Bass Inc., 1998), 10. We highly recommend this classic book to anyone who has not read it. Palmer offers an inspiring look into the interior world of the self we bring to teaching while challenging readers to develop an inner landscape that allows them to be the best teacher they are capable of being.

14 Robert J. Sternberg & Joseph A. Horvath, "A Prototype View of Expert Teaching," *Educational Researcher* 24, no. 6 (1995): 11.

4

Balancing With Pedagogical Wisdom

In the final scene of *Star Trek II: The Wrath of Khan*, as Spock prepares to sacrifice himself to save the Star Ship Enterprise, he and Kirk have the following exchange:

> Spock: Do not grieve, Admiral. It is logical. The needs of the many outweigh—
>
> Kirk: The needs of the few.
>
> Spock: Or the one...

Star Trek III: The Search for Spock picks up immediately after Spock's death as Kirk and the intrepid crew of the Enterprise risk life and careers to return Spock's body to Vulcan so it can be reunited with his spirit. Following the successful reunification, Spock says, "Why would you do this?" Kirk responds, "Because the needs of the one outweighed the needs of the many."

In the fictional *Star Trek* universe, Kirk and his crew have several days to balance the needs of the many and the needs of the one. Educators, immersed in the daily, unremitting flow of real-life practice, rarely have this luxury of time. With limited resources and a multitude of needs, what constitutes a fair and reasonable balance? Consider, for example, the following anecdote related by Sandy, a school administrator responsible for her small district's compliance with regulations for educational inclusion. Sandy had been working to arrange services for a girl with Down Syndrome who would be entering kindergarten at the start of the school year:

> I've been talking and talking with her parents. I thought we had the Individualized Education Plan worked out. I was so pleased that I actually found a

certified teacher to assign to the class as an educational assistant. It would be like having two teachers in the class. I really thought we had it all worked out. I walked into a meeting and there were twenty people in the room! The parents brought their lawyer, different advocates, and friends!

Everything I said, they didn't believe. They didn't believe I had found an educational assistant who was really credentialed as a teacher. I couldn't convince them of anything.

They wanted a special education teacher and a general education teacher assigned to the room along with an educational assistant assigned full-time to the child. I finally said to them, "Look, I have three hundred other children in the school to also be concerned about." The father looked straight into my eyes and said, "Well that's not *my* problem, is it? That's your problem." Then he turned to his lawyer and said, "Isn't that right? That isn't my problem, is it?" And the lawyer said, "No that's not our problem." I don't know where this is all going to lead. Our special education costs rose by $100,000 last year. By a fluke we were able to absorb it but we're not going to be able to continue. I really don't know what we'll do.[1]

Balancing the needs of the many with the needs of the one can be intellectually and emotionally exhausting for administrators and teachers. Intensifying this balancing act is a third component of educational endeavors—i.e., the purpose(s) to be accomplished. The pie shaped wedges in Figure 4.1 represent an equal balance among these three components. In practice, however, a multitude of forces continually exert varying degrees of pressure on one component or another. Given this, maintaining a steady state of equilibrium is impossible. Scholar-Practitioners understand that achieving balance is a dynamic process requiring Pedagogical Wisdom to move the group as a whole and each individual within the group toward the purpose.

Figure 4.1 - Components of Educational Endeavors

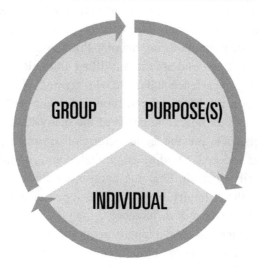

In this chapter, we highlight several pressure points that complicate this balancing act.

Pressure Point: Differentials in Engagement

Let us begin with the premise that learning is not limited to the confines of educational institutions. Individuals learn all the time in many ways from life experience. This natural or ordinary learning, however, differs from learning in formal institutional settings where experiences are designed to achieve particular purpose(s). Using our colleague Noreen Garman's term, we refer to these intentionally designed experiences as educational encounters. Regardless of institutional setting, age of students, scope of program, mode of instruction, and type of assessment, educational encounters are distinguished by the fact that they have been contrived—i.e., designed to achieve an intended purpose.

Ideally, every individual would be deeply and authentically engaged with the purpose(s) of the educational encounters in which they participate. Realistically, however, levels of engagement within a group can range from indifference or resentment to perfunctory compliance or game-playing to mild interest or genuine commitment. Differentials in engagement arise from a host of individual circumstances and capabilities, many of which are beyond the control of educators. This creates a pressure point requiring Scholar-Practitioners to balance their attention among those who are ready, willing and able to engage in the planned learning experience and those who are not. What is fair? What is possible within the limitations of time and resources? What are the consequences of sacrificing the needs of the many to the needs of the one or vice versa? Despite the facile rhetoric of "no child left behind" or "every student succeeds" finding an equitable and productive balance is extraordinarily difficult. Drawing upon one's Pedagogical Wisdom may not lessen the difficulty, but sometimes it points to a small opening that might make a world of difference.

Maria's mother was an elementary school teacher who tolerated no foolishness at home or in her classroom. Maria knew her mother was highly regarded by parents who fought to have their children assigned to "Mrs. P's classroom." Maria is fond of recounting the following anecdote:

> Mom brooked no failures. I imagined her sternly demanding that her young pupils pay attention, write neatly, and master the rudiments of reading and arithmetic. Decades after Mom had retired, I met Terry who had been a student in Mom's third grade class. A self-confessed wayward student at best, Terry fondly talked about the time my mother had visited my sister in Indianapolis. Knowing Terry's passionate interest in racecars, my mother brought him a flag from the Indianapolis Speedway. "It hung in my room until I left for college," Terry told me. "I loved that flag, and I thought it was so special she thought to bring it to me. I turned around after that. I became a much better student.

The "magic" of Terry's transformation did not emanate from the checkered racetrack flag, but from a teacher discerning and responding to a student's passionate interest. Pat recalls a similar incident from her days as a teacher of secondary English.

Eric rarely turned in assignments, was easily distracted, and participated in class discussions only when he could make a comment designed to elicit a laugh. I wondered what I could say to his eagerly attentive parents on parent-teacher night as they stood there, waiting to learn about their son's progress in 11th grade English. After sharing his grades and discussing his challenges, I felt I had to offer a positive, a strength their son had that might make their car ride home less bleak.

I felt really happy when I could honestly convey an impression I had had about Eric from the first day of class. "I wish Eric would use that wonderful speaking voice of his more effectively in class. His voice has such beautiful tone," I said." His parents looked happy and surprised, as if they had never consciously registered the sound of their son's voice. The day after the parent-teacher conferences, I couldn't help but notice that Eric stayed on task during class and participated in the classroom discussion as if he had read the assigned reading. I slowly realized that Eric really had read the story. After class, Eric came up to me and said with a huge smile on his face, "I heard what you told my parents about my voice. You like my voice." With that, he left the room to go to his next class.

Eric's story doesn't have a Hollywood ending; he didn't experience a complete change in his behavior and become a stellar student. But he did improve; it seemed as though he took himself a bit more seriously. For Pat, this was a pedagogical lesson on the importance of a student feeling seen and, in Eric's case, heard. Granted, such small gestures may never solve all of the difficulties presented by disengaged students, but small acts of caring may, for a moment, tip the balance toward authentic engagement.

Pressure Point: Disconnections Between Teaching and Learning

The work of designing educational encounters falls under the umbrella of curriculum and instruction. Scholar-Practitioners have a responsibility for offering well-planned curricula and instruction. Yet no amount of planning guarantees that students will take from an educational encounter what was intended. The potential for disconnection between what is taught and what is learned has given rise to several descriptors:

- The taught curriculum versus the learned curriculum
- The delivered curriculum versus the lived/experienced curriculum
- The intended curriculum versus the unintended curriculum
- The overt curriculum versus the covert/hidden curriculum
- The tested curriculum versus the learned curriculum

Curriculum scholar Dennis Sumara offers a vivid metaphor to illustrate the potential for disparities between intention and outcome. "Imagine," he says, "that you are releasing a huge container of water at the top of a mountain. It will follow many different courses as it flows down the crevices of the mountain. This happens, too, when we release a curriculum. It will flow in many directions within and among students." This multiplicity of pathways creates another pressure point, and one of the key issues for achieving balance is the extent to which Scholar-Practitioners acknowledge and value the individual variations. This point harkens back to the discussion in Chapter 2 about two different views of learning: learning as an observable change in behavior and learning as meaning-making. Here we elaborate a bit on these distinctions.

In the mid-20th century as behavioral theories of learning began to take hold, there was a shift from writing instructional objectives (what the teacher would do) to learning objectives (what the students would master). Driven by this perspective, the behavioral objective movement came into vogue. Educators were expected to state the purpose of an educational encounter clearly and precisely in terms of behavioral outcomes and the conditions under which the outcomes would be demonstrated. On the surface this appears to make a great deal of sense. It really isn't fair to turn educational encounters into a "guess my expectations" game. Clearly understanding expectations for learning would give students a greater sense of control and responsibility for their learning.

Unfortunately, the strategy of using behavior objectives to clarify intended educational purposes led to an infinite regress of sub-objectives. In other words, before mastering a broadly stated objective, it was necessary to master more specific, precursor objectives. When conscientious educators worked to make this hierarchy of objectives explicit, the number of objectives, sub-objectives, and sub-sub-objectives quickly became unwieldy. In addition, mastery of specific objectives often did not result in the ultimate goal of competent performance. To ameliorate that problem, the concept of "competencies" replaced the language of objectives. Unfortunately, a similar regression of sub-competencies occurred and movement from mastery of competencies to competence still remained elusive. More recently the concept of "skill sets" has emerged in an effort to foster integration of learning. It remains to be seen whether this change in language will have the desired outcome. In any event, the residue of behavioral objectives lingers in course evaluation questionnaires, program accreditation criteria, individualized education plans for students with special needs, and general lessons plans. This behavioral language reinforces the view that learning corresponds to teaching.

Anyone who has left a well-planned, well-conducted educational encounter feeling overwhelmed and disoriented recognizes the fallacy of the correspondence view. Anyone who has left an educational encounter thinking, "That was a complete waste of time!" understands the disconnection between what they were meant to learn and the value they place on it. Anyone who has worked tirelessly to help students understand a concept and seen misconceptions persist sees the gap between intent and outcome. Those who espouse a view of learning as a meaning-making process accept the inevitability that disconnections occur between what is taught and what is learned.

In London, as passengers exit the subway, a disembodied voice warns, "mind the gap" between the car and the platform. Scholar-

Practitioners understand the importance of minding the gap between what they hope students will learn and what they actually take away from an educational encounter. Only by minding the gap can they begin to draw upon their Pedagogical Wisdom to balance connections between intended purpose and lessons learned.

Pressure Point: Modes of Learning—Modes of Teaching

One outgrowth of the behavioral objective movement was growing attention to individual differences in learning style. Here the "road map" analogy came into play. Just as travelers can take many different routes to a given destination, students should have leeway to decide how best to reach intended outcomes. Lending support to this notion was the desire to ferret out best practices by identifying factors that might facilitate or impede mastery of objectives. Psychological studies soon documented individual variations in learning styles as one such factor. Within a few years, the number of learning style inventories mushroomed. A nursing colleague showed Maria a large file drawer from which she could pull inventories for everything from the Myers-Briggs Typology to external/internal locus of control to auditory/visual/kinesthetic learning preferences. "The problem is," she said, "what I should do with this information once I get it. I have 30 students in my smallest class and I'm teaching two, sometimes three, courses. Plus I'm in the clinic supervising student nurses several times a week. How can I possibly tailor my instruction to fit each person's style?" This conscientious nursing instructor voiced a subtle, but extremely important, shift in perspective. Initially, identification of learning styles was meant to give individual students more responsibility, control and freedom in their process of learning. All too often, however, teachers assumed that they were responsible for attending to individual differences. This creates an enormous pressure for already over-extended teachers. Consider, for example, the following exchange:

> At the completion of his student teaching experience, Mark along with fellow students gave a presentation on what he had learned. With great pride, Mark explained how he had accommodated individual student learning

styles. When he finished, a member of the audience asked, "You mean if you had 30 students in your class, you would write 30 different lesson plans?"

"Yes," Mark replied unequivocally.

Such an unrealistic expectation is a recipe for burnout—an unwise expenditure of scarce time in pursuit of an unattainable ideal. Pedagogical Wisdom calls for a balance between a "one size fits all approach" and individualized instruction matched to each person's learning style.

Another, sometimes overlooked, pressure point exists between the Scholar-Practitioner's instructional style and individual students' learning styles. Some instructors are brilliant lecturers. Some are geniuses at facilitating discussions. Some skillfully manage multiple project groups. Some exhibit a creative flair for incorporating visual, auditory, tactile, and/or kinesthetic modalities into instructional processes. Some use digital technology to great advantage. How should these variations in instructional style be balanced? Should teachers give up their strengths to accommodate student preferences? Should they strive to augment their preferred style with other, less "natural" styles? If a teacher's style fits the purpose of educational encounters, what is gained or lost by changing that style? Is there a value in helping students learn how to learn through a broader range of modalities? Developing Pedagogical Wisdom entails striking a balance among these individual, potential conflicting differences.

Another more insidious imbalance arises when too much credence is placed on the results of inventories.

One faculty member in a professional school became quite enamored of the Myers-Briggs Typology. After several frustrating years of trying to institute curriculum changes, the faculty member began to toy with the notion that the Typology could be used to screen out applicants who didn't match the profile of an idealized type of practitioner. In another professional program, several faculty members used the Myers-Briggs to label and pigeon-hole students. Pedagogical Wisdom is needed to safeguard against the misuse of inventory data that at best can only provide glimpses into the complex nature of any individual's learning process.

Pressure Point: Measurement Mania

From the moment we are born, we are measured. Height, weight, pulse rate, respirations, level of oxygen, IQ, EQ, test scores, grade point averages, math comprehension, reading comprehension, the list goes on and on. Such numeric descriptors in themselves are not particularly problematic. They are, after all, simply an objective indicator of some characteristic. However, when the measurements of individuals are aggregated and then used to categorize individuals along a continuum, a pernicious dynamic occurs.

Perhaps being judged "normal" is reassuring. The baby's height and weight are "normal." The oxygen level is within a "normal range." This is reassuring news to parents anxiously awaiting confirmation that their infant is "normal," i.e., healthy. Less reassuring is the news that we are "average." Those who fall on the "above average" end of the continuum may feel affirmed. But what of those deemed "below average?" Students who perform below average; teachers whose classes perform below average on standardized tests; schools that perform below average when compared to state and national norms—what damage is caused by these comparisons? Of course, the proponents of measurement will argue that such information is necessary. Without it, we will not know which students need help. Without it, we cannot hold teachers and school districts accountable. Those who do not realize they are below average may be complacent and lack the motivation to improve. Such rationalizations might be more persuasive if they resulted in greater resources to ameliorate "below average" performance. But they ring hollow when school budgets are cut, class size is increased, and teaching staffs are reduced.

Concern about grade inflation is another, ironic twist that arose when the behavioral objective movement called into question the logic of norm-referenced testing. If the intent of behavioral objectives is to make learning outcomes transparent and if every student is meant to master the objectives, then measuring student performance against a norm makes no sense. Performance should be criterion-referenced— i.e., measured against set criteria, and no student should be left behind; every student should achieve mastery. Teachers whose students achieved this idealized vision of mastery were suddenly suspect. How can every student in a class receive an "A?" How meaningful is an "A" if everyone has one? How can we tell the really outstanding (above average) students from those who just barely achieve the outcome (average/below average). The mania for measurement seems equal only to the mania for comparison.

It seems unlikely that this will change any time soon. Consequently, Scholar-Practitioners face enormous pressure to find a balance between assessment in service of student learning and measurement used to categorize students and hold teachers and school districts accountable for "failures." Let us be clear. We are not arguing against accountability. It is inevitable and to some degree necessary. However, preoccupation with narrow, episodic, and fragmented measurement has done great disservice—indeed damage—to many school districts, teachers, and students.

Scholar-Practitioners understand that many factors beyond their control complicate meaningful assessment of learning. The very structure of our educational institutions creates difficulties. Although human development experts know that both children and adults mature at different rates, individuals are expected to enter school at a specified age and achieve the outcomes specified for that school year. The arbitrary segmentation of time into school days, grading periods, and school years exacerbates the problems created by age-based, student cohorts. Despite individual differences in readiness to learn and pace of learning, everyone is expected to master content within the allotted period of time. Those who don't are "below average." When the culturally biased nature of standardized tests was recognized, their validity as a measurement of learning was called into question. How is the validity of assessments compromised when learning is affected by developmental differences, poverty, hunger, homelessness, violence, and other social difficulties?

At the heart of much thinking about assessment is the question, "How do we (teachers, parents, tax payers, policy makers, future employers) know that a student has actually learned?" Within a framework of measurement, most efforts to answer this question are couched in the language of science in which experimental design is seen as the way to determine the truth of a situation. Terms like "formative and summative evaluation" and "pre- and post-tests" stem from a desire to pinpoint what students knew before an educational experience and what they knew afterwards. With this information, teachers can hold students accountable for doing their job (i.e., learning); administrators can hold teachers accountable for doing their job (i.e., teaching); and policy makers can hold school districts accountable for doing their job (i.e., educating youth).

Asking how OTHERS know whether a student has learned excludes the most important person—the learner—from the assessment process. When assessment is embedded in the learning process, the emphasis shifts from "How do WE know that learning has occurred?" to "How do LEARNERS know what they have learned? As it became obvious that test-taking itself involves a number of skills, a multi-billion dollar, test-prep industry flourished. When the No Child Left Behind Act required school districts to demonstrate yearly annual progress, teaching students the skills to take standardized tests began to crowd out teaching of actual content. What seems lost in measurement mania is an understanding that tests (particularly standardized tests) are only one indicator of learning. Also lost is recognition that when learning is viewed as a meaning-making process, a very different set of skills is needed and those, too, must be learned.

When assessment is embedded within the teaching-learning process, Scholar-Practitioners can use multifaceted indicators to help students evaluate their own learning. Pedagogical Wisdom can guide Scholar-Practitioners as they work to establish the trust necessary for authentic conversations about learning. Through conversations, students can begin to discern, along with their teachers, what they understand and what remains to be mastered. Multiple forms of feedback can help students see where they stand—not in relation to others or some abstract norm—but in relation to where they started and where they want to go. Embedded assessments are not definitive measures of adequacy, but are directional signals pointing to new horizons of learning.

Balancing with Pedagogical Wisdom
and the *Telos* of Education

The issues raised in this chapter are complicated. Scholar-Practitioners need Pedagogical Wisdom to balance and rebalance the forces that either augment or undermine authentic engagement in learning. In this way, they can work toward the educative purpose of education.

Experience is one crucial source of Pedagogical Wisdom, but it alone is not enough. Also important is an understanding of the theoretical underpinnings of educational practice. Without theoretical understanding, Scholar-Practitioners lack the touchstones necessary for creating generative educational encounters. This is the quality we turn to in the next section.

REFLECTIVE PROMPTS

What thoughts and feelings are evoked by the ideas in this chapter?

In what ways do my responses to the ideas in this chapter contribute to my understanding of being a Scholar-Practitioner?

What questions are evoked by the ideas in this chapter? Where do those questions fit within my plan for continued learning?

What ideas do I want to incorporate into my evolving Scholar-Practitioner Narrative?

As I recall moments of learning that were especially powerful or especially frustrating, what insights do I gain into my mode(s) of learning?

In what ways do my modes of learning influence my modes of teaching?

NOTES

1 Micheline Stabile, *A Call to Conscience: Problematizing Educational Inclusion.* (Ed.D. Dissertation, University of Pittsburgh, 1999). UMI ProQuest Digital Dissertation #AAT9928088.

SECTION III

The Quality of Theoretical Understanding

Theoretical Understanding entails the capacity to draw upon theory to articulate a rationale for one's professional decisions and action.

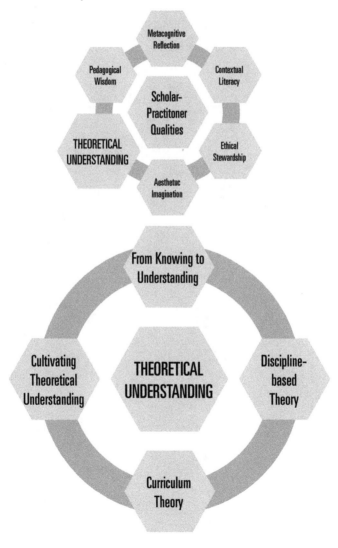

5

Theoretical Understanding in Pedagogical Moments

only known by few

The word "theory" can be off-putting. For some, it connotes highly abstract ideas that only super smart people can understand. For others, theory connotes esoteric, ivory-tower ideas with little relevance in the "real" world. Scholar-Practitioners, however, understand that theories provide lenses that bring pedagogical moments into clearer focus.

To convey the significance of lenses, we [have] used the metaphor of a foreopter, the piece of equipment found in ophthalmologists' offices that enables the doctor to determine through which set of lenses your vision is most clear. The ophthalmologist places the foreopter before your eyes and asks you to make a quick series of judgments regarding your vision. As she flips one new lens over another, the doctor asks repeatedly, "Is this better or is this better?" The foreopter is a trial lens method of ascertaining to what degree your vision changes from lens to lens and which lens gives better clarity. Sometimes it is difficult to discern differences from lens to lens; the differences in vision are so subtle. Yet, in the process of looking through the foreopter, of having choices about how you see, you incrementally decide which lenses enable you to focus. With the foreopter, movement toward visual clarity is gradual but, ultimately, dramatic.[1]

Theories give us a range of lenses for discerning issues more clearly. Therefore, in this chapter, we look at Theoretical Understanding in relation to pedagogical moments. First, however, we begin with a cautionary note about "common sense" theories.

A Cautionary Note

Scholar-Practitioners understand that all of us have informal, "common sense" theories of how the world works. Shaped by personal experience, working theories may or may not be consistent with formal theories. Scholar Virginia Richardson calls attention to the problem of mismatched conceptions about the nature of education:

> We have a unique situation in education. Nearly everyone has been a student, and on the basis of that experience, many claim knowledge of the field, perhaps even consider themselves to be experts. They act on unexamined beliefs and understandings that they gained simply through extensive experience as students in the educational system. Their beliefs are deep, strong, and often incorrect—or at least misguided and unworkable. Unfortunately, these beliefs often drive policy and practice in education.[2]

Shaking free of unrecognized, unquestioned assumptions can be difficult. Yet unearthing and examining these deeply held beliefs are crucial to on-going development as a Scholar-Practitioner. Pedagogical moments can be a valuable catalyst for this excavation process, prompting us to ask:

- What do I think?
- What is the basis for my thinking?

These questions lie at the heart of Theoretical Understanding. Taking them seriously is no easy task, because it entails recognizing one's preconceptions and taken-for-granted assumptions. It entails being open to the way others see the world. It entails a give and take of ideas so that new understandings can emerge.

From Knowing to Understanding

Often discussions of teacher competence stress knowledge of subject matter, instructional methods, and best practices. For Scholar-Practitioners such knowledge is necessary but not sufficient. The concept of knowledge connotes public repositories of codified information. The concept of understanding connotes an integration of knowledge into an individual's conceptual schema. As noted educator Lee Shulman puts it:

> [Understanding] includes knowledge, and it includes the ability to restate in one's own words the ideas learned from others...In contrast to knowledge and information, understanding connotes a form of ownership."[3]

Understanding allows for more sophisticated and nuanced use of knowledge within pedagogical moments. To illustrate this point, we return to Brianne, the relatively inexperienced, pre-school teacher who, when confronted by an angry mother, was unable to explain the educative value of play. At this stage in her development as a Scholar-Practitioner, Brianne may have thought, "This is what my professors taught, so this is what I'm supposed to do." When challenged, however, Brianne could not articulate the theoretical underpinnings of her pedagogical practice in a way that addressed the mother's fears. She did not yet "own" the ideas that shaped her practice.

As Scholar-Practitioners mature, they move from what Marcia Baxter Magolda describes as Absolute Knowing toward understanding as Shulman describes it. In reporting on her longitudinal study of students as they progressed through and beyond undergraduate school, Baxter Magolda described four different mindsets about knowledge:

> *Absolute knowing*, evident at the outset of college, involves viewing knowledge as certain. Learners with this way of knowing seek answers from authorities. *Transitional knowing*, prevalent in the middle years of college, involves acknowledging that some areas of knowledge are uncertain and require exploration

to decide what to believe. Learners with this perspective focus on learning how to decide or how to access others' perspectives. *Independent knowing,* a perspective that emerged for some students toward the end of college, entails viewing knowledge as largely uncertain. Learners with this perspective begin to think for themselves and make judgments based on their own perspectives or biases. *Contextual knowing,* a perspective that was rare in college, judges evidence in a particular context as a process that determines knowledge. Learners with this perspective use their knowledge when approaching a new learning situation, seek out persons who have developed expertise in the learning situation, and combine their own and others' expertise in learning.[4]

In moving from Absolute toward Contextual Knowing, Scholar-Practitioners recognize that knowledge assimilated in college cannot be taken for granted. They come to understand that knowledge is dynamically constructed and reconstructed within constantly changing contexts. What Brianne found sufficient within the context of her pre-school classroom proved inadequate within the context of a parent-teacher meeting. The idea of contextually constructed knowledge harkens back to Alan Alda's description of the mutual learning that can arise when individuals engage in conversations characterized by open listening, keen observation, and empathy. As each person draws upon his or her own repository of knowledge to address the topic at hand, possibilities for new understandings emerge for everyone.

In discussing Pedagogical Wisdom, we highlighted the importance of knowing the subject matter one is responsible for teaching. In moving from knowing to understanding, Scholar-Practitioners recognize that all subject-matter fields encompass multiple—often competing—theories. Maturing as a Scholar-Practitioner entails understanding the arguments underlying the various theories as well as their own theoretical position. Consider Marjorie Logsdon who we introduced in Chapter 3. Once she understood the theoretical difference between writing as product versus writing as process, she began to reshape her pedagogy. Another colleague, Pamela Krakowski, began to examine her own pedagogical approach within the theoretical frameworks that shaped early childhood art education—child-centered art education; discipline-based art education (art production, art criticism, history, aesthetics); art as social reconstruction.[5] Over time, almost all content areas have undergone similar transformations in approach.

Evolving theories about the way to teach subject matter knowledge are often put forward as "best practices." Reactions to newly espoused "best practices" provide insight into one's own maturation as a Scholar-Practitioner. Some teachers with entrenched views of how to teach may reject new best practices as the latest fad. Others may adopt them without question—either of their own volition or because they are pressured to do so by district mandate. Neither extreme is useful. Scholar-Practitioners examine the new practices AND their own practices. They consider the rationale for new practices and how that rationale informs their thinking. Through this process of questioning, Scholar-Practitioners may gain new insights for accomplishing pedagogical goals. Sources of confusion may dissipate when viewed through a new lens. At the very least, questions for further study and learning can arise. Carefully considering evolving best practices allows Scholar-Practitioners to augment the theoretical lenses through which they interpret the significance of pedagogical moments.

In addition to theoretical underpinnings of subject matter, Scholar-Practitioners draw upon theories from other disciplines to inform their thinking. In the following section we touch on several fields of study that provide lenses for looking at pedagogical moments.

Theoretical Understanding of Learning and Human Development

Because the aim of education is to engender learning, a fundamental question is, "What is the nature of learning?" This question has intrigued scholars from ancient to modern times. Greek philosopher Socrates thought that learning occurred as the individual's innate understandings were drawn out through the skillful use of questions by the teacher. For craftsmen and artisans, learning occurs through observation and practice under the watchful eye of those who have mastered their art. Psychologist B.F. Skinner thought of learning as a response to external stimuli with rewards or punishments reinforcing or extinguishing various behaviors. During the industrial revolution, learning came to be seen as a process akin to production—given the right in-puts and proper processing, raw materials (unformed children) could be transformed into desired products (school graduates with desired knowledge and skill). Social psychologist Jerome Bruner argued that learning occurs as individuals construct narratives to explain their life experiences. Computer technology gave rise to the view that the brain is an information processing mechanism and learning occurs as "data" are crunched through neural pathways. Today, the burgeoning field of Artificial Intelligence gives rise to new questions such as:

- Can computers learn?
- If computers are capable of learning, how is that learning similar to or different from human learning?

Ever more sophisticated imaging techniques allow scientists to see what areas of the brain light up during various types of learning activities. They can, with greater accuracy, understand where learning may be occurring and the neurochemical reactions during learning. Despite greater insight into the anatomical structures and physiological processes associated with learning, the essence of what it means to learn remains elusive. Why, for example, can individuals experience the same event but have widely divergent learning outcomes?

The puzzle of learning has given rise to a related set of theories about motivation. Why do rewards that work with some individuals fail with others? Why do some individuals persist in endeavors that are difficult, even painful, when no reward is apparent? What motivates some individuals to engage fully in learning and others to remain disengaged? Such questions have given rise to theories of intrinsic and extrinsic motivations. Psychologists, like Abraham Maslow, have theorized that humans have an innate drive to learn in order to satisfy developmental needs.

Theories of human growth and development also come into play as we strive to understand the nature of learning. Italian educator, Maria

Montessori stressed the inherent need of children to explore and master their environment. The Reggio Emilia school of thought emphasizes the multiplicity of ways that children interact with the world and learn from it. This view of learning echoes Howard Gardner's theory of multiple intelligences. In the early 1970s, Malcolm Knowles called attention to the differences between learning in children and learning in adults. Since the publication of *The Adult Learner: A Neglected Species* (now a classic), old assumptions about the inability of adults to learn have fallen aside. Indeed, whole industries have grown up around the learning interests of life-long learners.

Neuroscientific evidence has not only shown the capacity for lifelong learning, it has also challenged the view that intelligence is fixed. When children are exposed to neurogenic environments, new neural pathways can develop, creating greater possibilities for learning. School folklore abounds with stories of children who defy the labels that have been attached to them. Einstein, Bill Gates, Steve Jobs are among the iconic figures who have done poorly in school and gone on to brilliant careers. Individuals born without hearing have long seen themselves, not as disabled, but as members of a community with a rich and vibrant culture. More recently, those who are labeled "autistic" have been pushing back against the view that they have a disability and therefore a stunted capacity for learning and success. Such examples, underscore the dangers of judging students and giving them labels that follow them throughout school.

Victoria Sweet, in her memoir, *Slow Medicine*,[6] points to problems arising when physicians rely excessively on patient records as the source of data for diagnosis and treatment. In example after example, she illustrates how misdiagnoses can be passed from one doctor to another as patients are transferred from one hospital unit to another or from one hospital to another. Similar problems can arise when labels (e.g., ADHD, behavior problem, lazy, trouble-maker) follow students from year to year or school to school. From *To Sir with Love* to *Stand and Deliver*, mythic teacher-figures "redeem" students who have been written off by others. Looking beyond the labels, looking at individuals—really looking in Alan Alda's sense of the word—is the essence of Pedagogical Wisdom. Learning theory, motivational theory, and human development theory are lenses that help Scholar-Practitioners see their students and what they need more clearly.

Theoretical Understanding of Social and Cultural Dimensions

Our colleague Leonora Kivuva teaches English as a second language and works extensively with Somali refugees. One day she was contacted by a distraught kindergarten teacher who exclaimed, "I can't understand these kids. I give them a pencil and the next day it's gone. They keep stealing them; no matter what I do they won't stop. Today I lost it and yelled at them. Not my finest moment, but I'm just so frustrated. They've gone through a half a year's supply in a couple of weeks."

Within the micro context of the teacher's classroom, a struggle is escalating over something as seemingly mundane as pencils. From the teacher's perspective, she is providing adequate materials and is mindful of making her supplies last to the end of the school year. Perhaps she is tired of having to use her own money to supplement the school's meager supply budget. Looking at the situation through the lens of her life experiences, the children's behaviors made no sense. Labeling their actions as "stealing" connoted a criminalization of their behaviors that could set in motion a negative power dynamic for the remainder of the school year. Leonora provided a broader, macro lens to help the teacher to see that the children had lived in refugee camps where pencils were a rarity. Typically, they used small sticks to draw in the dirt. Further, the children never knew if, at any given moment, all of their possessions might be stolen or lost. Out of this life of deprivation, the children were hoarding pencils. Contributing to the cultural problem was the language barrier between teacher and students. In losing her temper and yelling, the teacher could have triggered the children's fear that they were in jeopardy of losing their new found home, especially in light of national initiatives to deport undocumented immigrants and deny entrance to refugees. Fortunately, the teacher knew Leonora and thought to reach out to her. Leonora's explanation helped the teacher to see the situation very differently and regain her equanimity in the classroom.

By running her conclusion past Leonora, the teacher separated the fact of hoarding pencils from her biased judgment of "stealing," recognized her misconceptions and let go of them.

As another example, let's revisit the confrontation between Brianne and the angry mother who felt her son was being cheated of a good education because he was "just playing." From Brianne's perspective, she was using sound knowledge of child development to guide her instruction. She loved her job and loved working with young children. She had rejected an offer from a fairly wealthy private preschool to teach in a blighted neighborhood where she felt she could make a difference in the lives of disadvantaged children. Given this, she was blindsided by the intensity of the mother's anger. What Brianne didn't understand was the depth of this African American mother's mistrust of white "do gooders" and a system of schooling that is perceived as oppressive. Given the large percentage of students who dropped out before graduation and the fact that very few graduates of the school district had gone on to college, the mother's fears for her son were understandable. Having a broader historical perspective of the contentious relationship between the social institution of schooling and minority communities might have helped Brianne to respond less defensively and to discuss how play as a mode of childhood learning aligned with the mother's hopes for her son.

Theoretical Understanding and the *Telos* of Education

Because education draws from so many disciplines for its theoretical underpinnings, it is often considered an applied field. In other words, the theories that educators need to carry out their work are generated by those in other disciplines and are passed along to educators who will apply them. To some extent this is true, but it does not paint a large enough picture. Educators, too, generate theories, in particular those that deal with the complexities of striving to educate many students within the time and space limitations of contrived educational encounters. Curriculum—with its focus on what should be taught and what structures and processes promote learning—can be considered as a field of study in its own right. This is the view we explore in the next chapter.

REFLECTIVE PROMPTS

What thoughts and feelings are evoked by the ideas in this chapter?

In what ways do my responses to the ideas in this chapter contribute to my understanding of being a Scholar-Practitioner?

What questions are evoked by the ideas in this chapter? Where do those questions fit within my plan for continued learning?

What ideas do I want to incorporate into my evolving Scholar-Practitioner Narrative?

When I reflect on my experiences as a student/learner in light of Baxter-Magolda's descriptions about knowing, in what ways have I moved from Absolute Knowing to Contextual Knowing?

What discipline(s) provide the theoretical underpinnings for my subject area(s)? With what schools of thought about my subject area(s) align most closely with my own thinking? What is the rationale for aligning with those particular schools of thought?

How would I characterize the developmental issues of the age group I teach? What pedagogical challenges do these issues raise?

What assumptions about motivation guide my practice?

How conversant am I with various perspectives about the role of educational institutions within society?

In what ways do cultural issues impact my practice?

NOTES

1 Marilyn Llewellyn, Patricia L. McMahon, & Maria Piantanida, "Of Foreopters and Fractals: A Scholarship of Educational Praxis for the 21st Century," *Spectrum* (Pittsburgh: The Carlow University Press, 2010): 26-27.

2 Virginia Richardson, "Stewards of a Field, Stewards of an Enterprise: The Doctorate in Education," in *Envisioning the Future of Doctoral Education: Preparing Stewards for the Discipline. Carnegie Essays on the Doctorate*, eds. Chris M. Golde, George F. Walker and Associates (San Francisco: Jossey-Bass, 2006), 258.

3 Lee Shulman, Making Differences: A Table of Learning. *Change* 34, no 6 (November/December 2002): 40.

4 Marcia B. Baxter Magolda, Post-College Experience and Epistemology, *The Review of Higher Education* 18, no. 1 (1994): 26.

5 Pamela Krakowski, *Balancing the Narrative and the Normative: Pedagogical implications for Early Childhood Art Education.* (Ed.D. Dissertation, University of Pittsburgh, 2004). UMI ProQuest Digital Dissertation #AAT3139692.

6 Victoria Sweet, *Slow Medicine: The Way to Healing* (New York: Riverhead Books, 2017).

6

Theoretical Understanding of Curriculum

Often when educators (and the general public) hear the word *curriculum*, they immediately think about courses—what content should be included; how it should be organized; what instructional methods will be used; how student learning will be evaluated. It is not unusual for a group of educators to talk about curriculum as though they all mean the same thing, when in reality, each may be thinking of curriculum in a slightly different way. Anyone who has served on a curriculum committee has likely encountered deep-seated and divergent opinions about what should be taught. For that matter, tacit assumptions about curriculum can surface at unexpected moments like the proverbial Thanksgiving dinner when Uncle Jim puts down his fork and asks, "Just what are YOU people teaching these days? Kids are coming out of school knowing nothing. In my day…" It seems like at the drop of a hat anyone and everyone has strong opinions about what should be taught. As Virginia Richardson pointed out, these views may be based on unexamined and potentially erroneous assumptions. Perhaps one of the most pervasive assumptions is that anyone who knows a subject can teach. Those who are committed to curriculum as a field of study understand that two questions precede decisions about what one can teach. These are:

- What is worth learning?
- Who gets to decide?

What is worth learning is often determined by the level at which decision making is vested. For example, does the decision rest with individual teachers who are presumed to have subject matter expertise? Or, as is the case in many districts, teams of teachers or formal curriculum committees provide the broad parameters for the curriculum and rely on individual teachers to develop specific courses or lesson plans. In some instances, curriculum decisions are made by those who select particular textbooks or instructional packages, placing teachers in the role of technicians who must follow specific scripts rather than professionals with decision-making discretion. In the past decade or so, as colleges and universities have competed for the best students, market forces have been reshaping decisions about curriculum. Curricula with low appeal to prospective students may be reduced or eliminated while curricula with broader market appeal are expanded. Consider for example, the following:

> The University of Wisconsin at Stevens Point has proposed dropping 13 majors in the humanities and social sciences…while adding programs with "clear career pathways" as a way to address declining enrollment and a multimillion-dollar deficit.
>
> Students and faculty members have reacted with surprise and concern to the news, which is being portrayed by the school's administration as a path to regain enrollment and provide new opportunities to students. Critics see something else: a waning commitment to liberal arts education and a chance to lay off faculty under new rules that weakened tenure.[1]

The University of Wisconsin is not alone in considering such fundamental curriculum decisions as higher education institutions across the country struggle with declining enrollments, escalating costs, and conflicting perceptions of their mission.

The general public has also been exerting greater pressure to modify curricula to conform to various ideological camps. Parents and elected officials have pressured teachers, administrators, and school boards to exclude information and ideas that conflict with their beliefs. Students choose colleges and universities where their deeply held assumptions will not be challenged. Teachers and professors are censured for presenting content that is "offensive" to one or more special interest groups. These pressures are creating deep fissures in the perceived purpose of education and what is worth learning. Vehement debates are raging at local, state and national levels. We suggest that a Theoretical Understanding of curriculum can help Scholar-Practitioners navigate complicated conversations about curriculum.

As is the case with any field of study, various scholars have put forward different theories of curriculum.[1] Rather than review and summarize these, we offer four lenses through which to view the underlying structure of curriculum. Although these structures have implications for Pre-K through secondary school, our focus is on undergraduate, graduate, and post-graduate education of professionals. Therefore, we invite readers to think about the following ideas through the lens of self-as-learner. (See Figure 2.2 in Chapter 2.)

Lenses for Viewing Curriculum Structure

discover or learn for themselves

FIGURE 6.1 - CURRICULUM STRUCTURES (A HEURISTIC)

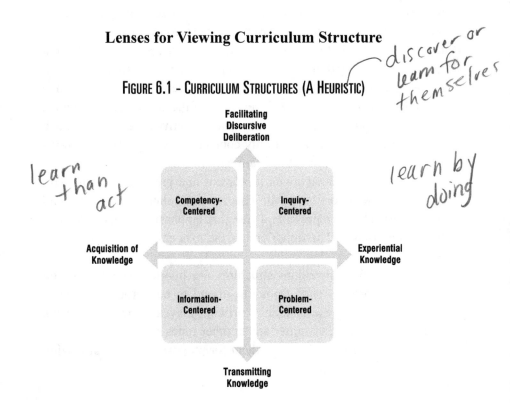

learn than act

learn by doing

Facilitating
Discursive
Deliberation

Competency-
Centered

Inquiry-
Centered

Acquisition of
Knowledge

Experiential
Knowledge

Information-
Centered

Problem-
Centered

Transmitting
Knowledge

Figure 6.1 is a heuristic representation of four curriculum structures shaped by the relationship between content and process. For the sake of distinguishing among these structures, we talk about the more extreme ends of the continua represented by the horizontal and vertical axes. However, as curricula are planned and carried out, they are rarely as cut and dried as these descriptions may make them appear. With this caveat in mind, let's consider the horizontal axis which focuses on the relative emphasis given to content and process. Those who lean toward the left-hand end of the continuum tend to conceive of curriculum as the delivery of formal bodies of knowledge. While those inclined toward the right-hand end of the continuum also value formal bodies of knowledge, they also place emphasis on contextualizing knowledge in experience.

"Learn then act" might be the motto of those who are drawn toward the left-hand side of the horizontal continuum. Mastery of existing knowledge is seen as an essential precursor to practical action. Successful students are those who are able to accurately reproduce, and eventually apply, formal knowledge. On the cover page for Section I, we quoted John Holt's view that we do not "learn and then do" but rather "we learn by doing," and this might be the motto for those drawn to the right-hand side of the horizontal axis. Successful students are able to immerse themselves in the experiences of the curriculum, deliberate with others, and construct individual and collective meanings. Through this process, they acquire not only content knowledge, but also skills for experiential and contextual learning.

The relative weight given to content and process leads, in turn, to different roles for those who enact a curriculum. The bottom end of the vertical axis represents a role that emphasizes transmission of formal knowledge. The upper end of the axis emphasizes facilitation of process.

Again, most curriculum structures are hybrids where focus on content and process shift from foreground to background and back again. Similarly, those enacting curricula may at times assume the role of knowledge transmitter and at other times process facilitator. It is, however, useful to delineate them for purposes of conceptualizing overarching curriculum structures.

Those who assume that subject matter is the centerpiece of curricula may assume that other approaches are unstructured. In reality, curriculum structure is shaped not only by the sequencing of content but by the allotment and use of time, the arrangement of space, and relationships between teacher and student(s) and among students. These facets of curriculum structure are often so ingrained that they go unnoticed until something unexpected takes place.

Maria is reminded of a professor from a dental school who was participating in a multi-disciplinary faculty workshop aimed at developing courses on the care of geriatric patients. To begin what would be an extended deliberative process, workshop participants were seated at round tables and invited to introduce themselves and talk a little about their school's current curriculum. At the end of the day, the dental school professor commented, "I was totally freaked out. I didn't know what was going to happen next. Were we going to be sitting on the floor beating drums?!" For this professor, the shift from impersonal, auditorium seating to round tables signaled a disorienting change in curriculum structure. Gina experienced a similar disorientation when Marjorie stepped out from behind the podium and entered into a conversational circle with her English literature students. The angry mother who accused Brianne of cheating her son out of a serious education may also have been caught in a misconceived assumption that play, with its appearance of free-flowing action, could not possibly be educative. Rather than narrowly equating curriculum structure with the organization of information, it is useful to consider the organizing principles that shape various curriculum structures (Figure 6.2).

The issue is not whether one structure is inherently superior to others. Trade-offs must be made no matter which approach is taken. Which tradeoffs are necessary or acceptable often come down to curriculum decision-makers' beliefs about what is worth learning. In the following section we look a bit more closely at each structure.

FIGURE 6.2 - ORGANIZING PRINCIPLES

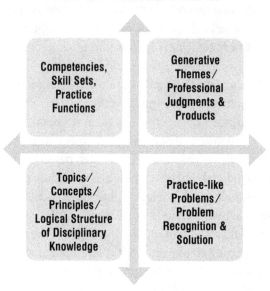

Information-Centered Structure

FIGURE 6.3 - INFORMATION-CENTERED CURRICULUM STRUCTURE

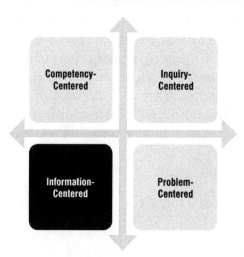

Information-Centered curricula are typically organized by topic areas that are meant to help students grasp important facts, concepts, and principles within formal bodies of disciplinary knowledge. Well into the twentieth century this curriculum structure dominated secondary and post-secondary education.

Often a building-block metaphor is used to describe curricula structured through the delivery of chunks of information. Well-organized curricula move systematically from simpler, more basic information blocks to increasingly complex and abstract knowledge. Advocates for the Information-Centered structure argue that students need an in-depth grounding in the basics in order to think about complex problems they will encounter in the future. As students proceed through successively more challenging curricula, they are socialized into a discipline's or profession's way of thinking.

In the Information-Centered structure, teachers are expected to deliver substantive, accurate content in an organized, manageable, and understandable manner. Students are expected to attend carefully to the information presented, commit it to memory, and recall it as needed. Paulo Freire critiqued this curriculum structure using a banking metaphor which presumes that students are empty vessels into which knowledge is deposited.[3] In the age of the Internet students enter classrooms as anything but empty vessels waiting to be filled. Further, with the speed of information-access, students may not be as willing to acquiesce to the pace of learning set by teachers.

Another difficulty associated with Information-Centered curricula is the potential mismatch between the teacher's conceptual organization of knowledge and the student's capacity to receive it. Since her days of working with faculty in a school of pharmacy, Maria has been fond of characterizing this mismatch as a lack of receptor sites. In order for medicines to be effective, they must bind with specific cells. If the body lacks those receptor cells, the medicine can't do its job. Metaphorically, when students lack receptors for the knowledge being presented, they may not be able to retain it. The more psychological metaphor for creating receptivity is "cognitive scaffolding," an apt allusion to the building block view of knowledge acquisition. The use of advanced organizers is also meant to increase receptivity.

Traditionally, the lecture has been the dominant mode for delivering content in Information-Centered curricula. Indeed, the lecture is often used synonymously for this curriculum structure. With the advent of technology, lectures have been augmented with slides, films, and videos. Still, the underlying intent is the transmission of knowledge. Currently, the most ubiquitous media enhancement for lectures is PowerPoint. Ironically, teachers steeped in the lecture tradition often end up reading word-for-word from their PowerPoint slides even when they have provided students with a verbatim handout. The assumption seems to be that if the teacher doesn't say it, the students can't grasp the information.

Historically, reliance on the lecture made sense. Before printed books became widely available and affordable, those who wanted to learn had to rely on those with more advanced knowledge. In this day and age, however, information can be delivered through multiple modalities including assigned readings, on-line course platforms, Internet-accessible videos, etc. In an ironic turn, textbooks have become so expensive many students do not buy them. Instead, they rely on lecture notes, which they argue, are more relevant for test preparation. This latter sentiment points to another limitation of the Information-Centered curriculum structure. When students do not have sufficient understanding of how the information may ultimately be useful, successful performance on tests can become an end in itself. If passing a test marks the closure of a learning episode, knowledge may not transfer from one course to another. Nor may knowledge blocks from multiple courses be integrated and transferred beyond school settings.

In an effort to offset these limitations, teachers working within an Information-Centered structure may use a variety of techniques to illustrate and reinforce the significance of knowledge. Class discussions and recitation sessions, for example, may give students a chance to exchange their understanding of lecture material. Case studies may illustrate situations in which knowledge is applied.

Before considering the next curriculum structure, we want to say a few words in defense of lectures. While information-transmission as an overarching curriculum structure has significant limitations, lecture as an instructional modality can have strategic uses. A well-presented lecture may serve as an advanced organizer, alerting students to areas of learning that lie ahead. Lectures can also be a source of inspiration as more than one student has said in effect, "I fell in love with this subject because of my professor's lectures"; or "She brought the subject alive for me"; or "That lecture just triggered something in me. I became fascinated and couldn't get enough of it." Lectures can also be an expeditious way to gain insight into a subject as for example TED Talks, the Great Courses packages, and community-based lectures by noted authors. Lectures can also play a vital role in helping students cope with information overload. Even a short Google search can provide a barrage of information on virtually any subject. Lectures can offer insights that help students to sort through this wealth of information, analyze the merits of various sources, and put the bits and pieces into a bigger picture.

Competency-Centered Structure

FIGURE 6.4 - COMPETENCY-CENTERED CURRICULUM STRUCTURE

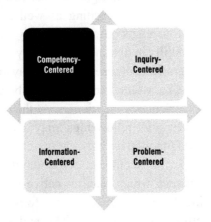

In an effort to ameliorate some of the limitations of the Information-Centered curriculum structure, Competency-Centered curriculum began to emerge. As mentioned previously, the behavior theory of learning shifted attention from <u>instructional</u> objectives (what a teacher would do) to <u>learning</u> objectives (what students would demonstrate). This shift contributed to a reformulation of curriculum structure organized around clusters of increasingly complex cognitive and psychomotor skills related to functions of practice.

In the Competency-Centered Structure, teachers (or curriculum developers) generally retain responsibility for deciding both the substance and sequence of the curriculum. A major difference, however, is shortening the time between the presentation of information and students' demonstration of skill sets associated with that information. In this structure, teacher responsibilities often include demonstrations of techniques and procedures as well as coaching students as they practice skills. The coach-student roles take on the attributes of the master craftsman-apprentice model as novices progress under the watchful eye of those who have already attained an advanced level of proficiency.

Within the Competency-Centered structure, a variety of instructional strategies may be used to support student learning. Lectures may be used to explain the theoretical underpinnings of particular competencies. Case studies serve not only to illustrate practical application of knowledge and skills but may also allow students to practice applying their knowledge to specific types of situations. Learning groups may include opportunities for peer coaching as well as for the practice of team-work skills. Site visits/observations may be incorporated so that students can see skills in action. Vocationally oriented secondary curriculum and undergraduate degree programs may include practicums and internships where knowledge and skills can be applied under the guidance of more experienced practitioners. At the post-graduate level specialized residencies and fellowships may extend Competency-Centered learning into practice settings.

One strength of the Competency-Centered structure is the emphasis on performance which requires active student engagement. Curriculum building blocks often take the form of modules with well-defined objectives, resource materials, and assessments. Such modules create opportunities for greater flexibility in terms of the time students need to complete them and the opportunity to review previous modules if misunderstandings occur. When accompanied by preliminary assessments, students may be able to skip modules focused on material they already know. Students might also have greater self-determination in choosing the order in which they study the modules, including opportunities to move back and forth among them rather than being locked into a prescribed sequence. All of these possibilities have exploded with advances in computer technology and the resulting proliferation of cyber-based schools and distance education programs. In spite of these strengths, the Competency-Centered structure does have some limitations.

One limitation has been mentioned previously. Namely, the mastery of specific skills or competencies does not necessarily add up to competence. In short, competence is more than the sum of the parts. A second limitation is lack of transfer of competencies. Because teachers still structure the times and situations in which students apply knowledge/skills, students may not, on their own, recognize when particular skill sets should be put into play. Further, just because students have mastered a skill does not mean they willingly use it. A classic example is youngsters who demonstrate reading skills in school but avoid any type of voluntary reading. Another limitation tends to be student reliance on teachers to plan and organize learning processes. They may be honing learning skills that serve them well in formal educational settings, but lack the skills necessary to learn through experience. Explicit attention on "learning to learn" is one quality that distinguishes the right-hand side from the left-hand side of the horizontal axis. We return to this point momentarily, but first we consider the issue of assessment in the Competency-Centered structure.

At its best, Competency-Centered assessment allows for a developmental approach to learning. If students are expected to master competencies, then incremental assessments can provide feedback on how students are progressing toward that goal. Various schema have been proposed for tracking skill development. One differentiates among the following:

- Unconscious incompetence—a stage when students don't know what they don't know. Students who see no relevance in curriculum content or disparage the importance of certain types of knowledge may be stuck in this stage.

- Conscious incompetence—a stage when students know, at least broadly, what they don't know and demonstrate a willingness to engage in the learning necessary to gain knowledge and skills.
- Conscious competence—a stage when students attend deliberately, often self-consciously, to specific aspects of a particular competence. Performance may be awkward or halting. Frequent reminders from coaches may be needed.
- Unconscious competence—a stage when students have internalized the competencies and are able to perform them smoothly and automatically as needed.

The classic example of movement from Conscious Incompetence to Unconscious Competence is learning to drive a car. The would-be driver knows there is much to learn (e.g., rules of the road, braking distance, acceleration, parking, 3-point turns) and is willing/eager to learn. At first careful attention is given—have I adjusted the rear-view mirror; have I released the parking brake, have I put the car in gear; have I signaled a change of lane; do I have the right of way or does that other car have it? With practice, these routines become automatic. Philosopher of science, Michael Polanyi, called this tacit knowledge.[4] The tools (and knowledge) we use become so ingrained we no longer notice them unless something unexpected or unusual calls them back to mind. For example, experienced drivers usually do not have to give much thought to the clearance needed to pass other cars. However, more attention might be required if one is driving a U-Haul truck.

Another developmental approach to assessment has the following stages:

- Non-readiness—a stage akin to Unconscious Incompetence
- Readiness—a stage akin to Conscious Incompetence
- Developmental—a stage requiring a great deal of coaching
- Practice—a stage when learners are continuing to master skills, but are able to do so more independently; they are able to articulate questions and ask for help when they need it; mistakes are fewer apart and learners are able to catch and correct them on their own.
- Demonstration—a stage when learners are ready to have their skills formally assessed; the results of the demonstration may

indicate a need for further practice or that an adequate threshold of performance has been attained.

- Mastery—a stage akin to Unconscious Competence
- Skillful artistry—a stage of on-going learning in which proficiency and nuance continue to develop

The process of learning to read exemplifies these stages as youngsters advance from recognizing single letters to seamlessly reading books. This example points to one of the difficulties with assessment in Competency-Centered curriculum. Theoretically, students should have as much time as necessary to move from readiness to mastery. Unfortunately, structuring formal education into semesters and school years puts limits on how much time learners have. If they require more than the "normal" time allotted for learning, they have failed. There is a difference between failing to master skills within an arbitrarily designated time and being a "failure." Yet, too many students do not make this distinction and begin to internalize the self-image of "failure."

Despite the downside of time-limitations, assessment of skills can reduce the guesswork of gauging one's progress. Rubrics and check lists specify sequences of skills thereby providing insight into where more practice is needed. When shared with students, rubrics can promote more accurate self-assessment. Increasingly sophisticated computer simulations allow for assessment of integrated, rather than fragmented, skills sets. They can also provide almost instantaneous feedback to guide further learning. At their best, competency-centered assessments can increase learner engagement and autonomy. They can also help students prepare for professional certification and licensing examinations. At their worst, passing assessments may become an end in itself as happened during the testing-mania associated with No Child Left Behind.

Problem-Centered Structure

FIGURE 6.5 - PROBLEM-CENTERED CURRICULUM STRUCTURE

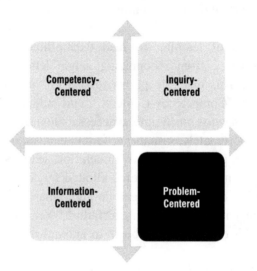

One reason faculty in professional schools began to shift from a Competency-Centered to a Problem-Centered structure was the lack of knowledge-transfer from school settings to the world of practice. In addition, research on expert practice began to reveal that expert practitioners draw upon a repertoire of problem-patterns when confronted by practice situations. Given this, immersion in a sequence of problem-solving experiences serves as the organizing principle for the Problem-Centered curriculum structure. When curricula are organized around frequently encountered problems, students can begin to develop a repertoire of patterns from the outset of their education. With this organizing principle, learning is going on at two levels—the technical content to be mastered and the skills associated with problem solving. In terms of teacher education, a Problem-Centered curriculum might be structured using sequences of thorny pedagogical moments.

The Problem-Centered structure entails a reconfiguration of teacher and student roles. Typically, students work in teams on problems developed by the teacher. They are expected to analyze the problem, identify information needed to address it, use available resources to gather the requisite information, and formulate a response to the problem. Curricula structured in this way tend to promote Contextual Knowing because team members must take each other's ideas and perspectives into account and develop an integrated response. Thus, this curriculum structure promotes team-working skills (e.g., communication, planning, organizing) and the type of collaborative knowledge generation commonly required in work settings.

Because so much time is spent working within teams and doing research, it can seem as though teachers are "missing in action." Indeed, the apparent passivity of the teacher's role in Problem-Centered curricula may cause teachers to feel that they are "doing nothing" and that their wealth of knowledge is "going to waste." A common student complaint is voiced as, "I'm not paying all this money to sit around and talk with students who don't know any more than I do. I'm paying for you experts to tell me what I need to know."

In reality, teachers are anything but passive. Rather than being transmitters of knowledge, they become problem-designers. For problem scenarios to be educative, they must be richly textured and evocative in two ways. First they must create a virtual context in which to immerse students. Second, they must evoke questions that catalyze the students' search for relevant knowledge. Over the course of an entire program of studies, students move through increasingly complex problems. Problem-scenarios rather than topics become the backbone of the curriculum. Well-constructed problems typically require knowledge from multiple disciplines, which in turn, requires cross-disciplinary collaboration both in designing and teaching courses. The need for collaboration can be a significant limitation if teachers fear loss of autonomy as well as encroachment on their already limited planning time. Rewards that may accrue from such collaborative deliberation are likely to occur only after one experiences such a process. So, just as students must have faith that the inductive problem-centered approach will "pay off" in the end, teachers must have faith that their joint efforts will be worth it. Whether the potential benefits of either process are realized depends on the extent to which individuals are willing to risk authentic engagement.

Once a Problem-Centered curriculum is initiated, teachers serve as process-guides, information resources, and debriefing coaches. These roles entail sophisticated pedagogical skills as well as a willingness to be vulnerable and spontaneous. Likewise, the student role of problem-solver entails a high degree of engagement, tolerance of ambiguity, willingness to be vulnerable, and risk-taking. Students who have been successful in Information-Centered and Competency-Centered curriculum structures may become highly anxious within a Problem-Centered structure. To alleviate their anxiety, they may seek out those who have already dealt with the problem-solving scenarios to find out the "right" answer. If a body of folklore about the problems is passed from one cohort of students to another, the intent of the Problem-Centered curriculum is undermined. This also creates an additional burden on teachers as they must constantly generate new problem-scenarios. Despite these difficulties, teachers and students who are willing to experience these different roles often come to value the vitality of the learning experience.

It may seem that lectures have no place in a Problem-Centered curriculum. This is far from the truth. However, lectures play a very different role. Rather than front-loading information for use at a later time, lectures often come after the students' problem-solving experience. Having heard and observed the students as they engaged in problem-solving, the teacher is able to identify and address points of misunderstanding. Once students have experienced contextualized problem-solving, they can be more attuned to additional information presented through lectures. Another critical difference is that lectures are only one of many sources of information that students are expected to use. Textbooks, library and Internet searches, prior experience, interviews, trial and error, etc. become key sources of information.

Some might argue that this approach is less efficient and more time-consuming than the Information-Centered structure. This is a valid argument when only the time of knowledge-transmission is considered. However, if the transmitted knowledge is not transferred and utilized beyond the classroom, then one can argue that the time has been wasted. In addition, the structure of the Information-Centered curriculum tends to promote a unidimensional use of time. In other words, each segment of instructional time is devoted to covering a narrow, perhaps singular, chunk of content. In the Problem-Centered structure, instructional time is used to immerse students in an experience that can lead to multidimensional learning (e.g., content from multiple disciplines, problem-solving skills, team work skills).

Assessment in the Problem-Centered structure presents several issues. On the plus side, a key criterion for assessment can be the adequacy of the problem-solution. In the world of practice, competence is not measured by artificial tests but by results. Debriefing problem solutions can help students assess how well they understood the problem, how thoroughly they addressed it, the efficacy of their proposed solution, and any unintended, and potentially damaging, consequences. They can weigh the merits of information gleaned from various sources. As students accumulate a repertoire of problem patterns and responses, they can begin to extrapolate underlying principles that provide both structure and flexibility for dealing with future problems. Proponents of the Information-Centered structure might say this is a wasteful exercise in "re-inventing the wheel." If experts have already formulated principles to guide practice and if researchers have determined "best practices," then why not just relay these to students? Why put them through all the time-consuming effort to figure it out for themselves? It goes back to the receptor sites. The contextualized experience of problem-solving creates sites where students can anchor knowledge in a way that makes sense to them. This, in turn, allows them to retain and retrieve the knowledge when needed. In short, they come to own and understand it.

Because teamwork is so integral to the Problem-Centered structure, it can create assessment difficulties, especially when it comes to grading. Students might argue that they should be assessed only on their content knowledge. If they have been assigned to a dysfunctional team, they should not be penalized. Why should marginally contributing team members benefit from the work of others? Will students who are used to working collaboratively in teams be handicapped when they have to take credentialing exams on their own? These issues are not easily resolved, but the key to thinking about them lies in how one answers the question, "What is worth learning?"

As teachers gained experience with the Problem-Centered structure, several limitations became apparent. Because problems are pre-designed and assigned, students may be inclined to look for a "right" answer—i.e., "right" in the eyes of the teacher as accepted authority. More significant is the limitation of presenting "well formed" problems. As discussed in Chapter 3, contexts of practice are messy, and problems rarely appear in clearly identified packages. Thus, problem-solving competence entails a capacity to discern a problematic situation and to frame it in a way that leads to a satisfactory resolution. To promote the development of these capacities, some teachers began to design "ill-formed" problems. Such problems are not sloppily conceived. Rather they are fraught with ambiguities that can be framed in many different ways. This can promote the "what if" thinking associated with contextual knowing. What can I do if I frame it this way? What can I do if I frame it another way? Ideally, "what if" thinking becomes generative as students begin to pose questions for themselves. The capacity to generate significant questions is important in the Problem-Centered curricula; it lies at the very heart of an Inquiry-Centered curricula.

Inquiry-Centered Structure

FIGURE 6.6 - INQUIRY-CENTERED CURRICULUM STRUCTURE

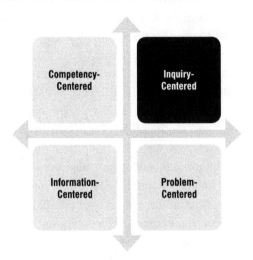

Inquiry-Centered curricula aim to engender proficiency with the type of learning outlined in Chapter 2—i.e., learning as

- experiential,
- meaning-making,
- relational,
- situated (contextualized),
- recursive,
- discursive,
- deliberative, and
- reflective.

"Learning to Learn" fosters Contextual Knowing which better serves professionals than Absolute, Transitional and Independent Knowing. "Learning to Learn" supports the transition from *knowing* to *understanding* in Lee Shulman's sense of the word.

The building block metaphor commonly associated with Information-Centered curricula evokes an image of a craftsperson carefully laying one block upon another until some edifice is constructed. The edifice is the craftsperson's creation which others can enter but not alter. Entering a well-constructed building (i.e., curriculum) can be very reassuring. The boundaries are clear. The path from one "room" to the next has been laid out. Guesswork is reduced, if not eliminated. Someone is at hand to provide directions or signs may be posted with arrows clearly pointing "this way."

Another popular metaphor, often used with the Competency-Centered curriculum, is the road map. This is akin to the American Automobile Association's "Triptik." The traveler has a specific destination in mind and the helpful agents at AAA provide a detailed map of how to get there.

Both the building block and road map versions of curriculum can be comforting in that uncertainty is minimized and effort is not wasted. But this can be confining, even oppressive. There is little sense of adventure, wonder, excitement, serendipity, or discovery. For this reason, we offer a different metaphor for Inquiry-Centered curricula—a journey. The image of *journey* suggests a more leisurely pace with time for exploration, side trips, even alternations in the final destination. The point of a journey is the experience of the journey itself. It is not simply a necessary means to some end point. Curriculum scholar Dennis Sumara echoes this metaphor when he describes curriculum as "laying down the path while walking." It is the walker who creates the journey.

The journey metaphor calls to mind the origin of the word "curriculum" which derives from the Latin *currere* meaning to run, to run the course of. The connotation of curriculum, then, is the course or path one's mind runs on. Inquiry-Centered curriculum is predicated on the notion that individuals are pursuing matters of interest and concern to themselves. These matters set the journey in motion and, in the course of the journey, individuals may enter formal education programs. The structure of Inquiry-Centered curricula is meant to support—not prescribe—each traveler's journey.

In Chapter 3 we introduced Jenny who entered a formal teacher education program to learn exactly what she needed to know so that she would, at all times, do exactly the right thing. Imagine her confusion, consternation, and anxiety upon entering an Inquiry-

Centered curriculum. Imagine her crying in desperation, "It's so unstructured! Will somebody just tell me what I'm supposed to do?" Imagine a teacher responding, "You are supposed to learn how to learn. You are supposed to take charge of your learning. You are supposed to engage authentically in the experiences of the program. In the end, you are supposed to produce a product that will represent what you have learned from these experiences." In all likelihood this response would escalate Jenny's anxiety into full blown panic, because nothing in the response fits with her preconceived notion of the way education is supposed to be.

Like many who have excelled in Information-Centered and Competency-Centered curriculum structures, Jenny has no receptor sites to hold on to what the teacher is saying. She has well developed receptor sites for acquiring Absolute Knowledge, but few, if any, for grasping the concept of Contextual Knowledge. One might say Jenny is at the readiness (or non-readiness) stage of unconscious incompetence. She is trying to make sense of this experience in light of what she has already experienced. What Jenny doesn't realize is that she has come to a cross-road on her path to becoming a teacher. As Robert Frost would say:

> Two roads diverged in a yellow wood,
> And sorry I could not travel both
> And be one traveler, long I stood
> And looked down one as far as I could
> To where it bent in the undergrowth...[5]

The poignancy of Frost's image lies in the realization that where each path ultimately leads is unknown. Jenny has a choice. She can retreat to the familiar or she can move forward into a new paradigm of learning. What characteristics can help those like Jenny understand this new paradigm?

First is the use of generative themes to provide an overarching structure for the curriculum. Typically, such themes would convey major areas of learning related to the functions and responsibilities of a profession. These themes encompass subthemes which become the focus of specific contrived educational encounters. Consider the Scholar-Practitioner quality of Pedagogical Wisdom. At the broadest level, the generative theme might be "responding with Pedagogical Wisdom." Under this theme might be themes such as:

- Planning engaging lessons,
- Mastering instructional techniques,
- Creating safe spaces for learning, and
- Balancing authentic learning assessments with required accountability assessments.

Dealing with peer and cyber bullying might be subsumed under "creating safe spaces for learning." Successfully completing an anti-bullying workshop does not bring an end to learning about creating safe spaces nor to cultivating Pedagogical Wisdom. Thus, the Inquiry-Centered structure does not preclude educational programs with specific outcomes. Those outcomes, however, are seen within a broader framework which affords greater flexibility in pursuing further learning. For example, after an anti-bullying workshop, a special education teacher might want to explore the ways in which various social-emotional disabilities affect the nature of bullying and responses to it. A museum educator, on the other hand, might want to pursue different issues related to safe spaces in her context.

Because it is the learner who is laying down the path within the broader parameters of generative themes, the outcomes from one experience can engender a desire to explore the next turn in the road. In short, generative themes promote questions, curiosity, and desire for more learning. Once students grasp this point, they can more confidently take charge of the path their mind runs on. We are reminded of Aisha who announced in class, "I was at an in-service workshop yesterday. It was pretty Mickey Mouse. I mean it might have been helpful for others, but for me it was a waste of time. Then I had an epiphany. I realized that I have to go to district in-service programs, but I don't have to rely on the district to provide instruction on what I want to know. I can find other resources to answer my questions." Aisha radiated such a sense of empowerment as she shared her "ah hah" moment that other students could clearly see the wisdom of her insight. Engendering this sense of agency is a major aim of Inquiry-Centered curriculum. Often this is referred to as self-directed learning. Maria offers the following anecdote to illustrate that self-directed learning can be fraught with difficulty.

> As part of my doctoral coursework, I was required to take a course on statistics. Having never been very proficient in math and having no intention of using quantitative research methods for my dissertation, I resented having to "waste my time" on this course. It was clear to me, that the course instructor was fairly new to teaching. He exuded an aura of uncertainty and hesitancy. (Perhaps he was as unhappy as I was to be caught in this educational encounter.) Sensing his vulnerability, I used my newly acquired knowledge of self-directed learning to brow-beat the instructor into letting me do "my own thing." I no longer remember what "my own thing" was. I do vividly remember how years later, when I was teaching an introductory course on qualitative research, I desperately needed an understanding of statistics. Students that I was teaching were struggling to understand the difference between qualitative and quantitative research. I was struggling to make the difference clearer. In the pedagogical moments of that course, I realized that even a rudimentary knowledge of statistics would have helped me respond to student questions.

As laudable as it is for students to have a sense of agency for their own learning, when trapped in the stage of unconscious incompetence or non-readiness, opportunities for learning can be missed. For this reason, we have reservations about defining Inquiry-Centered curriculum as self-directed learning. Instead, we see it as involving both student and teacher in a discursive and deliberative relationship. Thus, the inquiry lies at the heart of the learning, not an isolated individual left to his or her own devices. This changes the roles of teacher and student.

Those planning and enacting an Inquiry-Centered curriculum are responsible for creating educational experiences that evoke issues and questions related to one or more generative themes and/or subthemes. They are meant to help students reflect on prior life experience in relation to the subject at hand and begin to identify avenues of inquiry they find meaningful to pursue. There is an expectation that the avenues of inquiry relate in some way to the themes/subthemes under study. In many instances, however, students may not be able to articulate that relationship until the end of the experience. At the outset, their efforts may be guided more by intuition and instinct than clearly specified goals, objectives or outcomes. This ambiguity can create anxiety not only in students but also in teachers. When Gina asked Marjorie, "Where's all this going?" the truthful answer is, "I don't know, but I have faith in you and this group that we will end up some place interesting, useful, and educative."

Over a course of study, students are immersed in a series of experiences—some devised by the teacher; others devised by the student(s); others spontaneously encountered in the course of daily life. The experiences contextualize issues related to the theme(s) under investigation. Learners are encouraged and supported as they examine these experiences through multiple lenses and from multiple perspectives. The experiences are not channeling everyone toward a pre-determined end. Each experience lays down a bit of the path allowing students and teacher to discern the next bend in the road.

Of necessity, there must be sufficient flexibility in the structure to accommodate adjustments as the curriculum unfolds. Communication is essential. So, too, are trust and faith in one's self, in the community of learners, and in the process. Trust and faith are earned as the journey proceeds, so entering into an Inquiry-Centered curriculum requires a willingness to risk involvement. This sense of risk is experienced by teachers as well as students, because everyone is vulnerable. Think back to the difference between formal and improvisational theater. Everyone in the improvisational scenario is vulnerable, because they don't know exactly what will happen next. They are "on the spot" to respond in ways that move the scene forward and readjust if a gambit doesn't work as hoped. All of this is done in front of an audience. Trust among the acting troupe (the community of learners) can develop only as individuals move beyond superficial pleasantries and self-protective, self-promotional conversations.

For those unfamiliar with Inquiry-Centered curriculum, its highly process oriented nature can create the impression that anything goes. What if, as was the case in Maria's ill-founded rejection of the statistics course, students "go off track"? And, how on earth is learning assessed; especially if everyone is doing something different? These are, indeed, serious concerns. Several checks and balances are inherent in well-planned Inquiry-Centered curricula. As mentioned above, conversation is essential. This is not casual conversation or ritualized class discussion. Nor does it mean (as the dental instructor feared) that students are baring their souls or revealing deep-seated secrets. Rather, it means individuals come together with a willingness to think together about substantive issues and do the hard work of discursive deliberation. It becomes a process of thinking together, perhaps on the same topic; perhaps on a variety of topics based on each learner's area of inquiry. The intent is to help students cultivate their capacity for Contextual Knowing; for learning as meaning-making; for pursuing their journey.

It would be erroneous to assume that lectures have no place in Inquiry-Centered curricula. As is the case in Problem-Centered curricula, lectures (or more often mini-lectures) can serve a variety of purposes: posing an educational conundrum; catalyzing reflection; reframing questions; challenging simplistic interpretations; debriefing aspects of the inquiry process, etc. Giving lectures can be especially tricky as the teacher doesn't want to reassert her or his role as AUTHORITY, yet has information worth sharing.

Learning Groups play an important role in Inquiry-Centered curricula. Although such groups comprise an arbitrary collection of class members, they serve as "surrogate" Communities of Practice. In other words, professionals are often required to work with groups of colleagues in practice settings. Contributing productively to group endeavors entails capacities that can be developed within the relative safety of contrived educational encounters. At their best, members of course-based groups can forge collegial relationships that continue beyond any given educational encounter. Such relationships can evolve into an important professional network.

The outcomes associated with Inquiry-Centered structure are represented by the final products that students create. Those products provide evidence of engagement in the learning process and the understandings that result from it. Above we mentioned that one aim of Inquiry-Centered curricula is to engender capacities for the type of learning described in Chapter 2 (experiential, discursive, deliberative, etc.). Another aim is engendering a sense of agency for one's learning. A third aim is to engender the students' capacity to make professional judgments and to evaluate the quality of those judgments. To be congruent with these aims, students must be able to exercise their judgment about the form and substance of their learning products.

As originally conceptualized, the portfolio is an example of a student-designed learning product. We say "as originally conceptualized" because within a few years of gaining popularity, the intent of portfolios was subverted. Because assessment of individualized portfolios is extremely labor-intensive, many teachers began to specify what should be included and to use standardized (and somewhat superficial) rubrics for evaluation. The idea of portfolios was borrowed from art and photography where they take the form of "working portfolios" and "best-works portfolios." The former contains work in progress and perhaps sketchy ideas for future projects. The latter showcases the creator's talents. Both forms have tremendous potential for assessment in Inquiry-Centered curricula. Working portfolios can provide a place for students to organize materials and try out various ways to represent ideas. They can be shared with teachers and peers as part of on-going discursive deliberation. And they can provide flexibility when the rigid time structures of grading periods make it unrealistic for students to create "best works portfolios."

As the name suggests, best works portfolios include samples of the creator's work. An artist, for example, might include samples of water color and oil paintings or pictures of sculptures, ceramics, or fabrics. Photographers might include black and white and color photographs of landscapes, people or events. Those in the performing arts use videos and audio recordings to showcase their talents. The point is that the artist decides what best represents her or his talents in a particular art form or medium. These portfolios are submitted as part of job interviews or competitions or shows. As such, the quality of the product (and by inference the capabilities of the artist) can be evaluated.

To return to our journey metaphor, portfolios contain artifacts of the journey and an explanation of why those artifacts are significant. A student's working portfolio, for example, might include drafts of papers, book summaries, field observation notes, or other such materials-in-process. A student's best work portfolio would include finished products (e.g., a completed research paper, a reflective essay about a practicum experience, an elegantly conceptualized lesson plan, a video of a classroom activity, a manuscript for publication). There is virtually an endless variety of products that students might choose to recount their journey and demonstrate what they learned from it. The flexibility afforded by digital portfolios can make the process of maintaining and updating materials far more user-friendly. The key point is that the <u>student chooses</u> and in so doing claims ownership of her or his learning.

Of course, this idealized view does not always play out in practice. One example still troubles us. Lindsey was part of a cohort enrolled in a five semester graduate program that the three of us co-taught. During the first four semesters she did not talk with us about the feedback she was receiving. She simply tried to guess what would "make us happy" so she could <u>be given</u> a high grade. By the fifth semester, when she finally expressed what she was genuinely thinking and feeling, the journey was rapidly drawing to an end. Even so, the journey need not be wasted. For example, she could have used a framework like that in Figure 2.2 (Chapter 2) to trace her journey toward a more authentic self-as-learner.

We elaborated on the idea of portfolios because they stand in contrast to assessment methods drawn from science (i.e., standardized tests). Curriculum structures in the left-hand quadrants of Figure 6.1 tend to align with the view that learning outcomes can be scientifically measured and that there is a value in comparing individual performance against group norms. Emphasis is on verification of what Donald Schon described as "rational technical knowledge."

Curriculum structures in the right-hand quadrants of Figure 6.1 aim to promote practical wisdom. Although there are undoubtedly scientifically inclined scholars who believe that wisdom can be measured, others would argue that efforts to measure wisdom would undermine its very nature. That said, it is still possible to evaluate learning that aims toward wisdom.

Decades ago, Elliot Eisner[6] pointed out that evaluation comprises two steps. The first is description—what is this thing we are evaluating. The second is judgment—what are the merits, worth or value of this thing. Within an Inquiry-Centered curriculum, students have a responsibility to describe their learning process and outcomes. This may be in the form of a traditional research paper, a portfolio, an article for publication, a grant application, curriculum modules, the possibilities go on and on. With this description in hand, it is possible to make a judgment about its merits. In contrast to "objective" measurement done unilaterally by a teacher, evaluation in an Inquiry-Centered curriculum calls for inter-subjective judgment by teacher and student. When both student and teacher have been open to authentic learning and have developed a trusting, discursive relationship, they can deliberate together on the value of what has been gained from the journey. A major criterion of value is the extent to which the learner was able to accomplish what he or she set out to do. Has the effort come to fruition? If not, what is missing; what remains to be learned? If so, what are the next horizon(s) for learning? At this point in the journey, the generative themes can be revisited to set directions for the next phase of the journey. In this way, learning becomes self-perpetuating throughout the span of one's professional life.

Curriculum Theory and the *Telos* of Education

As we said at the outset of the chapter, each curriculum structure has its strengths and limitations. Each structure presents specific challenges to both teachers and students. The preceding discussion barely touches the surface of the issues inherent in each. Indeed, one can spend a professional lifetime honing an understanding of and ability to enact any of the structures. Hopefully the thumbnail sketches in this chapter have peaked readers' curiosity and generated questions.

If, as Parker Palmer contends, we teach who we are, then weighing the tradeoffs among the various curriculum structures must take into account what we believe to be worth learning and, in turn, worth teaching. As we sort through our beliefs, it is crucial to keep in mind that the choices we make have ethical implications. One touchstone for considering the ethical implications of our choices is Dewey's concept of educative experience—i.e., experiences that promote the individual's desire and capacity for further learning. Another touchstone is Dwayne Huebner's view of learning as the journey of the self or soul. Whatever one chooses, our ethical obligation is to support, not undermine, the learner's journey. As Scholar-Practitioners cultivate their theoretic understanding, they are better able to articulate the rationale for their decisions. In the next chapter, we consider several strategies for cultivating theoretic understanding.

REFLECTIVE PROMPTS

What thoughts and feelings are evoked by the ideas in this chapter?

In what ways do my responses to the ideas in this chapter contribute to my understanding of being a Scholar-Practitioner?

What questions are evoked by the ideas in this chapter? Where do those questions fit within my plan for continued learning?

What ideas do I want to incorporate into my evolving Scholar-Practitioner Narrative?

Which of the four curriculum structures have I experienced? What was the experience like? Which curriculum structure(s) seem most conducive to my learning?

As I think about myself as a maturing Scholar-Practitioner, what do I consider worth learning? Have my ideas about this changed over time and if so, in what ways?

As I think about my role as educator, which curriculum structure(s) seem most congruent with my beliefs and values about "what is worth learning"?

When I think about the six Scholar-Practitioner qualities, in what developmental stage would I place myself?

NOTES

1 For extensive reviews of various schools of thought about curriculum see: *Understanding Curriculum: An Introduction to the Study of Historical and Contemporary Curriculum Discourses,* 5th Edition by Pinar et al.; *The Curriculum Studies Reader* by Flinders & Thornton; and *What is Curriculum Theory?*, 2nd Edition by Pinar. See the Bibliography for complete citation.

2 Pittsburgh Post-Gazette, March 22, 2018, p. A-4

3 Paulo Freire, *Pedagogy of the Oppressed.* 50th Anniversary Edition. Translated by Myra Bergman Ramos (New York: Bloomsbury Academic, 2018).

4 Michael Polanyi, *The Tacit Dimension* (Garden City, NY: Anchor Books, 1967).

5 Robert Frost, "The Road Not Taken," in *The Bedford Introduction to Literature: Reading, Thinking, Writing* 5th ed., Michael Meyer (Boston, MA. Bedford/St. Martin's, 1999), 976.

6 See Elliot W. Eisner, *The Art of Educational Evaluation: A Personal View* (Philadelphia: Falmer Press, 1985) and Elliot W. Eisner, *The Enlightened Eye: Qualitative Inquiry and the Enhancement of Educational Practice* (New York: Macmillan Publishing, 1991).

7

Cultivating Theoretical Understanding

In Chapter 5 we discussed the importance of having multiple theoretical lenses through which to interpret pedagogical moments. In Chapter 6, we presented four different theoretical lenses for thinking about curriculum structures. We have also mentioned that for any area of study, multiple theoretical perspectives are likely to co-exist. Given all of this, it can be daunting to sort through answers to the following questions:

- What do I think?
- What is the basis for my thinking?
- Where does my thinking fit within a broader landscape of ideas?

These questions lie at the heart of Theoretical Understanding. Taking them seriously is no easy task, so we urge Scholar-Practitioners, especially those early in their careers, to be patient with themselves. Literature on professional competence suggests it takes ten years for practitioners to acquire sufficient mastery to feel confident in their work. Being able to look at pedagogical events through multiple theoretical frameworks is challenging under the best of conditions, let alone when one is immersed in the urgent demands of daily practice. Setting realistic expectations, giving oneself time and remaining open to ideas are crucial attributes for the cultivation of Theoretical Understanding. This is no sprint toward a finish line. It is a journey across a professional lifetime.

It is also a journey through some messy terrain, because it entails letting go of Absolute Knowing and recognizing that knowledge is:

- socially constructed within communities of discourse,
- dynamic and continually evolving,

- contested,
- value-laden, and
- political.

When one is hip-deep in the swampy lowlands of practice, it is easy to lose one's way. Our intent in Chapter 7 is to offer some touchstones for maintaining one's sense of direction.

Discourse Communities—Fields of Study

In the popular imagination, theories seem to pop into the minds of solitary geniuses. Newton sitting under a tree is hit on the head by a falling apple and suddenly formulates the theory of gravity. Darwin sailing from the Galapagos Islands on The Beagle suddenly formulates the theory of evolution. Einstein has an "aha" moment and formulates the theory of relativity. While it is true that key intellectual figures have insights that advance (and even alter) our understanding of the world, they do not work in isolation. They are members of discourse communities dedicated to understanding particular aspects of our world.

Clusters of discourse communities studying related questions constitute a field of study. As we suggested in Chapter 6, curriculum is a field of study within the broader field of education. Within any given field of study, individuals are drawn to ask certain types of questions. Consider how questions about curriculum structures might differ among educators working within these various sub-fields:

- Early childhood, elementary, middle level, secondary, and post-secondary education,
- Professional education in teaching, educational administration, the health and human sciences,
- Special education as related to students with visual or hearing impairments, cognitive challenges, attention deficit/hyperactivity disorder, autism spectrum disorders; psychomotor difficulties,
- Multicultural education, culturally relevant/responsive pedagogy,

- Educational testing, measurement and evaluation,
- Community education such as museum education, leisure learning, corporate-based in-service education, and
- Educational policy and financing.

This list only skims the surface of fields of study under the umbrella of education.

Touchstone 1 flags the importance of (1) knowing that one is working/studying within a field, and (2) what field(s) lie at the heart of one's passions. The first point might seem too obvious to warrant mention. If, however, one considers curriculum, it is not uncommon for teachers to think of curriculum as a series of design tasks. As suggested in Chapter 6, how one approaches design tasks is shaped by broader conceptions of curriculum. These broader conceptions represent positions within curriculum as a field of study.

Figure 7.1 - Touchstone 1: Know the Field(s)

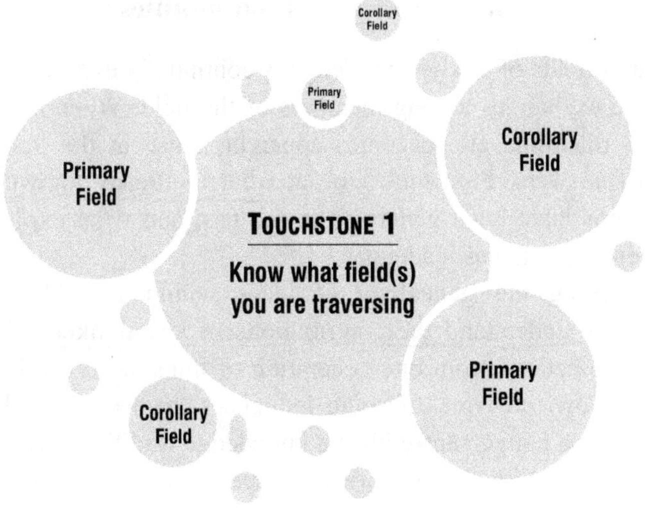

The central circle in Touchstone 1 represents the major field with which a Scholar-Practitioner identifies. As indicated by the smaller circles, Scholar-Practitioners may have corollary interests that take them into related fields of study. The outlying circles represent areas or fields of study that may be of moderate interest or fall into the category of "someday I'd like to learn about that."

Having in mind one's central and corollary fields of study can help Scholar-Practitioners remain oriented. As new information and ideas are encountered, they can be placed within a field and given some priority for learning. Understanding one's field provides anchor points (receptor sites) for information.

As a side note, we mentioned in Chapter 6 that lectures can provide useful glimpses into ideas that may not be central to one's interests. The peripheral circles for Touchstone 1 illustrate this point. Take the small circle in the lower left side of the figure. If it represents an area of interest that one has no time to pursue, wouldn't it be terrific to hear a lecture by an expert in the field who can provide at least a glimpse into that world of ideas?

Dynamic Knowledge Constructed
within Discourse Communities

Within fields of study, knowledge is continually evolving through discursive exchanges among members of the field. When a problem, question, dilemma, etc. becomes apparent, those in the field go in search of answers. First they look at what is already known—what explanations have been generated in the past and what explanations have been discarded as inadequate.

By tracing the genealogy of ideas within a field, Scholar-Practitioners understand the contributions of key thinkers; they can see the connections from one generation of thinkers to another; they recognize how the work of some influences the work of others. In short, they are conversant with the knowledge traditions within their field of study. With this historical perspective, they can weigh the significance of current questions and issues. They can also gain insight into potentially useful avenues of investigation and avoid unproductive cul-de-sacs.

When Scholar-Practitioners encounter a question or problem, Touchstone 2 comes into play. The circles in Touchstone 2 represent several points. First, the small circles can be seen as troubling little thoughts or occurrences happening randomly over time. At some point, enough of these thoughts coalesce into the realization that something is going on. It may take some time and a little digging around to finally formulate a specific question—to think "this is what I want to know."

FIGURE 7.2 - TOUCHSTONE 2: KNOW THE HISTORY

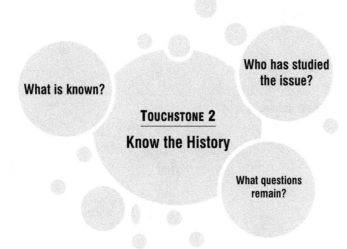

If Scholar-Practitioners are conversant with Inquiry-Centered processes, they are able to relate a key question to one or more generative themes and do a quick mental inventory of what they might already know. A Google search is often another quick way to start exploring what is known about the question. For Scholar-Practitioners, however, delving into discourses within the relevant field of study is imperative. This means reading scholarly literature.

This is the point at which the discursive nature of knowledge becomes apparent and potentially disorienting. We have met many students (even at the doctoral level) who approach a field of knowledge in search of THE answer to a question or problem. Such a quest is fruitless, because multiple schools of thought exist within and among communities of discourse. Often it takes quite a bit of time to sort through what various scholarly groups have proposed as answers to a question. As Touchstone 3 urges, Scholar-Practitioners need to develop strong information literacy strategies. While it goes beyond the scope of this chapter to discuss all the skills and strategies associated with information literacy, we offer thumbnail sketches of three: strong reading, concept mapping, and processing information.

FIGURE 7.3 - TOUCHSTONE 3: DEVELOP INFORMATION LITERACY

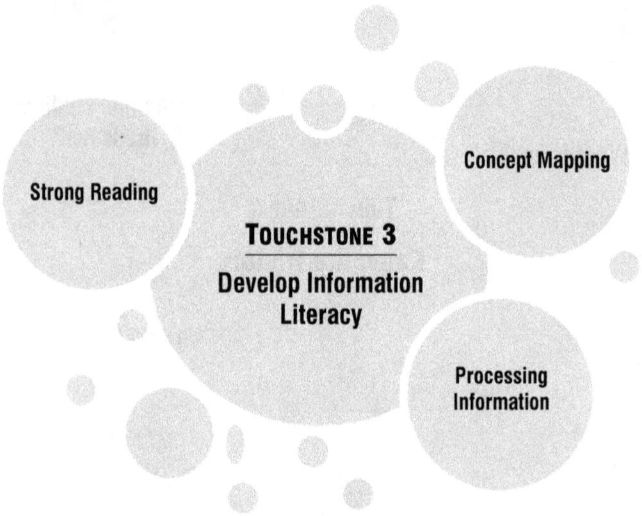

Strong Reading as David Bartholomae and Anthony Petrosky describe it

> ...can be the occasion for you to put things together, to notice this idea or theme rather than that one, to follow a writer's announced or secret ends while simultaneously following your own. When this happens, when you forge a reading of a story or an essay, you make your mark on it, casting it in your terms. But the story makes its mark on you as well, teaching you not only about a subject...but about a way of seeing and understanding a subject. The

> text provides the opportunity for you to see through someone else's powerful language, to imagine your own familiar settings through the images, metaphors, and ideas of others.[1]

This type of reading goes beyond casual perusal of an article or book and requires active engagement with the text. Bartholomae and Petrosky suggest that one can read both *with* and *against* the grain of an author's ideas. The former allows one to "read generously, to work inside someone else's system, to see your world in someone else's terms...It is a way of working *with* a writer's ideas..." The latter approach encourages one "to read critically...to ask questions they believe might come as a surprise, to look for the limits" of the author's vision and "find examples that challenge" the author's argument.[2]

Strong reading allows Scholar-Practitioners to discern various discourse communities that illuminate their educational practice. The more one reads, the more attuned one becomes to the multiple voices engaged in the discourse. Inevitably, one tends to gravitate more towards some voices than others. In this way, it is possible to situate one's thinking within the broader knowledge landscape.

One obstacle to cultivating theoretic understanding is an all too human impulse to accept ideas based on whether we agree or disagree with them. Two versions of **Concept Mapping** can help to curb this impulse. The first is a **Concept Map of Discourses**.[3] In creating such a map, the purpose is not to find the right answer to one's questions. Nor is it to find those with whom one agrees and dismiss everyone else. Rather, the purpose is to discover the various schools of thought embedded in a field of study. As a map is constructed, it illuminates the relationships among those schools of thought.

In discussing the Theoretical Understanding of curriculum, we underscored the importance of asking, "What is worth learning and who decides?" In higher education, university professors—either individually or collectively; consciously or tacitly—decide how newcomers to a field will be introduced to various schools of thought. Often, students do not recognize this curricular purpose and, if they are seeking only validation of their existing ideas, very sticky pedagogical moments can arise. Consider an incident that made headlines when a male student enrolled in a religious studies program objected to a professor's showing of a TED talk by a transgendered speaker in her course on "Sin, Self, and Salvation." The professor then specified that women in the class would have the opportunity to speak first during the discussion. It is not clear from the media reports whether the male student objected to the content of the TED talk, the professor's instruction that female students would speak first, or some combination of the two. His reaction was fueled by what he deemed the "constant misuse of intellectual power in universities" apparently related to the presentation of ideas about gender that contradicted his own. The situation got out of hand, the professor wanted to bar this "disruptive" student from the course, and the student threatened to sue for violation of his first amendment right to free speech.[4] Here is a situation in which a Concept Map of Discourses within Religious Studies would have been useful. As much as the male student might object at a personal level to the professor's choice of instructional materials and discussion guidelines, he could have recognized them as representative of ideas within the field he had chosen to study. He might have created a map anchored by "traditional" religious perspectives and "feminist" religious perspectives. He could then have listed scholars in the field as aligned more with one position or the other—putting into perspective his professor's position and his own. Although this is no guarantee that civil discourse and insightful deliberation would have ensued, it had the potential to be more educative than the debacle that occurred. Or perhaps not, because knowledge claims grounded in different world views can be vehemently contested. Our point is simply that understanding the schools of thought encompassed within one's field of study can be difficult and Concept Maps of the Discourses can be useful in generating questions for further study by asking what accounts for various schools of thought. We also underscore the point that choosing to study a field carries with it a responsibility to learn the field rather than ratifying one's preconceptions and assumptions.

A **Personal Concept Map** creates a picture of one's evolving understanding of a question or issue. To create a map, one simply takes a blank sheet of paper, draws a circle in the middle, and writes a concept (or question or issue) in the circle. Then one brainstorms as many associated ideas as come to mind. Relationships among ideas are depicted by connecting lines. An advantage of this technique is delaying premature judgments about one's agreement or disagreement with ideas. Consideration is given to where the idea fits in relation to ideas one already has in mind.

Concept mapping can be a useful technique because it does not require linear thinking. It also allows for the incorporation of ideas and information without having to decide exactly where they fit. Repositioning individual ideas or clusters of ideas is relatively easy. Maps can be fashioned and refashioned to show different relationships among ideas. It's not unusual for initial maps to be fairly "thin," having few associated concepts and few connections among them. This can help to identify areas where additional learning is needed. Keeping successive versions of the map can illustrate how one's understanding is growing richer as more ideas and more connections are added.

Both forms of maps can provide a generative context for on-going learning. Such contexts can simultaneously affirm and challenge a Scholar-Practitioner's understanding. It is affirming to belong to a community where one can feel reassured that, "I'm on to something important. My questions are worth asking. My insights into those questions can be of value." At the same time, being in conversation with others who are thinking differently is a constant reminder that we cannot take for granted what we think we know.

Processing Information Concept mapping is one method for processing information as it is encountered. As mentioned above, it is a non-linear method for recording and playing with ideas. This is, of course, only one of many different ways that Scholar-Practitioners digest information to make it their own. Some keep journals which allow for greater elaboration of one's thinking. Our colleague Wendy Milne, an elementary art teacher, uses an artist sketch book because she thinks in pictures. She uses the term "reflective artmaking" to describe her process of creating sketches and then adding explanatory notes.[5] Another colleague, Doug Conlan, sketches cartoons as he encounters ideas. Our colleague, Noreen Garman, keeps note cards to jot down ideas as they occur to her. The point is that there are many techniques that Scholar-Practitioners can use to keep track of new ideas and their thinking about those ideas.

Knowledge as Value-Laden

The transition from Absolute Knowing to Independent, Transitional, and ultimately, Contextual Knowing brings Scholar-Practitioners into the territory where knowledge is uncertain and multiple schools of thought co-exist within a given field of study. When no one in the field has a good explanation for a particular phenomenon, competing explanations may be debated in a civil manner. Judgments are suspended in the absence of compelling evidence that one explanation is definitively better than another. Everyone is open to potential avenues for studying the phenomenon as they metaphorically scratch their heads and think, "What on earth is going on here?" The scientific community's response to new epidemics like AIDS, Ebola, and West Nile Virus is a good example of this state of knowledge uncertainty. Researchers in many fields and sub-fields were searching for answers and sharing information as it emerged.

At other times, however, knowledge is hotly contested, sometimes in most uncivil terms. Individuals in the field are arguing for the superiority of their school of thought over others. This can be confusing and frustrating to those who just want an answer to a practical question. As one student exclaimed in exasperation, "What am I supposed to think! What am I supposed to do?" This brings us full circle to the difference between knowledge *per se* and "owning" knowledge or understanding. It brings us to the value-laden nature of knowledge and the idea of world view. (Touchstone 4.)

FIGURE 7.4 - TOUCHSTONE 4: UNDERSTAND WORLD VIEW

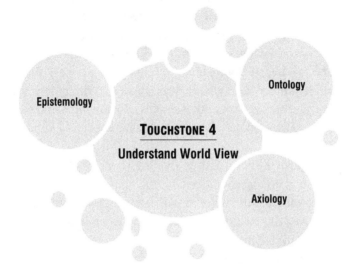

World view comprises the totality of what we believe, including beliefs about what is possible to know and what is worth knowing. These beliefs shape how we see ourselves and our world. They shape our actions. They are assimilated so early and are so ingrained that we may not even notice them until we encounter a jarringly different world view.

Since the 16th century, the dominant world view in Western Europe and the United States has been that of Newtonian science. This view was shaken by Eisenstein's theory of relativity, Heisenberg's uncertainty principle, and quantum physics.

The quest in Newtonian science is for certainty fueled by a belief that careful observation and measurement can get to the essence of a phenomenon as it exists apart from human subjectivity. Often this means reducing a phenomenon into its subcomponents. Just as a molecule can be subdivided into atoms, atoms can be subdivided into electrons, neutrons, and protons. This subdivision metaphor held sway until something disquieting happened. As atoms were further dissected, things became unexpectedly messy. Precise measurement was elusive.

Forces affecting Quarks in one location could affect other, distant Quarks. Light could be both a particle and a wave. Multiple universes could exist. The stuff of science fiction seemed closer to reality than we had ever imagined. These mysteries of the physical world jarred the Western world view of scientific certainty, causation, and even reality. The privileged dominance of science as the only method for generating legitimate knowledge was shaken. Within this space of uncertainty, discourses about other modes of knowing could emerge—including discourses on the ways in which knowledge of human affairs is generated.

What has all of this to do with cultivating Theoretical Understanding? Simply this. It is crucial to understand the nature of knowledge claims being put forward and the ways in which those claims are supported or warranted. Over the past decade or so, "evidence-based" has become the buzzword of choice in fields ranging from medicine to education. Usually "evidence-based" is shorthand for knowledge that has been generated and validated through a scientific method, through the world view of Newtonian science. Donald Schon[6] referred to this type of knowledge as rational technical. Barry Schwartz and Kenneth Sharpe describe it as rules. They go on to argue that:

> *best practices* Rules are aids, allies, guides, and checks. But too much reliance on rules can squeeze out the judgment that is necessary to do our work well. When general principles morph into detailed instructions, formulas, unbending commands—wisdom substitutes—the important nuances of context are squeezed out.[7]

Schon, Schwartz and Sharpe, and we are not arguing against the value of scientifically generated knowledge. We (and others) are arguing that scientific knowledge is necessary but not sufficient to understand human affairs. As Schwartz and Sharpe put it, "Rules can't tell practitioners how to do the constant interpretation and balancing that is part of their everyday work."[8] Thus, along with the knowledge claims of science are the knowledge claims of wisdom. Each form of knowledge is warranted by different forms of evidence. Each form of knowledge "generalizes" in its own way. Each form of knowledge has its own methods for "getting at" the nature of the phenomenon we are trying to understand. Collectively, these differences constitute distinctive world views—what C.P. Snow labeled "the two cultures"— science and art.[9]

Because the culture of science (Newtonian science to be more precise) has so dominated Western thinking, authors putting forward knowledge claims from this world view often do not make their assumptions about knowledge explicit. They work from the overarching belief that everyone shares their assumptions, in spite of the fact that this is not the case. Strong reading, therefore, entails a capacity to discern the assumptions that underpin the knowledge claims being put forward.

The small untitled circles in Touchstone 4 represent the myriad personal and social assumptions that can shape knowledge claims. To cultivate Theoretical Understanding, however, the most crucial assumptions are clustered under the concepts of epistemology, ontology and axiology—words that many students find intimidating. Indeed, their meaning is not easy to grasp, and at best this discussion gives only glimpses into the importance of these concepts.

Each concept considers a slightly different but interconnected question about knowledge. Epistemology focuses on the question, "What does it mean to <u>know</u> something?" Under this umbrella are assumptions about:

- the nature of knowledge,
- what counts as legitimate knowledge,
- what counts as evidence,
- criteria for judging the merits of knowledge claims,
- types of inquiry processes that generate knowledge,
- types of inquiry processes that cultivate wisdom,
- types of inquiry suitable for studying physical phenomena, and
- types of inquiry suitable for studying human affairs.

Ontology focuses on the question, "What is the <u>real or true nature</u> of a phenomenon we want to know?" Under this umbrella are assumptions about:

- the nature of human beings,
- the nature of our being in and relating to the world,
- what constitutes the essence of phenomena—their subcomponent parts or their holistic complexity,
- the role of human subjectivity and human consciousness in seeking the real/true nature of phenomena, and
- similarities and differences between physical phenomena and human affairs.

Axiology focuses on the questions,

- What is <u>worth</u> knowing?
- What forms of knowledge are valued?

As depicted in Touchstone 4, these clusters of assumptions are interconnected. To illustrate, let's briefly consider a question, "Why do some students succeed in school and other students fail?' Depending on one's epistemological, ontological, and axiological assumptions, one might tackle this question in different ways.

Those working in the field of educational psychology and holding assumptions embedded in the scientific tradition might think, "There is a psychological variable that accounts for this difference. If we can identify that variable, then we can predict which students are most at-risk for failing. Then we can devise interventions to modify that variable and help at-risk students succeed." Given this line of thinking, they might then select two groups of "subjects" to study—a group that has high grades and a group with failing grades. Then they might have both groups complete a battery of psychological tests. The results of the tests would be analyzed to determine any statistically significant differences between the two groups. If a particular personality trait (variable) stands out, that would become the focus for intervention and another round of research. One popular method for determining the effectiveness of an intervention is to give a pre- and post-assessment to the group under study. Another popular method is to have an experimental group that receives the intervention and a control group that doesn't. With either method, the hypothesis is, "If the intervention is effective, there will be a statistically significant difference either between pre- and post-assessment scores or experimental and control group outcomes." Despite the expenditure of millions and millions of dollars, this scientific approach to the question of student success or failure has yet to generate highly reliable knowledge claims. What is important to notice, however, is the ontological assumption that the essence (real cause) of the problem lies within individual psyches, and furthermore, within distinctive/specific psychological variables. An epistemological assumption is that valid knowledge would NOT be generated by asking students, parents or teachers to explain why particular students succeed or fail. This would be too subjective and idiosyncratic. The focus is on statistically substantiated patterns in groups of students. Further, for the knowledge claims to be considered legitimate, the results would have to be replicable across different groups of students and different contexts. Notice, also, that in this approach, students are treated as objects of study, the way one might study any other natural phenomenon. Other than their agreement to participate in the study, their in-put and reactions, thoughts and feelings, their life circumstances are set off as "limitations of the study." In this way, the risks of biasing results and undermining the legitimacy of the knowledge claims are minimized.

Now, let's consider the same question investigated by those holding a different set of assumptions. In this case, the starting ontological assumption is that student success and failure are rooted in socio-economic causes. The focus of study shifts from individual students to communities. Intra-psychic data give way to data about communities—some affluent, others economically distressed. Again, the identification of variables might drive the research. For example, it might be determined that children in affluent communities are more likely to attend pre-school and be better prepared to enter kindergarten than children in distressed communities. Having identified this variable, another round of research might begin; perhaps offering pre-school to children in distressed communities and then determining whether they are as well-prepared as students in wealthy communities or better prepared than those from distressed communities where pre-school was not offered. Here again is a search for cause and effect and an intervention that can reliably predict the efficacy of an intervention. Again, the assumption is that if we can find the patterns, identify the social variables, we can offer interventions that help individuals, ~~without having~~ studied individuals *per se*. Millions and millions of dollars have been invested in this type of research. As one result, compelling evidence exists to support the knowledge claim that providing pre-school through programs like Head Start can improve school performance for youngsters from low-income families. Ironically, however, the very discourse communities that lobby for school districts to comply with evidence-based teaching practices seem willing to cut funding for the evidence-based policy of universal preschool. This points to the contested nature of knowledge to which we return in a moment. First, let's consider a third scenario.

Here the starting ontological assumption focuses on the meaning of school for individual children. If we can understand what meaning the child makes of his or her schooling experience, then perhaps we can find ways to encourage and support more productive learning. To discern meaning, it is important to listen to students—listen in Alan Alda's sense of being fully present to the other. It is important to move past facile labels or debilitating stereotypes. This approach does not treat students as subjects (objects) of study, but as co-participants. Inter-subjectivity, not procedural objectivity, guides both the gathering and interpretation of information. Millions and millions of dollars have NOT been invested in this type of research. Rather, thousands and thousands (perhaps millions and millions) of teachers—Scholar-Practitioners—carry out these intimate inquiries as part of their work with students. The aim is not to generate KNOWLEDGE or generalizable rules. Rather, it is an accumulation of "stories," the narratives that children tell themselves about who they are, what they want from life, what possibilities are open or closed for them, how the "journey of their self" will evolve. Attending to these narratives can yield wisdom to guide one's response in pedagogical moments, with the humbling recognition that there is no certainty, no predictability, and no objectively verifiable, replicable outcome. This view brings into sharp relief the axiological assumption of what is worth knowing. Some (like Harvard University professor Steven Pinker,[10] for example) would read this description of intimate knowledge and dismiss it as useless in the face of the big picture questions. Others, laboring in the messy lowlands might find such person-centered knowledge/wisdom to be valuable.

In delineating these three scenarios, our intent is not to privilege one over the others. Investigations guided by the assumptions of all three world views yield valuable knowledge. Of importance for Scholar-Practitioners is knowing "where they plant their feet" as our colleague Noreen Garman puts it. Understanding one's own world view contributes to strong reading by creating greater awareness of an author's epistemological, ontological, and axiological assumptions. For example, the language we have used throughout this book should give readers a fairly clear idea of the assumptions that underpin our thinking and writing. For some, this use of language may be jarring and evoke skepticism, even rejection of the ideas being discussed. Others might resonate with the language and the view of educational practice being put forward. With an understanding of world view, Scholar-Practitioners are better prepared to understand the theoretical perspectives of others and to see where those perspectives reside within their personal concept maps and concept maps of discourses.

Knowledge as Contested and Political

As indicated above, multiple schools of thought exist within any given field of study. At times, the views complement each other, adding an important piece to a bigger puzzle. At other times, however, the views are hotly contested among members within a field of study and among fields of study. Differences in world view can be a driving force behind such debates. For example, throughout much of the 20th century, publication criteria for research articles were based on the assumptions of science. If scholarly work did not conform to those criteria, it was likely to be rejected. For faculty, whose promotion and tenure depended on publication, the exclusion of work that appeared to be "non-scientific" was a source of frustration and anger. Some responded by trying to force-fit their work into the norms of the scientific world view. The terms "social and human sciences" reflect efforts to study human affairs according to the precepts of the natural sciences.

Others—particularly those who had historically been marginalized—began to challenge the epistemology and ontology of white, male, Western European science. From the margins, new fields of study emerged to reflect the world as experienced by women, persons of color, and a range of gender identities. Giving voice to these experiences required methods of inquiry aligned more with the humanities than science. Narrative, for example, emerged as a major alternative mode of inquiry. Yet, even the term "alternative" connoted the privileged position of scientific inquiry.

Movements for civil rights, justice, and equality within society at large, also played out among scholars who argued for the legitimacy and worth of their work. Just as the broader social movements evoked heated debate, so, too, did the movements among fields of study. The legitimacy of knowledge gave rise to questions such as:

- Legitimate in whose eyes?
- Who has the right and expertise to judge the work of scholarship that draws from the traditions of the arts and humanities rather than the natural sciences?
- What constitutes worthwhile knowledge if it doesn't conform to the criteria of science?
- How are research funds allocated and are "alternative" forms of research unfairly excluded from sources of funding?
- How can knowledge from the margins be incorporated into mainstream discourses?
- Whose interests are served by including or excluding knowledge from the margins?
- Whose interests are being served when some knowledge claims are given widespread attention and other claims are relegated to the sidelines?

These are politically charged questions, and responses to them can be quite heated. Let's consider the example of No Child Left Behind. As a rhetorical slogan, this conjured a vision of a society where every child would receive the education needed for success. Regulations for enacting the law drew upon scientific measures of reading and math to determine whether the intent of the legislation was being fulfilled. Allocation of federal funding for education became tied to standardized test scores, and districts were held accountable for making annual yearly progress. Districts, fearing the loss of funds, held teachers accountable for assuring adequate student test-performance. Many educational scholars, teachers and parents KNEW that standardized test scores provided only a limited and skewed view of student learning. But that knowledge DIDN'T COUNT. Only the test scores were considered legitimate. So what had sounded like a lofty, noble social value devolved into teaching to the test, encouraging poorly performing students to skip test-taking days, and falsifying test results. Not every teacher, classroom, or district did this. But enough did that the objections of those who understood the disastrous consequences hidden beneath the rhetoric were finally heard and accountability measures modified. Ironically, the original legislation did not include adequate funding to really achieve its stated purpose. A great deal of funding went to for-profit companies that administer standardized tests. Some of the most impoverished districts (those who were ostensibly supposed to benefit from No Child Left Behind) suffered the most under the draconian accountability imposed by legislators who believed they KNEW that our education system is flawed and how best to fix it. Even the view that the US educational system is failing is based on narrow indicators valued by specific discourse communities. We hope this example serves to illustrate the political and contested nature of knowledge and brings us to Touchstone 5.

FIGURE 7.5 - TOUCHSTONE 5: UNDERSTAND THE POLITICAL NATURE OF KNOWLEDGE

Follow the money

Whose power is being exercised?

TOUCHSTONE 5

Understand the Political Nature of Knowledge

Whose interests are being served?

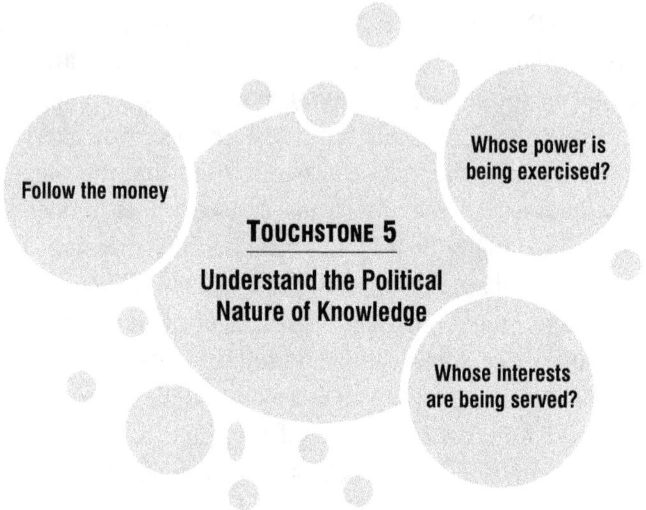

When knowledge is used to support a particular policy or to benefit a particular special interest group, the legitimacy of the truth claims can be suspect. For example, reports on the efficacy and safety of particular medications can be called into question if the pharmaceutical company that profits from the sale of the medicine has funded the research. Similarly, for-profit companies claiming the efficacy of their particular instructional package or supervisory technique or management system may draw upon knowledge claims that suit their purpose. Advocates and opponents of charter schools, educational inclusion, teacher-improvement approaches, standardized tests, or a myriad of other educational initiatives may be drawing selectively upon knowledge claims that support their particular agenda. When examining such claims, Scholar-Practitioners ask, "Who benefits? Whose interests are served? What type and source of knowledge are supporting or refuting the policy?" [11]

Cultivating Theoretical Understanding and the *Telos* of Education

Our aim in this chapter has been to illustrate the multifaceted, multi-vocal nature of knowledge within fluid, amorphous, and continually evolving educational discourses. Further, it has been to argue that Scholar-Practitioners need to enter into these discourses to understand the theoretical rationale for their decisions and actions. It is easy to become disoriented within the complex swirl of ideas. So of crucial importance is understanding the *telos* of education: understanding what it means "to educate." In this regard, scholars Walter Feinberg and Jonas Soltis offer distinctions among three world views:

> A functionalist perspective "…generally sees schools as serving to socialize students to adapt to the economic, political and social institutions" of society.

> A conflict theorist perspective "would generally view schooling as a social practice supported and utilized by those in power to maintain their dominance in the social order."

> An interpretivist perspective "…sees the social world as a world made up of purposeful actors who acquire, share, and interpret a set of meanings, rules, and norms that make social interaction possible."[12]

The language we use to talk about education points to underlying world views. Behavioral objectives, competency statements, and skill sets are conventions for expressing instructional intentions within a functionalist perspective. In contrast, Dwayne Huebner's interpretivist perspective sees education as a way to tend to the journey of the self or soul.[13] This view weds education to each person's struggle to realize his or her potential and to make meaning of her or his life. Certainly this view does not exclude the acquisition of knowledge and skills, or the cultivation of one's talents for the demands of work. But, it grounds education in a deeper existential reality that human beings are active agents in their own lives. Within this view, instructional intentions are more appropriately conveyed as learning opportunities or generative themes. The functionalist perspective translates into pedagogical approaches more akin to the scripted performances of formal theater. The interpretivist perspective supports improvisational pedagogy.

Schwartz and Sharpe offer this contrasting view of Rules Talk (the language of those who are seeking rational technical knowledge) and Wisdom Talk (the language of those seeking insights into the swampy lowlands of practice).[14]

RULES TALK...	WISDOM TALK...
...asks, What are the universal principles that should guide our moral choices?	...asks, What are the proper aims of this activity? Do they conflict in this circumstance? How should they be interpreted or balanced?
...tends to be about absolutes.	...is context talk—talk about nuance.
...sidelines, or even labels as dangerous, moral imagination and emotion.	...puts them at the center because they allow us to see and understand what needs to be seen and understood.
...ends with determining the right principle or rule to follow.	...ends with determining whether to follow it and how to follow it.
...marginalizes the importance of character traits like courage, patience, determination, self-control, and kindness.	...puts them at the center.
...urges us to consult a text or a code.	...urges us to learn from others who are practically wise.
...is taught by teachers in the classroom.	...is taught by mentors and coaches who are practicing alongside us

When considering the purpose to which they are committed, Scholar-Practitioners can begin by understanding whether they (like Pat's student Jenny) are seeking rules to follow or wisdom for enacting a moral practice.

As we draw this discussion to a close, we repeat our caution that Scholar-Practitioners be patient with themselves. Cultivating theoretic understanding takes time and serious study. It is a lifelong undertaking, not a task to be completed. It takes energy and commitment, an excitement for the world of ideas, a tolerance for ambiguity, an insatiable curiosity, a longing for deeper understanding of one's purpose within this complex human endeavor called education.

REFLECTIVE PROMPTS

What thoughts and feelings are evoked by the ideas in this chapter?

In what ways do my responses to the ideas in this chapter contribute to my understanding of being a Scholar-Practitioner?

What questions are evoked by the ideas in this chapter? Where do those questions fit within my plan for continued learning?

What ideas do I want to incorporate into my evolving Scholar-Practitioner Narrative?

How would I construct a Map of Discourses to represent my current understanding of various schools of thought within my field of study/ practice?

How can I represent my current understanding of myself as a Scholar-Practitioner through a Personal Concept Map?

How do I react when I encounter ideas that conflict with my own? In what ways do my reactions enhance or undermine my learning?

NOTES

1　David Bartholomae and Anthony Petrosky, "Introduction," in *Ways of Reading: An Anthology for Writers*, 5th ed. (Boston: Bedford/St. Martin's, 1999) 3-4.

2　Bartholomae & Petrosky, 11

3　For an example of a map of discourses see JoVictoria Goodman, "Confronting Authority and Self: Social Cartography and Curriculum Theorizing for Uncertain Times," in *The Authority to Imagine: The Struggle toward Representation in Dissertation Writing*, eds. Noreen B. Garman and Maria Piantanida, (Pittsburgh: Learning Moment Press, 2018), 85-102.

4　Bill Schackner, "Disruptive in Classroom Or Free Speech Denied," Pittsburgh Post-Gazette, March 14, 2018, A1-A2. Matt McKinney, "IUP Student in Free Speech Dispute can Rejoin Class," Pittsburgh Post-Gazette, March 20, 2018, C1-C2. For a more thorough discussion of these types of issues see *The Coddling of the American Mind* by Lukianoff and Haidt. Full citation in bibliography.

5　Wendy Milne, "Imagining Reflective Artmaking: Claiming Self as Artist-Teacher-Researcher," in *The Authority to Imagine: The Struggle toward Representation in Dissertation Writing*, eds. Noreen B. Garman and Maria Piantanida (Pittsburgh: Learning Moments Press, 2018).

6　Donald Schon, *The Reflective Practitioner: How Professionals Think in Action* (New York: Basic Books, 1983).

7　Barry Schwartz and Kenneth Sharpe, *Practical Wisdom: The Right Way to Do the Right Thing* (New York: Riverhead Books, 2010), 42.

8　Schwartz and Sharpe, 6.

9　C.P. Snow, *The Two Cultures* (New York: Cambridge University Press, 1998; First published 1959).

10　Steven Pinker. *Enlightenment Now: The Case for Reason, Science, Humanism, and Progress* (New York: Penguin Random House, 2017).

11　David C. Berliner, Gene V. Glass and Associates offer some interesting counterpoints to taken for granted assumptions about the failure of the U.S. educational system and approaches for fixing the problems. See *Myths & Lies that Threaten America's Public Schools: The Real Crisis in Education* (New York: Teachers College Press, 2014).

12　Walter Feinberg & Jonas F. Soltis. *School and Society* (New York: Teachers College Press, 1998), 6-7.

13　Dwayne Huebner, "Education and Spirituality." *Journal of Curriculum Theorizing*, 11 no 2 (1995).13-34.

14　Schwartz and Sharpe, 40-41

SECTION IV

Quality of Contextual Literacy

Contextual Literacy entails the capacity to read multiple contexts and understand how forces within those contexts affect educational practice.

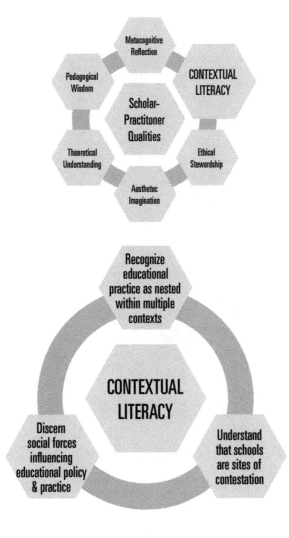

8

Contextual Literacy

CONTEXTS OF EDUCATIONAL PRACTICE

Megan's normally cheerful demeanor was noticeably absent as she entered our classroom one evening. "Are you okay," we asked.

"I just had the most horrible day," she replied, struggling for composure as tears welled up in her eyes.

"What happened?"

"My principal pulled me into his office and told me my students aren't performing well enough on the state's standardized tests. He made it sound like I wasn't doing a good job. I try so hard with these kids, but they come to high school barely able to read. How much can they really make up in a semester and a half?"

We were stunned to hear so much pain in Megan's voice. She is, in fact, a very accomplished English teacher with a sound grasp of her content and very creative ways of engaging students. Having known Megan during her undergraduate years at our university and during her student teaching experience, we had come to respect her dedication as well as her determination to teach in an urban school. After graduation she had accepted a position in one of the most economically disadvantaged neighborhoods in the city. She had returned to the university to pursue a Master of Arts degree in teaching. None of this matched with her account of the meeting with her principal.

"When I tried to explain how I work with the students and how much progress they are making, he just said, 'You've got to get them ready for these tests. That's what they're looking at.' What am I supposed to do? Spend all our classroom time drilling them on test taking? They're just going to turn off. How's that going to help them in real life? Right now I'm wondering if I really want to be a teacher if this is how it's going to be."

This brief scenario portrays a two-faceted pedagogical moment. On one side, Megan had been caught in a pedagogical moment, not with her students, but with her principal. In that moment, Megan's knowledge of her content area and pedagogical strategies was not sufficient to help her cope with the conversation. On the other side, as Megan's teachers, we were in a pedagogical moment and needed to respond to her obvious distress. Several options flashed through our minds:

- We could offer empathy, expressing our awareness of how painful her conversation with the principal had been.
- We could offer reassurance, letting her know that we think very highly of her and reaffirming her worth as a teacher.
- We could mirror her outrage and validate her anger and frustration toward her principal.

While these three responses might feel good in the moment, they would not be particularly educative in Dewey's sense of the word. How might we respond in a way that would help Megan to learn something from her moment with the principal and help her to be better prepared for similar moments in the future?

"Megan," we responded, "this must have been a really difficult conversation. It never feels very good to think your work isn't recognized or valued." Seeing some of the tension leaving Megan's face, we continued, "Would you mind if we talked about this conversation a bit more? It really touches on an important issue that we'd like everyone in the class to think about." With her nod of agreement, we said, "What do you think the principal meant when he said, 'That's what they're looking at.' Who are the 'they' he was referring to?"

A puzzled look replaced Megan's frown. Others in the class also looked puzzled. This gave us an opportunity to talk about the accountability measures that were being instituted in the aftermath of the No Child Left Behind legislation. At the time of Megan's conversation with her principal, the requirements for Annual Yearly Progress (AYP) were not widely known. The pressure being placed on school administrators to meet AYP goals was not widely appreciated. The 'they' we explained could have meant the principal's superintendent, the school board, the State Department of Education, the Federal Department of Education, or even the general, tax-paying public. Lacking awareness of how forces within the broader social contexts were impacting her school, district, and community, Megan interpreted the principal's comments as a personal attack on her dedication and competence. Undoubtedly, the principal might have done a better job of putting his comments into a broader perspective. He might have indicated that he was talking with all teachers in the building. He might have first acknowledged the progress that she had made with the students. He might have talked with her about the support she needed from him to improve the scores. In these ways the principal might have made this moment with Megan more educative. But Scholar-Practitioners understand that passively relying on others to contextualize conversations can engender feelings of helplessness or victimization. As Scholar-Practitioners become more experienced, they recognize that their work is nested not only within classroom contexts, but also within broader social contexts (Figure 8.1).

FIGURE 8.1. CONTEXTS OF PRACTICE

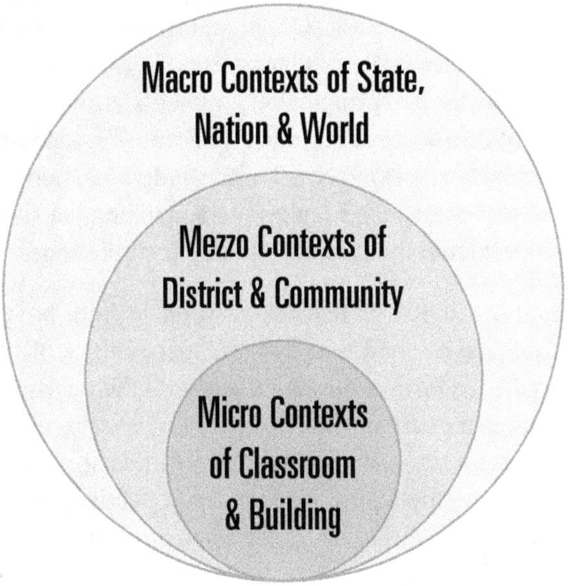

Macro Contexts of State, Nation & World

Mezzo Contexts of District & Community

Micro Contexts of Classroom & Building

Understanding multiple contexts allows Scholar-Practitioners to discern both the finely grained features of pedagogical moments as well as larger social forces impacting their practice. In discussing Pedagogical Wisdom, we stressed the importance of content knowledge and pedagogical strategies. In discussing Theoretical Understanding, we stressed the importance of bodies of knowledge that can inform content-pedagogy. Both Scholar-Practitioner qualities come into play within the micro context of classrooms where relationships between teachers and students and among students are central. If Megan had not been so shocked by her principal's comments, she might have responded with theoretical knowledge in support of her classroom practices. That, however, would not have adequately addressed her principal's concerns. To respond to those, Megan would need to take into consideration how her school district is situated within a macro context where underperforming districts like hers were coming under state and federal scrutiny. Beyond that, Megan would have to understand how standardized test scores were being used to hold teachers and districts accountable for student learning. Even more broadly, she needed to recognize that the scrutiny of her district was part of national effort to maintain the United States' competitive advantage in a global economy. Located in an economically distressed community, students in her district struggled with poverty, hunger, inadequate health care, and family stress. Drugs and gangs with their attendant violence added further stress to the students' lives. Given these forces, Megan's response to her principal's comments is understandable but not particularly useful, because those pressing for accountability did not take those factors into account when judging school and teacher performance. Unfortunately, Megan's personalizing the situation is not atypical. A report from the Learning Policy Institute states:

> Multiple studies of teacher attrition in high-poverty schools have found that teachers' perceptions of their school's leader is a dominant factor in the decision to remain in the school. Teachers working in schools with large proportions of low-income and minority students tend to rate their principals as less effective, and the impact of this rating on the decisions to leave is larger in such schools.[1]

As we mentioned in Chapter 1, school administrators serve at the interface of micro and macro contexts. They may feel as demoralized as Megan by an inability to buffer the effects of ill-conceived policy. Interestingly, Anthony Bryk argues that

> ...recognizing and wisely responding to these two issues—*systems complexity* and *variability in performance*—is key to any effort aimed at systematically improving the productivity of our educational institutions.[2]

Perhaps if The Carnegie Foundation and other school reform organizations begin to study the nested contexts affecting education, more useful indicators of performance will emerge. In the meantime, however, Scholar-Practitioners must continue to cultivate their capacity to read contexts beyond the classroom.

Reading Contexts—Discernment in Practice

In discussing the concept of a prototype expert, Robert Sternberg and Joseph Horvath argue that such an individual

> ...has knowledge of the political and social context in which teaching occurs. This knowledge allows the prototype expert to adapt to practical constraints in the field of teaching—including the need to become recognized and supported as an expert teacher.[3]

Education is not the only profession in which Contextual Literacy has become increasingly important. Over 30 years ago, the Association for the Study of Higher Education published the results of a study on the nature of professional education. Emerging from an examination of twelve professions (including education) were two major categories of outcomes—professional competencies and professional attitudes—deemed essential for competent professional practice. One of the six professional competencies was contextual competence—"Understanding the societal context (environment) in which the profession is practiced."[4] The authors elaborate on the nature of contextual competence, stating:

It refers not only to the professional's specific work setting, but also to the larger environments, both social and natural, within which the work is embedded. The acquisition of this competence implies that the student can examine the environmental context from a variety of vantage points: historical, social, economic, psychological, political, and philosophical. The capability to adopt multiple perspectives allows the student to comprehend the complex interdependencies between the profession and society, thus fostering both increased professional social awareness and more effective citizenship (Smith, Johnson, and Johnson 1981). *The achievement of contextual competence allows the student to transcend egocentric or parochial levels of thought in interpreting contemporary life.*[5] (italics added)

These views of contextual competence point to the relationship between the Scholar-Practitioners' grasp of theoretical constructs and their ability to read and interpret the contexts of their life journey. In naming the Scholar-Practitioner quality *Contextual Literacy*, we underscore the importance of discerning the nuances of experience. In discussing Theoretical Understanding, we introduced Bartholomae and Petrosky's concept of strong reading of written texts. Strong reading requires close attention to the author's intent as well as reading with and against the grain of the author's arguments. This is difficult enough to do in the close reading of stable written texts. Reading dynamic social-political-economic con**texts** presents even greater challenges. It entails a capacity discern the forces beneath the surface of particular circumstances. Thomas Schwandt, in discussing the concept of responsive evaluation, offers a useful explanation of what it means to be discerning:

Because all practices are mutable and indeterminate, the virtue of responsiveness demands plasticity— flexibility in attending to the salient features of each situation. This contrasts with a kind of attention that is directed by templates, procedures, rules, or habits and thus tends to be unmindful of concrete specifics. "But the salient features of a situation do not jump to the eye ready labeled for easy identification" (Pendlebury, 1995, p. 60); they must [be] picked out from among the blooming, buzzing confusion of details that comprise any action, person, or event that is the object of our attention. Thus responsiveness requires a particular kind of perspicuity—an ability to discern the relevant features of a case at hand. . . In other words, attention is not some easy categorization and description of contextual features as might be based, for example, on checklists, but a "seeing as"—*an ability to ascertain what is at stake in this or that circumstance.*[6] (italics added)

The ability to ascertain what is at stake in a particular circumstance relates to the qualities of Pedagogical Wisdom and Ethical Stewardship. Within the micro context of a classroom, what may be at stake is supporting the student's engagement with a particularly difficult subject. Within the context of a teacher-parent conference it may be explaining a particular pedagogical approach. Within the context of a community, it may be taking a stand against a proposed program that is not in the best interest of children. Reading the nuances of various contexts and understanding what is at stake allows Scholar-Practitioners to depersonalize their reactions and respond ethically and wisely in ways that care for the well-being of individuals and the profession.

Discerning what is at stake in macro-moments brings us back to Feinberg and Soltis' description of the conflict theorist perspective of knowledge mentioned in the previous chapter. Generally, those holding a conflict theory perspective view "schooling as a social practice supported and utilized by those in power to maintain their dominance in the social order."[7] It is the use of power to control what happens to and in schools that makes schools sites of contestation.

Schools as Sites of Contestation

Because public education is an institution meant to serve societal interests and because we live in a pluralistic democracy, Scholar-Practitioners understand that a wide range of stakeholders have vested interests in what happens in schools. Often these stakeholder groups disagree strongly. These disagreements waged at global, federal, state, and local levels make schools sites of contestation. Consider just a few examples.

- What is and should be the role of federal, state, and local government in setting educational policy?
- Who should control the curriculum? For example, should local school districts be allowed to teach creationism as an alternative to or instead of evolution? Should sex education be mandatory? Who decides what textbooks will be used?
- Are transgender bathroom policies or lack of such policies discriminatory?
- Should property taxes continue to be the source of funding for schools even though economic disparities among communities perpetuate inequitable educational opportunities?
- Is it fair for those without children to pay school taxes?
- Are scores on standardized tests a meaningful way to hold school districts accountable for the results achieved with the funds they receive?
- Do men's and women's sports deserve equal funding?
- Should affirmative action programs/policies be discontinued?
- Should foundations and corporations be able to influence educational policy to benefit their own ideological and financial interests?
- Do charter schools and vouchers offer alternatives to students who are not well served by regular public schools or do they siphon off money that is needed to support all students?
- Should students with disabilities be taught in separate, specially designed classes or included in classes with all students?
- Are schools preparing a work force that will maintain the United States' competitive power in a global economy? Should that be their primary purpose?

- Does tenure promote scholarly inquiry or protect incompetent teachers?
- Should teacher unions be disbanded?

Although these are highly complex issues, we have phrased most of the examples in "yes/no" and "either/or" terms to underscore the vehemence with which opposing camps argue for their position. Often it is the vehemence that signals one is caught in contested terrain. In the good old days, teachers could close the doors to their classrooms and shut out disturbances from the world at large. Whether this was really the case in the "good old days," today's teachers do not have even the illusion of this luxury. Like Megan, educators can find their daily work impacted by the push and pull of forces beyond the micro context of their classroom and school. To discern these forces, it is useful to start with Schwandt's question, "What is at stake in a given circumstance?" Wedding this question with the conflict theory of schooling gives rise to several questions that promote close contextual reading:

- Who stands to benefit? Who will lose?
- What are the ideological principles/values driving a particular position?
- Whose money is being used to influence decisions?
- What stakeholders are being included in and excluded from the decision-making process?

Figure 8.1 above depicts ever-widening contexts within which educational practice is situated. As depicted in Figures 8.2a and 8.2b, developing Contextual Literacy allows Scholar-Practitioners to discern forces and stakeholders at play within micro, mezzo, and macro contexts. This positions them to respond to the all too common phrase, "They say…" by asking, "Who says?" and "Where is it written?"

FIGURE 8.2A - STAKEHOLDER GROUPS IMPACTING EDUCATIONAL CONTEXTS

Stakeholder Groups

Macro Contexts of State, Nation & World

- General Public
- Elected Officials
- National & Multinational Corporations
- Foundations
- International Aid Organizations
- Military
- Professional Organizations
- Teacher Unions

Mezzo Contexts of District & Community

- Superintendent
- School Board
- Residents
- Elected Official
- Businesses
- Community Organizations

Micro Contexts of Classroom & Building

- Teachers
- Students
- Aides
- Parents
- Principal
- Specialists
- All Support Personnel

FIGURE 8.2B - SOURCES OF INFORMATION

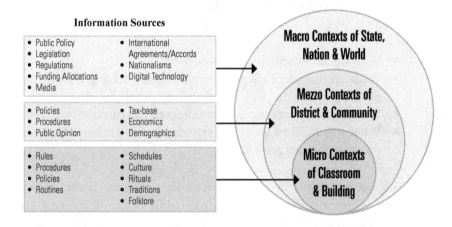

Information Sources

- Public Policy
- Legislation
- Regulations
- Funding Allocations
- Media
- International Agreements/Accords
- Nationalisms
- Digital Technology

Macro Contexts of State, Nation & World

- Policies
- Procedures
- Public Opinion
- Tax-base
- Economics
- Demographics

Mezzo Contexts of District & Community

- Rules
- Procedures
- Policies
- Routines
- Schedules
- Culture
- Rituals
- Traditions
- Folklore

Micro Contexts of Classroom & Building

Actually, the question, "where is it written" raises another thorny aspect of Contextual Literacy. Often, the official "story" recorded in formal documents co-exists with a multitude of unwritten, unofficial stories passed by word of mouth among various groups within organizational and societal contexts. The capacity to discern these multi-layered and potentially conflicting texts contributes to Contextual Literacy.

Reading Micro to Macro Contexts

As illustrated in Figures 8.2a and 8.2b, both explicit and implicit texts shape the nature of acceptable decisions and actions within the micro context of classrooms and school buildings. Consider, for example, how "everyone knows":

- Who are the easy graders and who are the tough disciplinarians;
- What maintenance person to go to if you need something to be fixed;
- Whether the anti-bullying posters reflect a culture of respect or are mere lip service;
- Where a "secret" stash of supplies can be found;
- Schools where it is a pleasure to be a substitute teacher and schools where it is dreadful;
- What is done to celebrate holidays;
- What is celebrated—winning a state-wide football championship or a state-wide debate competition;
- What is acceptable and unacceptable teacher-room talk;
- Whether teachers socialize outside of school; whether teachers and teachers' aides socialize;
- Who decides what can/should be announced over the school's intercom or published in the school's newsletter;
- How a new extra-curricular club is formed;
- What disciplinary action can teachers take; what must be referred to the principal;
- How are in-service topics selected and planned;
- How much time is allotted for family leave, sick days, bereavement;
- What are the fire and safety protocols; and
- Which building principals have a good working relationship with the school superintendent and which do not.

These examples don't even begin to scratch the surface of all that can be known about the micro context of classroom and building. Typically, teacher induction processes focus on explicit policies and procedures. Employee handbooks and school policy manuals are useful sources of information about the official version of micro-contexts.

However, only by living within a context do the nuances become apparent. Often these nuances reveal unspoken norms which may or may not coincide with official organizational information. When official and unofficial "stories" conflict, the response can range from benign amusement (Yeah, that's what they say, but everyone knows the real scoop.) to anger, frustration, resentment, and burnout or demoralization within toxic systems. Just as theories of learning, human development, and motivation can help Scholar-Practitioners discern the nuances of pedagogical moments, familiarity with theories of organizational systems and instructional leadership can provide useful lenses for discerning the nuances of school context.

Within Mezzo Contexts, the number and type of stakeholder groups who influence the world of teaching expands. Often the texts at this level can be found in the news media which both report on and influence education. Consider a few headlines:

- District superintendent submits resignation; the board has formed a search committee to find her replacement
- District schools ranked 99 out of 100 on state-wide assessment
- Teachers set to strike over salary
- Local foundation gives $500,000 grant to upgrade district's instructional technology
- School board considering a later start time for high school classes
- Citizens attend school board meeting to protest proposed cut in spending for arts-education
- District set to lay-off teachers' aides and clerical staff in the face of budget short-fall
- State mandates core curriculum and standardized assessments for all districts
- Poorly performing school put under Department of Education oversight
- District adopts new curriculum for math and science

Behind such headlines lies more detailed information that can give Scholar-Practitioners greater insight into forces that may impinge upon their practice.

Within Macro Contexts, a multiplicity of national and international forces can impact education. Consider, for example, several older and newer examples:

- The Supreme Court's decision in support of school integration
- Efforts to deport undocumented immigrants
- Restrictions on immigration
- Development of national testing standards
- Policy decisions by the U.S. Secretary of Education
- Legal decisions on the right of teachers to strike
- Efforts to undermine teacher unions and tenure
- The idea of spending federal money to arm teachers in the wake of school shootings as opposed to spending money to improve access to mental health services
- National and international perspectives on the quality of U.S. educational systems and their role in maintaining U.S. dominance in global markets

Although such issues may seem far removed from the daily demands of practice, they often exert subtle and not so subtle influence on how schools, teachers, and administrators function.

Considered together, the scope and significance of forces at play in the micro-, mezzo, and macro- contexts can seem overwhelming. How can individual Scholar-Practitioners possibly develop the Contextual Literacy necessary to discern the continually shifting issues that impact their work? In short, they can't. It is simply too much to keep track of. For this reason, we offer two suggestions. First, as suggested in Chapter 7, it is important to have reasonable expectations for oneself. Becoming familiar with both the overt and covert information about multi-layered contexts requires patient and careful observation over time. Second, we strongly urge Scholar-Practitioners to connect with Communities of Practice.

Communities of Practice

Communities of Practice are networks of individuals who share common interests and concerns. They may be as informal as voluntary study groups or as formal as unions and professional organizations. By joining one or more such communities, the work of scanning contextual forces can be shared. Inevitably, some individuals are drawn more strongly to understanding some issues than others. By pooling these individual interests, members of Communities of Practice can expand the range of issues that come to their attention. For example, unions and professional organizations have paid staff who track issues that can impact their membership. Through newsletters, briefing alerts, journals, meetings and conferences, the information gathered by staff is disseminated to all organizational members. Thus, Scholar-Practitioners can benefit from a great deal of time-consuming groundwork done by others.

Often, when Scholar-Practitioners are early in their professional journey, they lack the time (and perhaps the confidence) to actively participate in Communities of Practice. They may choose to "lurk" quietly as passive recipients of information. Over time, however, active involvement may take the form of attending meetings/conferences, serving on committees, or joining special interest groups at the local, state, national, or even international level. These more intensive involvements offer opportunities for an "inside look" at the ways policies are formulated and promulgated. Further, they offer opportunities for Scholar-Practitioners to help shape decisions that are impacting their practice. Deciding where to invest one's time and effort also entails the capacity for discernment—carefully "reading" which communities of practice are most closely aligned with one's professional values and conducive to one's professional/life journey.

Contextual Literacy and the *Telos* of Education

As Scholar-Practitioners develop their capacity for Contextual Literacy, they can begin to discern stakeholder groups that are competing for control of schools. Some of these groups may be seeking control in order to enhance the quality of education available to all citizens. Other groups may be seeking control to serve more personal agendas, perhaps at the expense of those who come to school to learn and work. Keeping in mind "who benefits" can help to sort through the myriad fragments of information available within micro- to macro-contexts. Beyond that, having a sound understanding of one's own theoretical and philosophical values about the purpose of education allows Scholar-Practitioners to align their interests with well-chosen Communities of Practice.

REFLECTIVE PROMPTS

What thoughts and feelings are evoked by the ideas in this chapter?

In what ways do my responses to the ideas in this chapter contribute to my understanding of being a Scholar-Practitioner?

What questions are evoked by the ideas in this chapter? Where do those questions fit within my plan for continued learning?

What ideas do I want to incorporate into my evolving Scholar-Practitioner Narrative?

What educational contexts have I experienced as a learner, teacher, parent, and/or visitor? How would I characterize the similarities and differences among them? What did I find most and least appealing?

What strategies have I developed to track forces that may be affecting my practice?

To what Communities of Practice do I belong? What is the nature of my participation in those Communities?

NOTES

1 Lelb Sutcher, Linda Darling-Hammond and Desiree Carver-Thomas. *A Coming Crisis in Teaching? Teacher Supply, Demand, and Shortages in the U.S.* (Paolo Alto, CA: Learning Policy Institute 2016), 67.

2 Anthony S. Bryk, "2014 AERA Distinguished Lecture. Accelerating How We Learn to Improve," *Educational Researcher* 44, no 9 (2015): 469.

3 Robert J. Sternberg and Joseph A. Horvath. "A Prototype View of Expert Teaching," *Educational Researcher 24,* no. 6 (1995): 12.

4 Joan S. Stark, Malcolm A. Lowther, and Bonnie M.K. Hagerty, *Responsive Professional Education: Balancing Outcomes and Opportunities*, ASHE-ERIC Higher Education Reports, Washington, D.C.: Association for the Study of Higher Education, 1986, 13.

5 Stark, Lowther, and Hagerty, 30-31.

6 Thomas A. Schwandt, "Responsiveness and Everyday Life," in *Responsive Evaluation: New Directions for Evaluation*, eds. Jennifer G. Greene, Tincke A Abma, (San Francisco: Jossey-Bass, Winter 2001), 77.

7 Walter Feinberg and Jonas F. Soltis. *School and Society* (New York: Teachers College Press, 1998).

9

Cultivating Contextual Literacy

In the preceding chapter we outlined the multiple contexts within which the practice of teaching is nested and flagged various forces and stakeholder groups that influence these contexts. Further, we suggested that careful observation helps Scholar-Practitioners discern both the official and unofficial messages that shape their experiences within micro- to macro-contexts. Discernment, however, is never objective. Inevitably, we read contexts through autobiographical lenses which shape what we are able to see, how we interpret what we see, and how we choose to respond to what we see. Scholar-Practitioners, we contend, are committed to understanding the values, assumptions, life experiences, biases, knowledge, feelings, etc. that constitute their autobiographical lens. Such self-understanding is not easy to come by. In this chapter, we suggest that the stories we tell—about ourselves, about education, about school, and about society—offer important insights into our capacity for discernment.

ability to judge well

A Note about "Story"

Because the idea of "story" is often associated with fiction, a word of explanation may be in order. In the latter half of the 20th century, psychologists, social psychologists, and sociologists began to challenge the idea that knowledge can be generated only through logical, scientific processes. They argued that human beings in their everyday life make meaning through a narrative mode of thinking—i.e., they construct stories that give meaning and coherence to their life experience. As educational scholar Laurel Richardson puts it:

> People organize their personal biographies and understand them through the stories they create to

narrative →

explain and justify their life experiences. When people are asked why they do what they do, they provide narrative explanations, not logico-scientific categorical ones. It is the way individuals understand their own lives and best understand the lives of others. Experiences are connected to other experiences and evaluated in relation to the larger whole. Something does not make sense when it does not fit in with the narrative. To make sense of the events in their lives, people reconstruct biography.[1]

All of us have stories about who we are, what our life has been like, our place in the world, what we believe the future will hold for us. Embedded within these stories of self are stories about the nature of the world we live in, including the nature of education, school, and society at large. When we encounter new experiences or unfamiliar ideas, we tend to accept those that fit easily into our stories and reject those that contradict them. Perhaps the most basic challenge in cultivating Contextual Literacy is slowing down this accept/reject impulse and dwelling in a state of cognitive dissonance. *lack of harmony*

Cognitive dissonance can engender anything from mild to extreme anxiety—never the most pleasant or welcome feeling. So we have choices. We can avoid to the greatest extent possible any experiences that might challenge our stories of self. Failing this, we can take steps to minimize the anxiety by rejecting the dissonant information. Or we can use the dissonance to raise questions for exploration and study. Choosing the third response can have a paradoxical effect of simultaneously increasing and decreasing anxiety. The possibility of discovering that one's story has been wrong all these years can be threatening, thereby increasing anxiety. On the other hand, tapping into one's curiosity and desire for greater understanding can keep the anxiety within tolerable and productive limits.

In the chapter on curriculum theory, we posed the question, "What is worth learning?" From our perspective, it is worthwhile—indeed essential—for Scholar-Practitioners to learn strategies for responding to cognitive dissonance. Reframing dissonant information from a threat to an opportunity for learning allows for the development of greater

Pedagogical Wisdom, deeper Theoretical Understanding, and more nuanced Contextual Literacy. In the following sections, we consider several themes that are inevitably embedded in stories about the world, education, school, and society.

Stories of a Changing World

Our parents were born in the early decades of the 20th century. When we pause to reflect upon the lives of these remarkable men and women, we are astounded by the social changes they witnessed: the ubiquitous use of automobiles and airplanes, the Great Depression, two world wars, the Korean War, the Vietnam War, waves of immigration from Eastern Europe, Asia, and the Middle East, the fall of the Iron Curtain, the Civil Rights movement, the moon landing, the women's liberation movement, homes with indoor plumbing and electricity, the invention of the television, private telephone lines and mobile phones, computers, and fast food restaurants. The list of small and large changes at both the personal and social level goes on and on. Despite the magnitude of changes, it seems (at least in retrospect) that the pace was slower, allowing for adjustment and adaptation. Today, however, the pace of change itself is a major force to contend with. Nowhere is this pace more intense than in the rise of technology that our parents could never have imagined.

Back in the 1960s only the government and a few industrial giants had access to computers. These massive machines occupied huge rooms and were used by specialists. Today, micro-processing technology has made computing power available in the form of smart phones, programmable televisions, coffee pots, and robotic sweepers. Wearable technology allows us to monitor health parameters that once were the province of doctors' offices. Smart houses with everything from temperature controlled zones to medication monitoring are already available. Each year (often more frequently) newer, more powerful personal computing devices hit the market, giving us more rapid access to more information. Round-the-clock media bombard us with an unending stream of "late breaking news" from around the world. Social media connect us 24/7 with the activities and thoughts of family, friends, and strangers. Inundated with this never-ending stream of information, it is hard to know where to focus and to discern what is significant.

One effect of living in a digital age saturated with information from around the world has been the erosion of isolating social boundaries. Daily, we are confronted by cultures with ideologies far different from our own. Forced to think on a global scale, we create stories about "the other." Some stories are fraught with danger, fear, and a desire to wall off any incursion by others who might challenge our way of life. Other stories challenge us to examine who we are, not just within our own nation, but as citizens of the much larger community of planet Earth. Even more disconcerting than these stories of where we fit in the global scheme of things are challenges to the very core idea of what makes human beings different from (superior to?) all other creatures.

In his book, *Homo Deus: A Brief History of Tomorrow*, historian Yuval Noah Harari argues that advances in artificial intelligence are pushing the boundaries of what it means to be "homo sapiens." Biomedical technology from gene manipulation to bionic body parts may, by the end of the 21st century, extend the human life span to 150 years or more. Just as Neanderthals became extinct, homo sapiens may be replaced by a carbon-silicon hybrid species with an intelligence more god-like than human. Further, he challenges the assumption that humans will remain the most highly evolved life form, speculating that self-aware artificial intelligence machines may supplant our species. Whether or not this vision of the future comes to fruition, it challenges our most fundamental assumptions about who we are as a species and our place in the world.[2]

At times the pace and enormity of change can all seem too much. So we tell ourselves stories about change, not just about its inevitability, but our reaction to it. For some, both the pace and nature of change threatens a sense of a stable and orderly world. When change overwhelms an individual's capacity to adapt and adjust, it may be viewed as a dangerous, disorienting disruption of "the way things are supposed to be." Unable to keep one's bearings, one can feel out of control and, in turn, anxious, angry, and frustrated. Within this story, change is an enemy to be resisted and advocates for change may be viewed with suspicion and resentment. A contrasting story frames change as exciting, as progress, as a source of opportunity. Rather than evoking dread, change is embraced with a sense of wonder and adventure. Those who resist change may be viewed with suspicion and resentment.

The above characterizations are, of course, simplified and extreme. Often the response to change differs depending on where change intersects with our self-interests. Some may see technological change as exciting but social change as threatening. For others, the response might be the exact opposite. Thus, when individuals come together in educational encounters, a kaleidoscope of change-stories can be at play. By understanding their own autobiographical story of change, Scholar-Practitioners are better prepared to discern the stories of others. This heightened discernment, coupled with empathy, helps Scholar-Practitioners forestall an accept/reject judgment of others' stories, thereby enhancing their capacity for Contextual Literacy.

Stories of Education

Interwoven within our stories about our changing world are stories about education. Throughout the book we have contrasted a behavioral view of education with an existential view. These views, however, tend to be the province of professional educators, psychologists, and researchers. At a more fundamental level are stories about the role of education in our lives. In some stories, education is meant to instill the values of one's family and the social groups with which one associates. In other stories, education is meant to challenge and broaden one's understanding of the world and one's place in it.

For generations of immigrants, education was seen as crucial for pursuing the American dream. Parents would sacrifice a great deal to assure their children of an education and a better life. The stories of education within such families tend to be positive. Yet, even within this positive view, were other stories of education as a threat to one's cultural heritage and cohesive family identity.[3]

As lifelong Pittsburghers, we witnessed the collapse of the steel industry. Depending upon the year and the way "job loss" was calculated, the specific number of unemployed steel workers varies. Nevertheless, in tracing the decline of the steel industry, John P. Hoerr paints a grim picture:

> The steel industry had been badly hurt by the 1981-82 recession, and it continued sliding downhill through the late summer and fall of 1982. Steel unemployment soared; by the end of the year 153,000 hourly workers, or 53 percent of the work force, were laid off. Many thousands of the jobless had run out of unemployment benefits, and hundreds had lost, or were on the verge of losing, their homes and cars in mortgage foreclosures.[4]

In the face of this dire situation and the steady closure of more and more steel mills, federal, state and local governments, philanthropic foundations, and labor unions began to offer educational opportunities for job retraining. The responses to these opportunities illustrate widely discrepant stories about education. Much to the surprise and consternation of funders and educational institutions, relatively few laid-off workers availed themselves of retraining. For example, in a follow-up study of job retraining, Robert W. Bednarzik and Joseph Szalandki comment:

> Approximately 3,400 dislocated workers were trained under publically funded programs from the mid-1980's to early 1990's in the Pittsburgh area. They ranged in age from 25 to 55 years and about one-third, or 1,100, were displaced steel mill workers, who were mostly men and slightly disproportionately black.[5]

Granted the authors were looking at the experiences of a select group, but in interviews with counselors, teachers, and funders, they discovered that many displaced workers resisted retraining because they believed (or hoped) that the mills would reopen (a story of educational irrelevance). Others resented training for jobs that would pay far less than their union wages in the mills (a story of educational resentment). Still others could not afford the ancillary costs (e.g., transportation, child care) associated with tuition-free programs (stories of educational inaccessibility). Perhaps less forthcoming were those who were afraid they were too old or to incapable of learning (a story of educational incompetence). These stories of education are still at play not just in times of economic upheaval, but when individuals see education as a threat to their sense of self-worth and competence.

Stories of educational avoidance stand in contrast to a pervasive story of education as a means for achieving a good life defined in terms of economic security, buying power, and social status. These stories look on education, particularly higher education, as an investment worth making only if it results in enhanced accessed to high paying, high status jobs. Such a pragmatic story of education is understandable given the cost of a college education. Yet, some individuals have a different story of education as a means of broadening one's understanding of the world, cultivating one's own sensibilities, and cultivating habits of mind that go beyond preparation for specifically defined jobs. Traditionally, these broader aims have been the province of the humanities and social sciences—fields often disparaged as too soft for competition in the high-powered, hardnosed world of technology, economics, business, and professions like medicine and law. Interestingly, this dismissive narrative of the humanities and social sciences is being challenged by emerging stories about the value of a liberal arts education.[6]

Another stereotype falling by the wayside is the assumption that older adults are either unable or uninterested in learning. With some regularity, a newspaper will feature the story of an octogenarian who has just completed requirements for a long-deferred high school diploma or college degree. Other stories focus on retirees who pursue the education needed to enter a second career or develop a talent put aside because of more pressing life demands. The leisure learning industry is booming as seniors enroll in informal courses that pique their interest. Yet, these stories in which education is valued as a means of diversion, socialization, or increased knowledge stand in contrast to those who say "jokingly" they would rather undergo a double root canal without anesthesia than walk into a classroom or sit through a lecture.

We hope these few examples serve to illustrate the wide range of stories that individuals incorporate into their stories of self—who they are and the role of education in maintaining, challenging, or undermining their sense of self. Again, our point is to underscore the importance of understanding one's own story of education in order to discern potential sources of tension during pedagogical moments when the stories of others come into conflict.

Stories of Schooling and Social Justice

In the preceding section, we considered the multiple stories that people tell themselves about education—about the act or process of learning. Often, however, these stories of learning are conflated with stories about schooling and schools as social institutions. In Chapter 3, we recounted the story of John, the young boy who was so fearful of school that he hid under his teacher's desk. Such anecdotes call to mind two conflicting stories of school and schooling. In one story, school is seen as a fearful, threatening place; a place where one's sense of self-worth is diminished. In another story, school is seen at least as a necessary social obligation where one "puts in one's time" to gain a credential. Still other stories frame school as a refuge or a means of escape from oppressive circumstances. Such variations at the individual level point to deeper systemic stories about the role of schools as an institution meant to serve societal goals. Although there are many ways to frame these goals, educational scholar David Labaree offers a useful description:

> The American language of educational goals arises from the core tensions within a liberal democracy. One of those tensions is between the demands of democratic politics and the demands of capitalist markets. A related issue is the requirement that society be able to meet its collective needs while simultaneously guaranteeing the liberty of individuals to pursue their own interests. In the American setting, these tensions have played out through the politics of education in the form of a struggle among three major social goals for the educational system. One goal is *democratic equality*, which sees education as a mechanism for

education

producing capable citizens. Another is *social efficiency*, which sees education as a mechanism for developing productive workers. A third is *social mobility*, which sees education as a way for individuals to reinforce or improve their social position.[7] (italics in the original)

These various goals of American education are embedded in value-laden world views of individual rights, social obligations, and social justice which play out in overarching cultural stories. As Laurel Richardson puts it:

> Participation in a culture includes participation in the narratives of that culture, a general understanding of the stock of meanings and their relationships to each other. The process of telling the story creates and supports a social world. Cultural stories provide exemplars of lives, heroes, villains, and fools as they are embedded in larger cultural and social frameworks as well as stories about home, community, society, and humankind.[8]

Richardson goes on to point out that, "The cultural story is told from the point of view of the ruling interests and the normative order.... Cultural stories, thus, help maintain the status quo."[9]

Standing in tension with dominant cultural stories are collective stories "that give voice to those who are silenced or marginalized in the cultural narrative." Richardson contends that collective stories have transformative possibilities both for individuals and society. The power of competing stories to change how we see ourselves and the broader social landscape makes schools, as social institutions, sites of contestation. Should the purpose of schools be to perpetuate existing cultural stories of class, race, gender, and nation as written by those in power? Should the purpose of schools be to challenge cultural stories creating opportunities for those who have historically been denied access to "life, liberty and the pursuit of happiness?" Underlying heated debates and vehement language lurk the often unspoken questions: whose life; whose liberty; whose happiness? Recall Feinberg and

Soltis' description of conflict theory in which some win at the expense of others. If one's fundamental world view is grounded in this win/ lose ontology, policy debates are really about what stories and whose stories, will prevail.

In *Moral Tribes: Emotion, Reason and the Gap between Us and Them*, Joshua Greene[10] draws a distinction among three levels of this win/lose dilemma. At one level is the individual self—the "me"—in which self-interest is paramount. A second is the individual as part of a social group—the "me" as part of "us." A third distinction is between "us" and "them." Greene contends that curbing total self-interest for the benefit of one's tribe (the "us") gave an evolutionary advantage to those capable of intra-group cooperation. Working together afforded more security in terms of basic necessities and protection from life-threatening forces. At the same time, tribes who viewed outsiders with suspicion may have gained evolutionary advantage by thwarting the efforts of those who might have encroached upon and usurped the resources necessary for survival.

Thus, we humans seem to hold in tension an innate inclination for cooperation and for competition that gives rise to an "us versus them" mentality. Should the purpose of schools and schooling, therefore, be to reinforce and privilege the differences between "us" and "them?" Or should it be to promote tolerance and understanding of "them?" Or should it be to expand one's view of who constitutes "us" so that "us" embraces others? The nightly news offers an unending stream of stories in which "us and them" play out in policy debates as far ranging voter identification, legislative redistricting, single payer health care, immigration reform, environmental and economic regulations, welfare reform, affirmative action, trade embargos, international treaties, military spending, and involvement in the civil affairs (including armed revolutions/insurrections) of other countries.

Over the last few election cycles, the "blue states" and the "red states" have come to symbolize a deep divide within U.S. society. Steven Brill, however, argues that the political divide is grounded in a more fundamental polarization that:

> ...has broken America since the 1960s: The protected versus the unprotected. Enhancing the common good

versus maximizing and protecting the elite winners' winnings.[11]

Sadly, it seems that education plays a role in this polarization. A pervasive American narrative celebrates education as a way for individuals to overcome poverty and for society as a whole to overcome an inequitable distribution of wealth. J.D. Vance, author of the bestselling memoir, *Hillbilly Elegy,* touches on the power of this narrative within the working-poor culture of his youth:

> A lot of other Middletown parents and grandparents must have felt similarly: To them, the American Dream required forward momentum. Manual labor was honorable work, but it was their generation's work—we had to do something different. To move up was to move on. That required going to college.

> And yet there was no sense that failing to achieve higher education would bring shame or any other consequences. The message wasn't explicit; teachers didn't tell us that we were too stupid or poor to make it. Nevertheless, it was all around us, like the air we breathed. No one in our families had gone to college; older friends and siblings were perfectly content to stay in Middletown, regardless of their career prospects; we knew no one at a prestigious out-of-state school; and everyone knew at least one young adult who was underemployed or didn't have a job at all.[12]

On one hand is the story of education as a pathway out of poverty; on the other hand, are systemic forces that create often unsurmountable hurdles to pursuing an education. Although educational scholar David Berliner and Gene Glass acknowledge that there are "legitimate reasons to believe that education benefits the individual and the economy" they also label as a myth the view that "education will lift the poor out of poverty and materially enrich our entire nation." They offer five reasons that shed light on the limitations of education as a force for overcoming individual and societal poverty. Of particular relevance, is their contention that:

...the nation's high unemployment rate is not going
to be substantially reduced because of education. The
economy, now and in previous eras, is typified by a
limited number of jobs at the top, so that only a small
percentage of workers are well-paid. But the economy
also has a large "bottom" made up by the working
poor, the underemployed, and the unemployed. To
suggest that education alone can flatten this centuries-
old labor market pyramid is not just unrealistic, but
would be actively fought against by those now at the
top of the pyramid...[13]

Brill summarizes the remarks of Daniel Markovits who told the
2015 graduates of Yale's Law School that

...their success getting accepted into, and getting a
degree from, the country's most selective law school—
long associated with progressive politics and public
service—actually marked their entry into a newly
entrenched aristocracy that had been snuffing out the
American Dream for almost everyone else.[14]

highest class heredity

Elites, Markovits goes on to explain, can spend what they need
to in order to send their children to the best schools, provide tutors
for standardized testing and otherwise ensure that their kids can
outcompete their peers to secure the same spots at the top that their
parents achieved. In common parlance, the rich get richer and the poor
are left behind, often blamed for their lack of success by those who
reach the top of the pyramid and then "pull up the ladder so more could
not share in their success or challenge their primacy."

According to Berliner and Glass, educational inflation is a fifth
reason that education alone does not lead to economic equality:

Educational inflation, which happens when more people, say, get
a college degree and subsequently the value of that degree is reduced,
decreases the potential for education alone to create higher incomes for
all.[15]

As Labaree explains:

...the role of schools in promoting democratic equality has declined because schools have simultaneously been aggressively promoting social inequality... [E]very move by American schools in the direction of equality has been countered by a strong move in the opposite direction. When we created a common school system in the early nineteenth century, we also created a high school system to distinguish middle-class students from the rest. When we expanded access to the high school at the start of the twentieth century, we also created a system for tracking students within the school and opened the gates for middle-class enrollment in college. When we expanded access to college in the mid-twentieth century, we funneled new students into the lower tiers of the system and encouraged middle-class students to pursue graduate study. The American school system is at least as much about social difference as about social equality. In fact, as the system has developed, the idea of equality has become more formalistic, focused primarily on the notion of broad access to education at a certain level, while the idea of inequality has become more substantive, embodied in starkly different educational and social outcomes.[16]

These are complicated issues and give rise to the question, "What is the role of public schools in helping citizens understand the complexity?" Again, multiple stories give very different answers to this question.

Contextual Literacy and the *Telos* of Education

The existence of multiple competing stories about self, education, schooling and society presents a conundrum for educators. In this historical moment, it seems that individual, cultural and collective stories are shouted across an ever-widening ideological divide. How is it possible to honor one's own values while respecting the values embedded in the stories of others? For Scholar-Practitioners, the starting point is cultivating a capacity for listening openly and with empathy to the stories of others. Marilyn offers a humbling insight into her own realization of the need for respectful listening:

> One of the tremendous challenges of teaching about persons who are oppressed is to not romanticize their lives or portray them as victims. The challenge for me as an educator is to develop the pedagogical frameworks that invite persons to understand the lives, culture and strength of persons in the margins while at the same time critically analyzing the dominant center that produces those margins (hooks, 1984). In my initial attempts at doing this, I failed miserably. At first I was very didactic in my approach. Consequently, I was met with incredible reaction and resistance from many of the persons in class. I judged them to be morally unenlightened and intellectually shallow because they did not share either my understanding of the situation of persons working as migrant farm workers or my rage at their oppression. The harder I pushed for their understanding the more they resisted. Finally, I asked them about it.
>
> A number of them told me that I was trying to shove things down their throats. I was very disturbed by the suggestion that I had created an oppressive environment through the way I was teaching about the injustices that existed in our society, where learners felt no freedom to interact or disagree. I had seen myself as very open. What I failed to acknowledge was the power I held in that classroom. I not only possessed the power to determine the curriculum, classroom structures, and grades, but also the power to control the ways ideas were shaped and shared.[17]

When education is seen as the journey of the self, then the story of that journey offers insights into the reasons individuals hold certain beliefs. Structuring learning environments where participants feel safe to share their views is, perhaps, the most difficult pedagogical aim to achieve. Responding in pedagogical moments where one's own beliefs and those of other learners are challenged requires a sensibility and wisdom that elevates teaching to an art.

Recently, we have encountered an intriguing approach to sharpening one's capacity to discern the biases embedded in one's autobiographical story. In *Visual Intelligence: Sharpen Your Perception, Change Your Life*, Amy Herman[18] stresses the importance of careful observation as a way to understand biases that are affecting one's perceptions. Herman majored in art history in college, but for a variety of reasons later decided to become a lawyer. As part of her law school experience, she did a "ride along" with police officers who were called to a scene of domestic violence. She was close enough to the action to be terrified. At the same time, however, she was struck by the way awareness of the smallest details could make the difference between a safe or deadly outcome. From this experience, she began to explore how viewing works of art—not just glancing at them but studying them in great detail—could enhance the capacity to read situations more carefully. Over the years she has used this arts-based approach to teach police officers, intelligence agents, doctors, teachers, lawyers, and many other professions how to sharpen their capacity for discernment. "To effectively observe, perceive, and communicate factual truths," Herman contends, "we must be able to account for our biases and, in many cases, overcome them." To do so, Herman suggests three rules:

- Rule 1: Become aware of our biases and boot the bad ones.
- Rule 2: Don't mistake biases for facts; instead use them to find facts.
- Rule 3: Run our conclusions past others.

Obviously, this is simply a shorthand reminder to remain alert to one's biases and to remain vigilant to their effects on how we interpret the contexts which we are reading. Cultivating this alertness entails reading one's own autobiography with and against the grain of broader cultural narratives of public education and schooling. Tracing the historical evolution of schools from pre-kindergarten through post-graduate education helps to put many of today's contentious issues in perspective. Teacher preparation courses like "Social Foundations of Education," "Education and Society," "Education and Culture," and "Education and Democracy" are valuable sources of insight into the forces that are shaping multiple narratives about school and education. Unfortunately, the relevance of such courses is often less apparent to teachers than courses that have immediate relevance to their work in the classroom. Yet, having an historical, social, political, and cultural perspective is crucial for discerning forces within the macro context that are impinging on the micro context. Weaving these broader understandings into one's own autobiography as learner and teacher contributes immeasurably to one's Contextual Literacy.

Amy Herman TED talk

REFLECTIVE PROMPTS

What thoughts and feelings are evoked by the ideas in this chapter?

In what ways do my responses to the ideas in this chapter contribute to my understanding of being a Scholar-Practitioner?

What questions are evoked by the ideas in this chapter? Where do those questions fit within my plan for continued learning?

What ideas do I want to incorporate into my evolving Scholar-Practitioner Narrative?

When I think about my own life's journey as student, learner and teacher, what stories about the purpose of education shape my perspectives of school, society and social justice? What life experiences have shaped those stories?

Have I experienced pedagogical moments (as a teacher and/or learner) in which my stories of education, school, society and social justice have come into conflict with those of others? If so, what was my response?

When I think about the rate and nature of change that human beings are experiencing, what is my reaction? What do I see as the role of education in helping me and others deal with change?

NOTES

1 Laurel Richardson, *Writing Strategies: Reaching Diverse Audiences*. Qualitative Research Methods Series 21 (Newbury Park: Sage, 1990), 23.

2 Yuval Noah Harari, *Homo Deus: A Brief History of Tomorrow* (New York: HarperCollins, 2015). Harari posits these ideas to invite speculation, not as predictions. Steven Pinker in *Enlightenment Now* argues that apocalyptic visions of artificial intelligence entities dominating or supplanting the human species still remain in the realm of science fiction. Read together, these two books offer interesting perspectives on where we have come as a species and where we might be headed in the future.

3 For two eloquent descriptions of the tensions created when one's pursuit of education draws one away from one's family culture and socio-economic group, see Tara Westover's *Education: A Memoir* (New York: Random House, 2018) and J.D. Vance's *Hillbilly Elegy: A Memoir of a Family and Culture in Crisis* (New York: HarperCollins, 2016).

4 John P. Hoerr, *And the Wolf Finally Came: The Decline of the American Steel Industry* (Pittsburgh: University of Pittsburgh Press, 1988), 19.

5 Robert W. Bednarzik and Joseph Szalandki, *An Examination of the Work History of Pittsburgh Steelworkers, Who Were Displaced and Received Publicly-Funded Retraining in the Early 1980s*. IZA DP No. 6429 March 2012. Retrieved from https://d-nb.info/1024171671/34 May 10, 2018.

6 See for example: George Anders. *You Can Do Anything: The Surprising Power of a "Useless" Liberal Arts Education* (New York: Little, Brown and Company, 2017) and Mark Edmundson, *Why Teach? In Defense of a Real Education* (New York: Bloomsbury, 2013).

7 David F. Labaree, *Someone Has to Fail: The Zero-sum Game of Public Schooling* (Cambridge, MA: Harvard University Press, 2010), 15-16.

8 Richardson, L, 24-25.

9 Richardson, L., 25.

10 Joshua Greene, *Moral Tribes: Emotion, Reason and the Gap between Us and Them* (New York: Penguin Press, 2013).

11 Steven Brill, *Tailspin: The People and Forces behind American's Fifty-Year Fall— and Those Fighting to Reverse It* (New York, Alfred A. Knopf, 2018), 7.

12 J.D. Vance,. *Hillbilly Elegy: A Memoir of a Family and Culture in Crisis* (New York: HarperCollins, 2016). 35-36.

13 David C. Berliner & Gene V. Glass and associates. *50 Myths and Lies that Threaten America's Public Schools: The Real Crisis in Education* (New York: Teachers College Press, Columbia University, 2014), 231.

14 Brill, 20.

15 Berliner & Glass, 230-232.

16 Labaree, 166.

17 Marilyn Llewellyn, *Spirituality and Pedagogy: Being and Learning in Sacred Spaces* (Pittsburgh: Learning Moments Press, 2017), 75-76.

18 Amy E. Herman, *Visual Intelligence: Sharpen Your Perception, Change Your Life* (New York: Houghton Mifflin Harcourt, 2016).

SECTION V

The Quality of Ethical Stewardship

Ethical Stewardship entails a capacity to act in the best interests of telos of the profession.

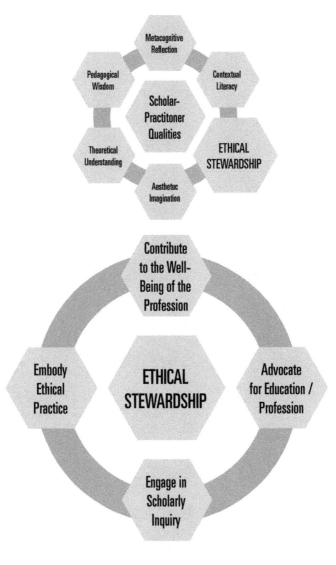

10

Ethical Stewardship

SCHOLAR-PRACTITIONERS AS STEWARDS OF EDUCATION

We take as our starting point for this discussion, work that began in 2003 when The Carnegie Foundation formed a commission to study the nature of doctoral education across the disciplines. Emerging from the Commission's deliberations was the concept of "stewards of the disciplines." Virginia Richardson who participated as a representative of the discipline of education explicated the concept of stewardship in relationship to the Ph.D. degree as follows:

> As stewards of the field of study, Ph.D.'s in education generate new knowledge, understand the intellectual history of the field, use the best ideas and practices in current work, and represent that knowledge to others both within and outside the field. Stewards have a respectful sense of the broader intellectual landscape, including paradigms and questions, and are able to speak about how the field can contribute important understanding to these larger questions. They have a sense of obligation to their field in helping preserve the best while promoting change and improvement.
>
> As they work within the enterprise of education, stewards of education have duties related to communicating and engaging in decisions concerning

the practice of education. In particular, they communicate normative as well as epistemic theory, research, and analyses to very different audiences so that decisions about the enterprise are made within strong analytical and morally defensible frameworks.[1]

In the aftermath of The Commission's work, a number of universities began to make distinctions between a Doctor of Philosophy (Ph.D.) with an emphasis on research and a Doctor of Education (Ed.D.) with an emphasis on practice. As stated at the outset of this book, we challenge this traditional dichotomy between scholar and practitioner. Indeed, the book rests upon the premise that all educators have the potential to embody the stance of Scholar-Practitioner and, in turn, serve as stewards of the profession. Educational Scholar-Practitioners may work as teachers or administrators in public or private schools or community-based organizations. They may be involved with educational policy, programs, and research endeavors to better meet the needs of individuals throughout the span of human development (e.g., from pre-K through graduate education through adult learning). They may be enrolled in formal degree programs or learning on the job. Whatever their primary role and context, Scholar-Practitioners are committed to three major dimensions of stewardship—ethical conduct, advocacy, and commitment to inquiry.

Before turning to a discussion of these aspects of Ethical Stewardship, let's consider an experience described by Annie, one of our graduate students.

Early one morning in October, during my first year of substitute teaching, I entered a fifth grade science classroom, eager to start teaching the first of a two-day assignment. Upon entering the classroom, I found the teacher's simple yet explicit plans: start the new lesson on organized systems, cover the material on these pages of the textbook, and have the students complete the questions for homework. I had 20 minutes to develop an engaging lesson that met the teacher's objectives. No sooner had I begun planning when the special education teacher stopped by to let me know that she would be in the room first period for inclusion science. She also notified me that the daily plan consists of reading from the textbook. Stunned, but feeling a need to show respect to the classroom teachers, I stopped planning and braced myself to have the students read from the book. Just as I began to call on students to read, the inclusion teacher interrupted, telling me I had to read the chapter, because science textbooks are too technical for students to read themselves. By the end of my five-period day, I was drained. And I still had to endure the following day of substitute teaching. I experienced this moment at a critical time in my teaching career, a time when I sought to understand my position, responsibility, and authority in the classrooms where I taught.

The special education teacher exemplifies what we might call an "anti-steward." Her conduct in relation to both the students and Annie is egregiously unethical—showing no respect for them as individuals; assuming none of them have anything worthwhile to contribute to the "lesson," and forcing everyone to endure a mind-numbing exercise devoid of meaning. More broadly, the special education teacher fails miserably as a representative of, and advocate for, the profession of education. Experienced teachers should serve as welcoming and supportive colleagues, especially of beginning teachers. In terms of commitment to inquiry, she apparently has no understanding of the pedagogical principles for teaching science, no awareness of STEM initiatives occurring around the country, and no curiosity about how to make science accessible to students who have special learning needs. Drawing from and contributing to the knowledge-base of the profession plays no part in her professional life. With this negative example as a backdrop, let's now consider the commitments for Ethical Stewardship inherent in the stance of Scholar-Practitioner.

Commitment to Moral/Ethical Conduct

In Chapter 4 we introduced the concept of contrived educational encounters to distinguish formal programs of learning from the learning that occurs more freely through daily living. These contrived encounters differ from the ordinary learning, because they are designed to achieve specific purposes. It is vitally important to recognize that when individuals enter formal, institutionally based educational encounters, they relinquish some degree of autonomy and control in exchange for achieving the purpose for which the encounter is planned. Whether acknowledged or unacknowledged, this *quid pro quo* arrangement constitutes a contract. The contract carries with it an obligation for all involved parties to behave responsibly and ethically.

When individuals <u>voluntarily</u> enter into an educational contract, the nature of the relationship is similar to that between clients and other professionals (e.g., doctors, lawyers, financial advisors). If clients are dissatisfied or unhappy, they are free to walk away from the situation. However, rightly or wrongly, a great deal of formal education is <u>involuntary</u>. Children are <u>compelled</u> by law to attend elementary and secondary school. Adults seeking professional credentials (e.g., licensure or certification) <u>must</u> complete required courses of study. Many adults are <u>required</u> to attend educational programs as a condition of employment. When individuals are compelled, required, forced, or coerced to enter into contrived educational encounters, they are cast (willingly or unwillingly) in the role of student. The role of student is imbued with vulnerability arising from limitations on the individual's freedom to walk away from unsatisfying situations. Vulnerability is exacerbated when students are subjected to judgments by those holding greater power and control. Thus, Scholar-Practitioners have a moral, as well as ethical, obligation to make judgments in the best interest of individuals who come under their purview.

Over the years, several educational associations have developed codes of ethics for teachers. For example, the first principle of the National Education Association's code of ethics for educators is a commitment to the student:

> The educator strives to help each student realize his
> or her potential as a worthy and effective member of

society. The educator therefore works to stimulate the spirit of inquiry, the acquisition of knowledge and understanding, and the thoughtful formulation of worthy goals.[2]

Similarly, the first ethical principle of the Association of American Educators is:

The professional educator accepts personal responsibility for teaching students character qualities that will help them evaluate the consequences of and accept the responsibility for their actions and choices. We strongly affirm parents as the primary moral educators of their children. Nevertheless, we believe all educators are obligated to help foster civic virtues such as integrity, diligence, responsibility, cooperation, loyalty, fidelity, and respect-for the law, for human life, for others, and for self.

The professional educator, in accepting his or her position of public trust, measures success not only by the progress of each student toward realization of his or her personal potential, but also as a citizen of the greater community of the republic.[3]

The National Association of State Directors of Teacher Education and Certification has developed a Model Code of Ethics for Educators that states the third principle as:

The professional educator has a primary obligation to treat students with dignity and respect. The professional educator promotes the health, safety and well-being of students by establishing and maintaining appropriate verbal, physical, emotional and social boundaries.[4]

The thread running through all these statements is the paramount importance of working ethically in the best interests of students. This harkens back to Aristotle's concept of *phronesis* as a particular form of knowledge necessary for practical activity:

> This is a form of activity that has to do with the conduct
> of one's life and affairs as a member of society. It
> is about doing the right thing and doing it well in
> interactions with fellow humans. It is an activity that
> leaves no separably identifiable outcome as its product,
> hence the end (aim) of the activity (i.e., being a "good"
> human being, teacher, doctor, lawyer, etc.) is realized
> in the very doing of the activity itself. . . This [practical
> wisdom] is neither a technical nor a cognitive capacity
> that one has at one's disposal, but rather is bound up
> with the kind of person that one is and is becoming.[5]

As Parker Palmer argues, WHAT WE DO as educators cannot be isolated from WHO WE ARE as human beings committed to a particular field of professional endeavor. WHO WE ARE as much as WHAT WE KNOW shapes our ethical sensibilities and, in turn, our decisions and actions.

Because Scholar-Practitioners work in complex, ever-changing contexts, many states have begun to provide on-line resources to support the cultivation of ethical sensibilities. In Pennsylvania, for example, the Department of Education website contains a guide which identifies eight areas for consideration:

- Private and Professional Lives
- Relationships with Students
- The Connected Teacher
- Teaching in a Diverse Society
- Improper Personal or Financial Gain
- Ethical Colleagues
- Fostering an Ethical School Climate

The website provides a brief explanation of each area, videos, recommended follow-up readings and case studies. Other states have similar resources.

To gain a sense of how these areas might arise in practice consider the following examples:

A teacher from a wealthy suburban school district took students on a summer excursion to England. Among the photos posted on his and the students' Facebook pages were shots of them drinking beer in an English pub. Although the age for drinking in England is lower than in the U.S., the parents were outraged that the teacher would allow (perhaps encourage) underage drinking. The teacher was fired.

A cashier at a local supermarket offered to charge a teacher less than the marked price for her groceries if she would give the cashier's son a higher grade.

A number of teachers and administrators were fired when it was discovered they had falsified the results of state and federally mandated standardized tests.

A student sued her university for taking her tuition money but not preparing her to pass a state licensure exam.

Teachers have been reprimanded (and sometimes fired) for posting "inappropriate" material on their personal websites. Teachers have objected, saying that what they do in their personal life (assuming it is not illegal) is none of the school's business. This argument has not held up as teachers are held to a standard of exemplary conduct and role models for children and teens.

At one university, collegial relationships among several faculty members were damaged when the confidential deliberations of a promotions and tenure commitment became grist for the rumor mill.

Such situations only begin to touch upon the many thorny circumstances that teachers and administrators may encounter. It behooves educators to familiarize themselves with their state's code of conduct and their district's policies. Beyond that, a sensitivity to the mores and norms of the community in which one works is vital both to Contextual Literacy and Ethical Stewardship.

Commitment to Advocacy for the Profession

Ethical Stewardship extends beyond safe-guarding the well-being of students to caring for the well-being of the profession and its purpose (*telos*) within a democratic society. As Golde et al. explain:

- By evoking the term steward, we intend to convey the sense of purpose that guides action. Self-identifying as a steward implies adopting a sense of purpose that is larger than oneself. One is a steward of the discipline, not simply the manager of one's own career. By adopting as a touchstone the care of the discipline and understanding that one has been entrusted with that care by those in the field, on behalf of those in and beyond the discipline, the individual steward embraces a larger sense of purpose. The scale is both temporally large (looking to the past and the future) and broad in scope (considering the entire discipline, as well as intellectual neighbors).
- A steward thinks about how to preserve the heart and essence of the field. But there are also important forward-looking meanings, as stewardship does not imply stasis. A steward is a caretaker who trains a critical eye toward the future. A steward must be willing to take risks and move the discipline forward.[6]

In fulfilling their stewardship responsibilities as advocates, Scholar-Practitioners need a clear understanding of how their own vision of education aligns with the vision of others. In concluding our discussion of Theoretical Understanding, we referenced Feinberg and Soltis' distinction among functionalist, conflict theorist, and interpretivist perspectives on the nature of schooling. Each of these perspectives has its own advocates who draw upon various theoretical and philosophical traditions. In exploring various conceptions of curriculum, we contrasted a behavioral perspective to an existential perspective. By understanding these perspectives and by drawing on their literacy of social contexts, Scholar-Practitioners are better prepared to discern what is at stake when contentious issues arise. This, in turn, allows them to advocate for positions congruent with the well-being of the profession.

One of the challenges facing educators is discerning when to support reform efforts and when to resist them. In the early 1990s, when studying teacher reactions to a newly imposed instructional supervision system, our colleague Noreen Garman analyzed the responses of 200 teachers to the initiative. Emerging from the analysis were responses ranging from unbridled enthusiasm to resistance (Figure 10.1). It is hard to imagine that 25 years have passed since that analysis. It is even harder to imagine how much greater the pressure has become to control the practice of education. In the face of often ill-conceived and oppressive reform measures, we see a need to extend the framework in Figure 10.1. As stewards of education, Scholar-Practitioners must weigh their ethical obligation to advocate for or against new initiatives. Which ones will preserve the best of the profession and which will move it forward?

Figure 10.1 - Responses to Reform Initiatives: A Heuristic

Zealot: Exhibits unbridled enthusiasm for the initiative; unable to hear objections or criticisms. Has blind faith & refuses to question any aspect of the initiative. Typical Comment: "This is an incredible experience. It will change your life." Level of Engagement: complete immersion.

Moderate: Open to the new possibilities offered by the initiative, yet maintains a critical stance; willing to weigh the worth of an initiative in relation to one's professional aspirations and educational goals in general; actively engages in the relevant discourse from various perspectives. Typical Comment: This may be a good opportunity for meaningful experience." Level of Engagement: balanced commitment.

Skeptic: Questions the worth and/or soundness of an initiative yet is open to discussion & information. Typical Comment: "Is this program really worth the effort?" or "Can the program really deliver what it promises?" Level of Engagement: conditional involvement.

Accommodator: Silent acceptance of initiative; responds to authority & considers that one is "acting professionally" in compliance; interprets colleagues who raise questions as "acting unprofessionally." Generally does not express a position in a large group. Level of Engagement: passive involvement.

Game Player: Attitude reflects the notion that the initiative is another bandwagon. Typical Comment: "Tell me what you want and I'll give it to you." Level of engagement: marginal investment; goes through the motions.

Cynic: Assumes that the initiative is not worthwhile & has no benefit; raises questions, not for information, but in order to mobilize opposition. Typical Comment: "It'll never work anyway!" or "Let me play the devil's advocate." Level of Engagement: invests in undermining an initiative.

Snark: Assumes that no program will have any worth or value. Typical Comment: "I've been here x number of years and I've seen these fads come and go. This one won't work either!" Level of Engagement: high level of negativity invested toward initiative defeat; often expressed through derision of committed colleagues.

Retiree-in-Residence: May exhibit characteristics of any on the above, but remains detached & marginally involved. Typical comment, "I only have x number of years before I retire. Why would I want to do anything different at this point?" Level of Engagement: marking time.

In Chapter 1 we cited Barry Schwartz and Kenneth Sharpe's argument that social and institutional forces are eroding the ethical obligation of credentialed professionals to make wise judgments in the best interest of their clients and (we would add) their profession. In discussing the field of education, Schwartz and Sharpe describe a group of teachers in Texas who resisted mandates that replaced creative lesson plans with sterile scripts and trivialized learning in the name of test preparation. A university professor who had been working with the teachers began to study how they responded to the test-driven curriculum:

> ...many of the experienced teachers fought back. They became canny outlaws, or creative saboteurs, dodging the "law," finding ways to cover the "proficiencies" with great efficiency and squirreling away time to sneak real education back in at the margins of the standardized system, sometimes even conspiring with their students or teaching them how to "game" the system.7

The idea of "canny outlaws" represents one way in which committed professionals serve as advocates. Sadly, Schwartz and Sharpe go on to say:

> But there were schools that closed down even this improvisation, using strict enforcement to prevent teachers from turning the scripts into guidelines. Open Court was introduced in California's Downer Elementary School in fall 2002. The first year, a number of teachers looked, quietly, for ways to work around some of its less workable rules. In 2003, enforcement tightened. Outside consultants, including trainers from McGraw-Hill, the company that sells Open Court, began entering classrooms at will, says Ms. Jaeger, then the school's literacy coordinator. Teachers' lessons were interrupted, and some teachers were chastised in front of their students. The principal threatened

disciplinary action against teachers who veered from the script. The administration grew rigid, "focusing on things like whether teachers had posted sound/spelling cards in the correct place." Most of the teachers spoke privately about their frustration. Ms. Jaeger and a few of her colleagues were more outspokenly opposed to Open Court, but they nevertheless offered to help with in-service trainings, with organizing student study teams, and with mentoring new teachers. They also tried to negotiate modifications in the curriculum. Their help was refused.

In October 2005, Ms. Jaeger and four other teachers wrote an open letter to their colleagues stating their opposition to particularly egregious aspects of the program and said they would no longer participate in these practices. They all received letters of reprimand, and two of them, including Ms. Jaeger, were removed from their classrooms and transferred to other sites. There were local protests from parents and teachers, and support from educators around the country.[8]

We have taken the liberty of quoting this anecdote at length because it illustrates so many points we have touched on including:

- the intrusion of external forces into the micro-context of classrooms;
- the role of principals and administrators in buffering these outside forces (or colluding with them);
- the issue of what is really at stake (e.g., student learning, the district's compliance with mandates, or McGraw Hill profits);
- the potentially high personal cost of taking an ethical stand to advocate for children and the profession; and
- the importance of working collaboratively within Communities of Practice.

This anecdote and others provided by Schwartz and Sharpe point to a sobering (and chilling) metanarrative about the failure of public education to meet the academic needs of our nation's children. Those with vested self-interests are using this metanarrative to exert control over the profession and educational institutions. Advocacy against these broader debilitating forces constitutes an ethical obligation of stewardship.

Even as Scholar-Practitioners remain alert to potential threats to the well-being of the profession and those it serves, they must remain open to new ideas and new possibilities. Knee-jerk rejection of any new initiative because past efforts have failed or other bandwagons have come and gone creates obstacles to potentially useful changes. Thoughtful or principled advocates are able to analyze the extent to which new ideas bring forward and extend the best of the profession, revitalizing it as a force for the future.

Commitment to Inquiry

A third aspect of Ethical Stewardship is a commitment to inquiry. In the discussion of Theoretical Understanding, we stressed the importance of using existing knowledge as lenses for discerning and interpreting complex dynamics of educational practice. That is one way in which a commitment to inquiry is demonstrated. Another way is engaging in inquiry that contributes to the knowledge base of the profession.

In Chapter 7, we introduced the concept of world view as shaped by epistemological, ontological, and axiological assumptions about the nature of knowledge and reality. Further, we suggested that understanding one's own world view in relation to the world views of others is a hallmark of Scholar-Practitioners. This self-understanding becomes particularly important when considering the ways in which one might contribute to the knowledge base of the profession.

Many different descriptors are used to distinguish among major research traditions. For our purposes, we will use scientific, interpretive, and critical theory. We look a bit more closely at each of these in the next chapter.

oneself + similiar others   happiness lab

the environment constrain· fundamental
our behavior.   attribution
                                      error

Ethical Stewardship and the *Telos* of Education

When education is seen as the journey of the self/soul, anything that impedes that journey violates the *telos* of education and the ethical principles that guide its practice. As in the case of the special education teacher in Annie's story, impediments can take the shape of uncaring, inept teachers, teachers who may not invest meaningfully in their own life's journey. As in the case of the "canny outlaws," impediments can take the shape of externally imposed mandates and retaliation against those who advocate for students and the profession. Anywhere within the micro, mezzo, and macro contexts of education, the use of power to serve one's own self-interest at the expense of students and colleagues results in unethical practices. Someone wins at the expense of others— be they students, teachers, administrators, or the public at large. The Scholar-Practitioner quality of Ethical Stewardship is a call for vigilance against such abuse of power and advocacy for humane and just engagement with others. It calls for the moral skill and practical wisdom to discern "the right way to do the right thing in a particular circumstance, with a particular person, at a particular time." It calls for a commitment to think beyond one's own career to the well-being of the profession and its purpose within our society.

REFLECTIVE PROMPTS

What thoughts and feelings are evoked by the ideas in this chapter?

In what ways do my responses to the ideas in this chapter contribute to my understanding of being a Scholar-Practitioner?

What questions are evoked by the ideas in this chapter? Where do those questions fit within my plan for continued learning?

What ideas do I want to incorporate into my evolving Scholar-Practitioner Narrative?

In what ways have I been or might become an advocate for the profession of education?

NOTES

1 Virginia Richardson, "Stewards of a Field, Stewards of an Enterprise: The Doctorate in Education," in *Envisioning the Future of Doctoral Education: Preparing Stewards for the Discipline. Carnegie Essays on the Doctorate*, eds. Chris M. Golde, George F. Walker and Associates (San Francisco: Jossey-Bass, 2006), 254.

2 National Education Association, *Code of Ethics,* adopted by the NEA 1975 Representative Assembly, retrieved from www.nea.org on October 13, 2017.

3 Association of American Educators, *Code of Ethics*, retrieved from www.aaeteachers.org on October 13, 2017.

4 National Association of State Directors of Teacher Education and Certification, *Model Code of Ethics for Educators*, retrieved from http://www.nasdtec.net on October 13, 2017.

5 Thomas A. Schwandt, *The Sage Dictionary of Qualitative Inquiry*, 3rd Edition (Los Angeles: SAGE, 2007), 242.

6 Golde, Chris M. "Preparing Stewards of the Discipline," in *Envisioning the Future of Doctoral Education: Preparing Stewards for the Discipline. Carnegie Essays on the Doctorate*, eds. Chris M. Golde, George F. Walker and Associates (San Francisco: Jossey-Bass, 2006), 13.

7 Barry Schwartz and Kenneth Sharpe. *Practical Wisdom: The Right Way to Do the Right Thing* (New York: Riverhead Books, 2010), 171,

8 Schwartz and Sharpe, 173.

11

Commitment to Inquiry

INTRODUCTION

The preceding chapter introduced commitment to inquiry as a dimension of Ethical Stewardship. This chapter considers what type of inquiry is suited to generating wisdom from practice. As discussed in Chapter 7, differences in world view can give rise to differing opinions about what is worth knowing, what constitutes legitimate knowledge and what methods are most appropriate for generating knowledge. In concluding the discussion of world view, we emphasized the importance of Scholar-Practitioners understanding where their own world view situates them within a broader intellectual landscape. This understanding allows for stronger reading of professional literature and for conceptual mapping of scholarly discourses. In this chapter, we revisit the concept of world view to differentiate among three broad approaches to educational inquiry—scientific, critical, and interpretive. We then argue that interpretive inquiry, particularly narrative, is well suited for generating practical wisdom.

Scientific Tradition

We extend our discussion of the scientific approach to generating knowledge by considering the concept of *ideal* theory. Social scientist Bent Flyvbjerg draws upon the work of Hubert Dreyfus and Pierre Bourdieu to discuss six defining characteristics of ideal theory:

> It must be *explicit* because a theory is to be laid out
> so clearly, in such detail, and so completely that it can

be understood by any reasoning being; a theory may
not stand or fall on interpretation or intuition. Second,
a theory must be *universal* in that it must apply in all
places and all times. Third, a theory must be *abstract*
in that it must not require the reference to concrete
example...A theory must also be *discrete,* that is,
formulated only with the aid of context-independent
elements, which do not refer to human interests,
traditions, institutions, etc. And it must be *systematic,*
that is, it must constitute a whole, in which context-
independent elements (properties, factors) are related
to each other by rules or laws...Finally, it must be
complete and *predictive.* The way a theory accounts
for the domain it covers must be comprehensive in
the sense that it specifies the range of variation in the
elements, which affect the domain, and the theory
must specify their effects. This makes possible precise
predication. Today, it is especially this last criterion
which in the hallmark of epistemic sciences.[1]

Those working in a scientific tradition assume that each
phenomenon has an essential nature that can be discovered by stripping
away extraneous variables. Ideally, scientific inquiry offers theories
that explain both the essential nature of a phenomenon and the factors
that constitute its nature.   clear, logical, convincing

The art of this inquiry lies in formulating cogent hypotheses and
elegant research designs to test the hypotheses. Cogent hypotheses
focus on anomalies that cannot be adequately explained by existing
theories. The practice of this inquiry tradition lies in the rigorous
attention to methodological procedures. Methodological precision
enhances confidence that theoretical explanations are valid and reliable
representations of a phenomenon. Confidence in the theory increases
when different researchers replicate methodological procedures and
obtain the same results. Confidence in the theory increases when the
same results are obtained regardless of the person conducting the
research or the context within which the phenomenon occurs.

Some educational Scholar-Practitioners are committed to this inquiry tradition. Often their quest is for best educational practices that will improve the quality of education in public schools. Because it is costly to carry out well-designed, statistically-meaningful scientific studies, such Scholar-Practitioners typically work in universities or research centers where they can compete for funding. However, public school-based Scholar-Practitioners typically do not have the time or financial resources needed to carry out scientific studies that meet the criteria listed above. Nonetheless, they can contribute to the knowledge base of the profession by accepting invitations to be participants in such studies. Researchers conducting science-based research often distribute survey questionnaires, conduct interviews, or engage in field observations. To gather data, they often depend upon the cooperation of those working in a range of educational roles and settings. Participating in such studies is one way in which Scholar-Practitioners can demonstrate the quality of Ethical Stewardship. So, too, is thoughtfully considering the results of such research and their implications for one's practice.

As mentioned earlier in the book, the scientific tradition has dominated much of western thinking since the days of Sir Isaac Newton and has given us tremendous understanding of the physical world. In some ways, it has also given great insight into the world of human affairs, including education. However, inquiry into the nature of human affairs is always complicated by social and cultural complexity and the infinite variability of human beings. Within the scientific tradition, such complexity and variability present a problem. No matter how carefully researchers try to control for it, the variability still seems to undermine the certainty of theoretical explanations of human affairs. That is a reason why scientific findings are often reported in terms of probabilities—how likely is something to be true. Researchers also describe limitations and delimitations of their studies, meaning they specify the parameters within which a study was conducted and caution that the findings might be limited to the population or circumstances of the study. Even so, scientific researchers hold to the value of seeking ideal theories that transcend specific contexts. Their quest may never be fully realized, but their intent remains steadfast. This is a pivotal point that differentiates those working in the scientific tradition from those working in critical and interpretive traditions. In these traditions, different world view assumptions underpin inquiries into the nature of human affairs.

Critical Tradition

The critical tradition has its roots in Marxist thinking and is concerned with social, cultural, political, and economic forces that privilege some groups over others. It assumes that conflict is inherent between groups with competing interests and that when one group wins, another group loses. Within this tradition, scholars focus attention upon a macro or structural view of life in schools and are critical of the oppressive nature of schooling.

Schooling is viewed as a major instrument for maintaining and legitimating the domination of one group over others. It is seen as a social practice supported and utilized by those in power to maintain their dominance in the social order. Students learn to be workers and consumers who are necessary to the "boss" class. This embeds educational systems within broader social conflicts between social classes, between rich and poor, between workers and capitalists, between the powerful and the powerless, between the protected and the unprotected.

Educational practices like tracking are seen as magnifying social inequality by sorting individuals according to their socio-economic class and thereby determining how they will fit into and serve our capitalist economic system. Similarly, funding public schools through property taxes promotes wealthy districts where students have a wide array of advantages and choices and impoverished districts where students may not receive even the most basic education. The injustice of such educational practices and social forces are the focus of those working in the critical tradition.

Over the years, many different strains of critical theory have emerged as various groups have challenged the dominance of the scientific tradition and its claims of objectivity, value-neutrality, and context-free generalizability. These critical theorists assert that the scientific tradition rests on epistemological, axiological, and ontological assumptions embedded in a Euro-centric, affluent, white, male world view. Critical race studies, feminist inquiry, Latino/Latina studies, "queer" studies, etc. offer insights into the ways schools (and other social institutions) marginalize and silence various classes of people. Underpinning the critical tradition are epistemological, axiological, and ontological assumptions that aim to reveal the structural inequities of society (and schooling), and thereby, raise consciousness, engender resistance, and lead to liberation of the oppressed.

We recall a comment by Jack during an introductory course on modes of inquiry. Upon hearing about critical theory, he declared, "That is my inquiry tradition. I'm a very critical person." At the same time, he was very dismissive of articles written by critical theorists because they used arcane "jargon," convoluted sentence structures, constant references to the works of French philosophers like Foucault and Derrida, allusions to postmodernism, poststructuralism, and deconstruction. "How is any of this stuff useful? Why do they keep going on about social class, capitalism, and social justice? I just want to know how to do a research project. When are we going to learn about specific methods so I can get on with my Master's thesis?" In giving a keynote address at a qualitative research conference, Elizabeth Adams St. Pierre offered a counterpoint to such complaints:

> One of the problems we've found in these critiques…
> is that those who protest the loudest seem to be those
> who have not read much in the literature. Like any other
> bodies of knowledge and practice, postmodernism,
> poststructuralism, postfoundationalism, deconstruc-
> tion, and so forth, have their own complex histories,
> their own languages, their own contradictory and
> competing discourses, their own structures of
> intelligibility.[2]

St. Pierre studied with Laurel Richardson whose work we cited in relation to understanding cultural and collective narratives. In her keynote remarks, St. Pierre mentions the following experience:

> I enrolled in her [Richardson's] 800-level advanced
> feminist theory course with absolutely no background
> in feminist theory. She looked me in the eye and said,
> "Would you enroll in an advanced physics course with
> no prior knowledge of physics? What makes you think
> you can do that with feminist theory?"

As we noted in discussing Theoretical Understanding, close reading, with and against the grain, is crucial for grasping the meaning of texts. To this view of reading, we add St. Pierre's admission that "I'm a more humble reader these days, and I don't expect the text to rush to greet me."

One of the reasons we have stressed the importance of understanding one's own world view is to help Scholar-Practitioners gain a sense of resonance with various research traditions. Our student Jack, for instance, might be a critical person, but whatever his sensibilities for inquiry might be, they do not draw him to critical theory. In our own experience, we have found that many practitioners are drawn instinctively to modes of inquiry within the interpretive tradition.

Interpretive Tradition

Those with a scientific ontology, axiology, and epistemology strive for research designs that can control for human variability and yield generalizable, explanatory, and predictive theories. Those with an interpretive ontology, axiology, and epistemology take human variability arising from human consciousness as an existential reality. Rather than stripping away the variability, interpretive researchers seek to understand its nuances. Interpretive researchers assume that human affairs are fraught with dilemmas that are irresolvable. Inherent in a dilemma is a choice, not necessarily between a good option and a bad one, but between options which have tradeoffs between what is gained and what is lost.

The issue of educational inclusion is an example of such a dilemma. If we respect the worth and dignity of each human being, then children with special needs should be included within the social fabric of regular classrooms. Yet children with special needs often require more support and attention from classroom teachers, leaving less attention for other children. As a result, the learning of these children may not reach its full potential. If more funding were available, perhaps the dilemma could be resolved. Yet funding alone may not be a solution because there are often tradeoffs between funding education and funding other social services such as public safety, affordable housing, and universal health care.

In the end, there is no best practice to resolve a dilemma. The most we can hope for is the wisdom to understand the tradeoffs we are making as well as the moral and ethical implications of those tradeoffs. Thus understanding and wisdom are the aims of interpretive inquiry. This makes the interpretive inquiry tradition well suited for practitioners who want to study the dilemmas inherent in educational practice.

Interpretive studies are "intimate" in the sense that they look closely at dilemmas within micro contexts. Typically, they do not require large scale funding. Practitioners with a heightened capacity for discernment are well-positioned to engage in such inquiries. Previously, we have cited Alan Alda's concepts of seeing and listening as crucial to discernment in pedagogical practice. Scholars Kirsch and Royster describe such *deep listening* as an "inquiry strategy

> ...geared toward facilitating a quest for a more richly rendered understanding—listening to and learning from [those we are studying], going repeatedly, not to our assumptions and expectations, but to [those we are studying]—to their writing, their work, and their worlds, seeking to ground...inquiries in the evidence of [their] lives...[3]

Each new student, each new class, each new school year represents a "recursive turn," allowing practitioners to carry forward the insights already gained and to probe them more deeply. One might ask, "Why bother if I've already gained good insight?" This is where ontology and axiology come into play. If we believe that individuals make meaning within their unique life journey and our role as educators is to support those existential journeys, then there is always more to understand. If we are committed to attaining the full measure of our own unique potential, then the more we strive to understand, the more we learn and grow as individuals. Committing to this process is a matter of axiology—what one values.

One might also ask, "If these intimate studies yield no generalizable truth or best practice, then of what value are the results of interpretive inquiry? Why bother sharing them? What would even be shared?" The results of interpretive inquiries are often presented as heuristics— conceptual constructs that help to name previously unnoticed dynamics, reduce ambiguity, reveal tradeoffs, and touch universal chords of human experience. Unlike scientific inquiries where precautions are taken to guard against researcher bias/subjectivity, interpretive research assumes that the researcher is the instrument of inquiry. The researchers offer the meaning they have made of the dilemma under study. There are no preset formulas for how the meanings are represented. Each researcher creates a form that simultaneously represents both the process and results of the inquiry. This is a highly creative act, making interpretive inquiry more congruent with the arts and humanities than with the sciences. Therefore, it calls for a shift in criteria for judging the legitimacy of knowledge offered by the inquirer.

Various scholars writing about interpretive inquiry have offered a number of criteria for judging its merits. Among those commonly mentioned are:

- Self-awareness. Often this is referred to as "positionality." It means that inquirers are aware of the position from which they are observing and interpreting experience. Aspects of positionality include world view, social class, ethnicity, gender, disciplinary training, personal values, assumptions, etc.
- Reflexivity and Discernment. This refers to a capacity to reflect on experience and one's self to discern previously obscure or unnoticed features. Often this entails recognizing and examining one's own preconceptions and taken-for-granted assumptions.
- Deliberative. This refers to the breadth and depth of thinking the researcher brings to bear on the phenomenon under study. The researcher avoids premature, superficial, simplistic, self-congratulatory interpretations of events. The researcher's understanding and interpretations are informed by and situated within existing scholarly discourses.

[handwritten margin note: discover, learn for oneself]

- Contextualized. The researcher renders a vivid and compelling description of the experience within which the phenomenon has been studied.
- Aesthetic. This does NOT mean that the research report is merely decorated with artistic touches. Aesthetics refers to the elegance and power of the thinking that is represented in the final account of the inquiry. The mode of representation provides a compelling account of how the researcher has investigated the question under study and results are portrayed persuasively—not persuasive in the sense that everyone should now think the same way or that the results are universally applicable. Rather, the persuasiveness leads a reader to say, "Given what the researcher did, I can see how the researcher reached his/her conclusions and the conclusions are well-warranted."
- Useful. This refers to the utility of the inquiry results. They contribute meaningfully to scholarly discourses; enhance pedagogical wisdom and theoretical understanding, and advance the knowledge base of the profession.

The elegance and artistry of scientific inquiry lie in the formulation of the hypothesis and the research design. The rigor lies in careful adherence to the design procedures. In interpretive inquiry, the elegance and artistry lie in the inquirer's capacity to resonate with significant experiential moments. The rigor lies in the thoughtfulness and thoroughness with which the researcher probes such moments for meaning. Since the mid-1970's a variety of research methods have evolved to support such probing for contextualized meaning within the Interpretive Tradition. To touch even briefly on these many modes of inquiry goes beyond the scope and purpose of this book. However, we do want to focus a bit on narrative for three reasons. First, over the years it has become prominent in the discourses on teacher inquiry. Second, it aligns closely with the human proclivity for making meaning through story.[4] Third, regardless of which interpretive method is used, it is necessary to tell the story of the study: what prompted the study; why is it important; how was it conducted, and what was learned.

Narrative as a Mode of Interpretive Inquiry

Human beings are storytellers. Often we think of stories as fiction
that immerses us in imaginary worlds. Stories, however, play a
deeper, more profound role as human beings make sense of and give
coherence to their lives through the construction of stories. Writing *sensible*
in 1986, social psychologist Jerome Bruner contrasted paradigmatic
knowing to narrative knowing. We take the liberty of quoting him at
length, because he expresses so well the difference between the two
modes of thought:

> There are two modes of cognitive functioning, two
> modes of thought, each providing distinctive ways
> of ordering experience, of constructing reality. The
> two (though complementary) are irreducible to one
> another. Efforts to reduce one mode to the other or to
> ignore one at the expense of the other inevitably fail to
> capture the rich diversity of thought.
>
> Each of the ways of knowing, moreover, has operating
> principles of its own and its own criteria of well-
> formedness. They differ radically in their procedures
> for verification. A good story and a well-formed
> argument are different natural kinds. Both can be
> used as a means for convincing another. Yet what they
> convince *of* is fundamentally different: arguments
> convince one of their truth, stories of their lifelikeness.
> The one verifies by eventual appeal to procedures for
> establishing formal and empirical proof. The other
> establishes not truth but verisimilitude.[5]

the 'appearance of being true or rea [

Scholars writing in the field of education began to draw upon
Bruner's work to argue for the value of narrative as a mode of
educational inquiry. Among the earliest proponents of teacher narratives
were Michael Connelley and Jean Clandinin:

> Narrative inquiry is increasingly used in studies of educational experience. It has a long intellectual history both in and out of education. The main claim for the use of narrative in educational research is that humans are storytelling organisms who, individually and socially, lead storied lives. The study of narrative, therefore, is the study of the ways humans experience the world. This general notion translates into the view that education is the construction and reconstruction of personal and social stories; teachers and learners are storytellers and characters in their own and other's stories.[6]

Note that Connelley and Clandinin call attention to both individual and social narratives. The idea of a Scholar-Practitioner Narrative introduced in Chapter 2 is an example of an individual narrative. It is a mode of writing that allows Scholar-Practitioners to integrate new ideas and new ways of thinking into their personal and professional life's journey. The very process of constructing and reconstructing one's narrative can lead to learning, growth, and development. This is one reason we stressed the importance of listening carefully and respectfully to the stories that students bring to their experience of schooling. Through generative educational encounters, students have opportunities to change their stories of self and the stories that others have written for them. This is the pedagogical power of individual narratives. Social narratives constructed through more formal inquiry hold the potential for generating practical wisdom for the benefit of the profession. Thus, engaging in narrative inquiry is one way Scholar-Practitioners can enact their responsibility for Ethical Stewardship.

Bruner observes, "Narrative deals with the vicissitudes of human intentions."[7] Vicissitudes—troubles—give rise to a narrative impulse and serve as the engine to drive narrative. Awareness of trouble generally surfaces when strong feelings are evoked by a particular experience. We refer to such evocative experiences as "moments." For Scholar-Practitioners, troubling moments may arise at the micro-, mezzo-, or macro-level.

change of circumstances

The idea of "moment" suggests the concept of time—perhaps a brief instant; perhaps a more extended period or sequence of connected events, perhaps an era. Thus, moments can be as fleeting as a single classroom encounter or as prolonged as a multi-year reform initiative. Moments can arise from interactions with others or from reading or from news accounts. Whatever jars us from our sense of the expected or expectable; whatever disrupts the normal flow of life can constitute a moment potentially worthy of study. At the core of all narratives is the premise, "Life was going well, I was minding my own business, when suddenly this occurred." The narrative then traces the events surrounding the disruptive moment and what comes of it. Thus pedagogical moments can serve as a rich source of practice-embedded, narrative inquiry. The Scholar-Practitioner qualities of Metacognitive Reflection and Aesthetic Imagination encompass capacities at the heart of narrative and other forms of interpretive inquiry.

Metacognitive Reflection and Narrative Inquiry

After Donald Schon published *The Reflective Practitioner: How Professionals Think in Action*, "reflection" became a buzzword in educational discourses. Teachers were encouraged to keep reflective journals and create reflective portfolios. Rubrics for assessing teacher reflection soon followed. Eventually, the term became so overused (even trivialized), its meaning as described by John Dewey was often obscured. As one teacher educator exclaimed during a discussion about reflection, "I just want my students to learn skills that they can actually use in their classrooms." The implication that reflection isn't useful is unfortunate, because as Dewey maintains, reflection on experience is integral to the process of learning.[8] If teacher educators and teachers dismiss reflection as irrelevant, how then, can they nurture this capacity in their students?[9] A great deal of educational rhetoric stresses the importance of critical thinking and learning how to learn. A capacity for Metacognitive Reflection underpins both of these educational goals.

Reflection in Dewey's sense means more than casual musings on events. Pat, in an essay on narrative inquiry, offers the following elaboration of this point:

Polkinghorne (1997) tells us that "narrative transforms a mere succession of actions and events into a coherent whole in which these happenings gain meaning as contributors to a common purpose" (13). But attaining coherence from the spontaneity of an educational encounter is possible only if the teacher regards those learning moments as the epicenter of her research. "The sense of coherence," Bochner (1997) reminds us, "does not inhere in the events themselves. Coherence is an achievement, not a given" (429). The teacher becomes the conduit for coherency when "the meanings of events flows [sic] from their appearance in the researcher's reflections on them from the perspective of what has happened" (Schon, 1983, cited in Polkinghorne, 1997, 15). My ability to reflect on classroom interaction is crucial, then, to my understanding the significance of what has occurred.[10]

In other words, narrative allows us to incorporate the insights gained through reflection into our evolving life story. Through narrative we bring past meanings forward into the present and project current meanings into an anticipated future. As Deborah Britzman observes:

Learning to teach is not a mere matter of applying decontextualized skills or of mirroring predetermined images; it is a time when one's past, present, and future are set in dynamic tension. Learning to teach—like teaching itself—is always the process of becoming: a time of formation and transformation, of scrutiny into what one is doing, and who one can become.[11]

Meaning-making through reflection and narrative entails capacities for immersion in experience, careful observation, interpretation, and conceptual representation. For Scholar-Practitioners, these capacities come into play in the normal course of professional endeavors and in the course of formal inquiries. In the next chapter we look more closely at the quality of Metacognitive Reflection.

Commitment to Inquiry and the *Telos* of Education

From micro to macro contexts, education is fraught with complexity. Davis, Sumara and Luce-Kapler make an important distinction between complex and complicated systems. Briefly stated, complicated systems assume that "most phenomena in the universe are...mechanical—that is, that understanding 'how things work' and predicting their behaviors is a matter of reducing them to their fundamental parts."[12] In contrast:

> Complex systems can never be reduced to their parts because they are always caught up with other systems in a dance of chance. Complex unities are...spontaneous, unpredictable, irreducible, and contextual, and vibrantly sufficient—in brief, they are adaptive...Complex systems are systems that learn.[13]

Through a commitment to inquiry, Scholar-Practitioners help to illuminate the complexities of education for their own learning, for the improvement of the profession, and for the benefit of society. As David Labaree contends, educational scholarship can serve

> ...to develop research...--concepts, generalizations, theories—that make sense of educational processes across contexts and offer them to teachers and other practitioners. The idea is not to pretend to make claims about teaching and learning that are universal in a literal sense, but instead to provide a theoretical mirror, which teachers can hold up to their own problems of practice in order to see the ways that their problems are both similar to and different from those facing teachers in other settings. In this sense, then, theory allows teachers access to a community of practice that is otherwise often denied them by the tyranny of the self-contained classroom.[14]

By embodying a stance of inquiry, Scholar-Practitioners understand that substantive educational issues are embedded in the "stories" of educational practice—their own and others'—and so the focus of scholarly engagement is not so much on problem solving as it is on "deep listening" and problem framing. This perspective honors the complexities that teachers and learners experience as they cope with dilemmas of daily practice. When commitment to inquiry is connected with Contextual Literacy, Scholar-Practitioners can serve as stewards of the profession by contributing to broader deliberations on school improvement.

After analyzing reasons for the failure of so many school improvement initiatives, Anthony Bryk concluded that more nuanced forms of data are needed to formulate courses of action and a wider range of evidence is needed to evaluate those actions. Therefore, he argues for the involvement of practitioners in Networked Improvement Communities (NICs):

> To be clear, responding effectively to issues of task and organizational complexity does not mean imposing some seemingly arbitrary standards from outside or delivered from above. Rather, it entails an education improvement community that actively creates them through its disciplined inquiries. *Practitioners need to engage fully with researchers* and others in developing, testing, and enhancing the clinical work of schooling.[15] (Italics added)

Bryk's belief in the value of practitioner involvement is significant because he is president of the Carnegie Foundation for the Improvement of Teaching which exerts a great deal of influence on how school improvement efforts take place. At the end of Chapter 8, we suggested that Scholar-Practitioners participate in Communities of Practice to support their own learning. The influence of such communities tends to be at the micro-level. In contrast, NICs focus on educational issues at mezzo and macro levels.

Scholar-Practitioners who have an understanding of interpretive inquiry and Contextual Literacy are well positioned to participate in NICs or, through their scholarly writing, contribute to the deliberations of such networks. These are avenues through which they can serve as stewards of the profession.

REFLECTIVE PROMPTS

What thoughts and feelings are evoked by the ideas in this chapter?

p. 192

In what ways do my responses to the ideas in this chapter contribute to my understanding of being a Scholar-Practitioner?

What questions are evoked by the ideas in this chapter? Where do those questions fit within my plan for continued learning?

What ideas do I want to incorporate into my evolving Scholar-Practitioner Narrative?

reflection

NOTES

1 Bent Flyvbjerg, *Making Social Science Matter: Why Social Inquiry Fails and How It Can Succeed Again*, trans. Steven Sampson (New York: Cambridge University Press, 2001), 38-39.

2 Elizabeth Adams St. Pierre, "Working the Ruins: Qualitative Research in the Postmodern," (Keynote Address Presented at QUIG, January 4, 2002).

3 Gesa E. Kirsch and Jacqueline J. Royster. Feminist Rhetorical Practices: In Search of Excellence. *College of Composition and Communication*, 61 no 4 (2010): 649.

4 For an interesting account of the human affinity for story telling see: Jonathan Gottschall, The Storytelling Animal: How Stories Make Us Human, Boston: Mariner Books, 2013.

5 Jerome Bruner, *Actual Minds, Possible Worlds* (Cambridge , MA: Harvard University Press, 1986), 11.

6 F. Michael Connelly & D. Jean Clandinin, "Stories of Experience and Narrative Inquiry," *Educational Researcher*, 19, no. 5 (1990), 2.

7 Jerome Bruner, 16.

8 John Dewey, *Experience and Education* (New York: Collier Books, 1938).

9   Notice how this issue of "practical skills" versus reflection is a manifestation of differing theoretical perspectives of learning. The rhetoric of skills is often situated in the discourses of behaviorism. Reflection is situated in the discourses on learning as meaning-making.

10 Patricia L. McMahon, "Narrative Yearnings: Reflecting in Time through the Art of Fictive Story" in *The Authority to Imagine: The Struggle toward Representation in Dissertation Writing*, eds Noreen B. Garman & Maria Piantanida (Pittsburgh: Learning Moments Press), 242. For a more detailed explication of the role of fictive story in practice-embedded inquiry see, Patricia L. McMahon, "From Angst to Story to Research Text: The Role of Arts-Based Educational Research in Teacher Inquiry," *Journal of Curriculum Theorizing* 16, no 1 (Spring 2000): 125-146.

11 Deborah Britzman, *Practice Makes Practice: A Critical Study of Learning to Teach* (Albany, NY: State University of New York Press,1991), 8.

12 Brent Davis, Dennis Sumara, Rebecca Luce-Kapler, *Engaging Minds: Changing Teaching in Complex Times*, 2nd Edition (New York: Routledge, 2008), 55.

13 Davis, Sumara, and Luce-Kapler, 77-78.

14 David F. Labaree, "The Peculiar Problems of Preparing Educational Researchers," *Educational Researcher* 32, no 4 (2003), 20.

15 Anthony S. Bryk, "2014 AERA Distinguished Lecture. Accelerating How We Learn to Improve," *Educational Researcher* 44, no 9 (2015): 473.

SECTION VI

The Quality of Metacognitive Reflection

Metacognitive Reflection entails a capacity
to theorize from experience.

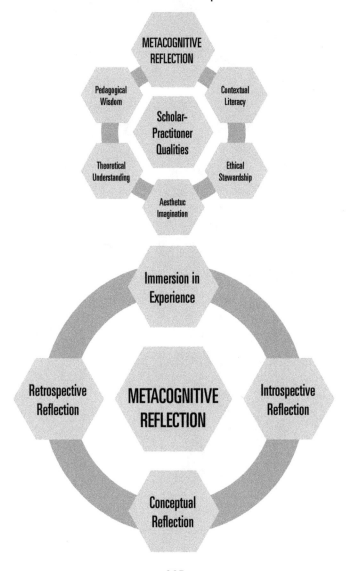

12

Metacognitive Reflection

Throughout this book, we have contrasted a behavioral view of learning to an existential view. Even when educational encounters are structured around specific behavioral outcomes, those encounters and the outcomes have existential meaning for participants. Often these meanings are incorporated without much thought or awareness into the stories we tell about ourselves, about school, about education, and about learning. Metacognitive Reflection entails giving deliberate, conscious attention both to the meanings we construct from our experiences and to the thought processes through which we construct those meanings. In short, Metacognitive Reflection is thinking about thinking. Through Metacognitive Reflection, Scholar-Practitioners construct personal, typically private, narratives. As ethical stewards of the profession, however, they have a responsibility to construct and publicly share narratives that contribute to the knowledge base of the profession. Thus, Metacognitive Reflection serves as a process for individual learning and formal narrative inquiry. In the remainder of this chapter we look more closely at Metacognitive Reflection as comprising three interconnected forms of reflection—Introspective, Recollective, and Conceptual.

Introspective and Recollective Reflection

Metacognitive Reflection often begins introspectively with an uneasy feeling (perhaps mild, perhaps intense) that something has gone awry. Such feelings may arise in a classroom (where one is a teacher or a student); they might occur as one reads and encounters new ideas; they might occur serendipitously in the course of daily living. What distinguishes these moments from others is their power to demand our attention. They nag at us, even haunt our dreams. They are like an annoying pebble in a shoe; in short, such moments signify some trouble that may be worthy of closer examination. This is where Introspective and Recollective Reflection come into play. Introspectively, we ask ourselves, "What am I feeling?" Recollectively, we ask, "Where did this feeling come from?" These questions set one on the path of inquiry. The path begins with a recollection of situational details including the answer to the following questions:

- When did the moment occur? How long did it last?
- Where did the moment occur?
- Who was involved in the moment?
- What was my role in the moment?
- What happened; what actions occurred; what was said and by whom?

In *Dragnet*, the precursor to today's police procedural television shows, Detective Sargent Joe Friday would inevitably say, "The facts, ma'am, just the facts." He wanted to screen out impressions, speculations, and emotional reactions that would impede his investigation. Recollective Reflection is similar in the recall of the "who, what, when and where" details of a moment. In Metacognitive Reflection, however, "subjective facts" are equally important. Through Introspective Reflection questions such as the following are taken into consideration:

- What are my impressions of the moment?
- What aspect of the moment triggered the trouble or feeling? What is the nature of my feelings?
- What does this moment tell me about my expectations and assumptions?
- What shaped these expectations and assumptions?
- Could this moment have gone more smoothly if I had known more about x, y, or z?

While a moment is still fresh, it is important to record as many of these details and impressions as possible. However, over time, additional situational details may emerge. So, too, may additional impressions in the form of metaphors, dreams, and speculations.[1] Sometimes a song, a poem, a play, a story, or cartoon comes to mind. Perhaps memories of another, seemingly unrelated, experience pop up. While these musings would have no place in Sargent Friday's crime scene investigations, they play an important role in Metacognitive Reflection and should be recorded. Often we assume that the record of Reflective and Introspective Reflections will be only verbal. But the record may also include sketches, pictures, or images[2]—whatever helps to capture a moment and one's responses to it.

At first, the significance of a moment may be nebulous; buried in one of those swampy, lowland messes that Donald Schon described. The act of recording responses to the types of questions listed above can help to clarify the source of trouble. So, too, can talking with colleagues. This is one reason it is so important to be part of one or more Communities of Practice. As trust and respect develop among community members, a safe space is created where nebulous, troubling thoughts can be explored. Through writing and conversation, issues embedded in the moment may begin to come into focus. Some issues may be of marginal interest; others may be sufficiently compelling to warrant further investigation. This represents a shift into Conceptual Reflection.

Conceptual Reflection

Through Conceptual Reflection, Scholar-Practitioners begin to explore the significance of moments within a broader intellectual landscape. Instead of relying on their immediate or instinctive interpretation of events, they turn to discourses to see who else might be thinking and writing about issues that have surfaced through Recollective and Introspective Reflection.

One immediate source of information are Scholar-Practitioners' existing stores of theoretical understandings gained over time through immersion in their field(s) of study. This calls for a blending of Recollective, Introspective, and Conceptual Reflection as the Scholar-Practitioner considers the question, "What meaning can I make of this ᴗᴍent when I look at it through various theories with which I am already familiar?" Returning to our foreopter metaphor, this review of one's reservoir of theoretic understandings gives rise to questions such as:

- Which lens brings issues into sharper focus?
- Which lens allows me to see more clearly what was at stake in the moment?
- Which lens gives me the most useful insight?
- What kept me from drawing upon this theoretic lens in the heat of the moment?
- What can I do to make this understanding more readily available to me in future moments?

When one's existing store of knowledge yields few, if any, insights, a next step is turning to additional discourses. Potentially useful information can be gained through a range of resources including:

- Books
  - Single Author
  - Edited Collections
  - Handbooks & Encyclopedias

- Journals
  - Research articles
  - Conceptual/theoretical essays
  - Book reviews
  - Editorial pieces

- Government Publications
  - Statistical compilations

Laws, rules, regulations

- Organizational Documents
  - External—annual reports, newsletters, position papers
  - Internal—memos, minutes of meetings, policies & procedures

- Individual and Organization Websites
- Wikipedia

- Blogs
- Facebook

Fortunately, digitalization makes many of these resources easily accessible. Scholar-Practitioners, however, understand that all sources of information and ideas are not equally useful or credible. In a pre-digital age, individuals who wanted to have their work published would submit a manuscript to a book publisher or journal. The manuscript would be sent for review by experts in the field who would critique the piece in terms of relevance, significance, quality of research/thinking, etc. Only if the manuscript received high reviews would it be published. This gave readers some assurance that what they were reading met at least minimum standards and could be considered credible. In today's digital world, individuals who want to share their ideas can do so directly. On one hand, this allows for the free exchange of ideas and reduces barriers to information access. On the other hand, this increases the risk of promulgating inaccurate information, ill-formulated opinions, and unsubstantiated knowledge claims. Consequently, reading critically is crucial. To read critically does NOT mean to criticize what others have written. Rather, as mentioned in the discussion of close reading, it means:

- Understanding the conceptual arguments or points the author is making;
- Analyzing the nature and adequacy of the warrants that the author uses to support an argument;
- Comparing and contrasting one author's perspective with those of other authors who are writing on the issue;
- Identifying the discipline, school of thought and/or discourse community within which the author's work is situated;
- Surmising the author's world view; and
- Reflecting on connections between the author's ideas and one's own thinking.

It may seem that immersion in discourses could quickly become overwhelming as one path leads on to another and another. This is potentially true, but there are several ways to think about this aspect of

Metacognitive Reflection. First is being mindful of setting boundaries that are reasonable within the time available to explore an issue. Often revisiting the catalyzing moment and the issue embedded in it can serve to anchor one's thinking. Again, introspective reflection comes into play as one checks potential sources of feelings:

- Am I going astray? Have I lost focus? Have the suggestions of friends and colleagues diverted my attention?
- Am I simply overwhelmed because this is a new process for me and I'm still learning how to manage it?
- Am I immersed in Conceptual Reflection that demands time, patience, and tolerance for ambiguity so I don't come to premature closure?

Second, when Scholar-Practitioners are following a line of inquiry because it is personally compelling to them, they may have no particular deadlines to meet. Therefore, they can engage in various activities as time permits. Annie, for example, could interview other substitute and regular teachers that she meets on subsequent teaching assignments. Or she could send out a request for job descriptions while on an assignment, but save the analysis until she has a break. If she is enrolled in an academic program, she may be able to do a review of literature as part of a class project or use that opportunity to gather information from classmates. Metacognitive Reflection allows Scholar-Practitioners to capitalize on the work they are already doing for sources of material and new insights.

A third way to cope with seemingly overwhelming avenues of inquiry goes back to the idea of curriculum as the track one's mind runs on and the notion of generative themes. Sometimes inquiries run their course. Whatever intellectual need catalyzed the inquiry has been satisfied. Other times, however, inquiries become so compelling they begin to shape and direct one's professional journey. The three of us, for example, are endlessly fascinated by what it means to be a Scholar-Practitioner. Even as we finish this book, we have begun to consider the next turn in our path—exploring how we might create a cyber-based community of Scholar-Practitioners. When one embraces the stance of Scholar-Practitioner, the results of one inquiry often contain the seeds of the next. Because inquiry aligns with one's professional passions, it is not an externally imposed burden, but a way of continually forming and transforming one's sense of self.

Conceptual Reflection on the ideas encountered in broader discourses can lead to several different outcomes. A perspective so strikingly different from one's own might precipitate a whole new round of introspective reflection—why did the experience evoke such strong feelings in me and a similar situation was inconsequential to my colleague? This might call for further Recollective Reflection— what did I miss in my recollection of events; what cues could I have noticed; what in my prior experiences primed me to respond as I did? These recursive turns generate more ideas and suggest alternative interpretations of an experience.

Alternatively, a Scholar-Practitioner may discover that the issue has already been thoroughly studied and a great deal of information is available in the professional discourses. In becoming familiar with these discourses, Scholar-Practitioners gain insight into the issue and reconstruct the meaning of a troubling moment in a way that deepens their reservoir of wisdom and knowledge. In other words, Conceptual Reflection has enriched the individual's personal narrative, but offers nothing substantially new to the knowledge base of the profession. That said, there may be situations in which this personal learning can be helpful to others. For example, if colleagues are discussing a problematic situation, a Scholar-Practitioner might be in a position to say, "You know, I had a similar situation. It bothered me so much, I began to do some reading and found a lot of people have been studying this issue. What was particularly helpful was something I read in an article by _____. It said…" Such acts of sharing, although small, are part of being a steward of the profession.

Another potential outcome of Conceptual Reflection may be the discovery of concepts that help the Scholar-Practitioner gain a new perspective on a troubling moment. Because others have not yet formally connected these concepts to the specific issue being explored, the Scholar-Practitioner has an opportunity to offer new insights. As we have suggested earlier, narrative inquiry lends itself to moving personal, private learning into a broader, public arena. These are instances in which Scholar-Practitioners can contribute to the knowledge base of their profession thereby fulfilling the Ethical Stewardship responsibility of inquiry.

In reviewing various discourses, a Scholar-Practitioner may discover that his or her particular perspective has not been given much attention. This represents an opportunity to make the current discourses more nuanced and, in some cases, to offer a counterpoint to a prevailing narrative. For example, Doris Santoro, the teacher educator we referenced in Chapter 1, expanded the discourses of teacher burnout by introducing the concept of demoralization. In doing so, she reframed the issue from the failure of individual teachers to failures within mezzo and macro contexts. This has significant implications for school reform efforts and creates new avenues for research.

During the course of reviewing discourses, a Scholar-Practitioner may discover that little has been written about the issue embedded in the troubling moment. Consider, for example, the availability of literature on the issue of school shootings and what might be appropriate deterrents to such tragedies. A Scholar-Practitioner searching for discourses after the shooting at Columbine might have found very little. Now, in the aftermath of so many shootings, a robust discourse is emerging. However, a great deal of this discourse is taking place in real time"—e.g., in news media and on-line. The discussions about school violence are evolving so rapidly, it is difficult to get a bird's eye view of all the positions represented by various stakeholder groups (e.g., teachers, students, victims and their families, law enforcement officials, and politicians). A Scholar-Practitioner who feels strongly about this issue could contribute to the profession's knowledge base by sharing the results of his or her investigations with broader Communities of Practice.

For a variety of reasons, a Scholar-Practitioner may decide that the lack of information in the existing discourses represents an opportunity for formal investigation. In such situations, a Scholar-Practitioner might embark on a process of information gathering through interviews, questionnaires, observations, etc. This type of investigation often becomes more structured as an inquiry plan is formulated. If the plan will be carried out within an organization or under the auspices of an organization, the Scholar-Practitioner may need to submit a proposal for institutional review and approval. Typically such a review process includes a review to assure that the investigation will be carried out in an ethical manner and assuring protection for anyone asked to participate in it. In the following section, we offer two examples of how a Scholar-Practitioner might move from a situational moment to a plan for inquiry.

From Moment to Inquiry

Example 1: To illustrate the process of formalizing an inquiry, let's revisit the moment experienced by Annie, the substitute teacher who was told to read the textbook to her students. Her Introspective and Recollective account of the moment was described in Chapter 10, where she stays close to the details of the situation including her exhaustion at "teaching" in this way. After some additional Introspection and Recollection, she might summarize the moment more briefly:

> As a substitute teacher I felt de-energized and frustrated when directed to read to students by a special educational teacher. I felt forced to ignore or abandon educational principles that I value as a foundation for authentic teaching.

Notice the difference between these two accounts of the moment. In the Chapter 10 version, Annie gives a more robust picture of the moment including her feelings, but already touches on the "troubling pebble in her shoe." Through conceptual reflection, Annie is able to clarify the issue signaled by her feelings and frame it into a question for study:

Issue: Teaching authentically as a substitute teacher

Question for Study: In what ways is it possible to teach authentically within the scope of responsibility and authority of a substitute teacher? (Even though this is

worded positively, Annie would have to hold open the
possibility that it may not be possible for substitutes to
teach authentically.)

Once Annie has framed the question, a number of subsidiary
questions can be posed. Each points to a different source of information
and a different method of accessing the information.

How are the responsibilities and authority of substitute
teachers described in the educational discourses?
(Literature review)

How are the responsibilities and authority of substitute
teachers detailed in the job descriptions of various
districts? (Content analysis of multiple job descriptions
representing districts of varying size and location)

How do other substitute teachers think about the
responsibilities and authority of their role? Have they
experienced moments of authentic and inauthentic
teaching? (Interviews with other substitute teachers or
survey questionnaire)

How do full-time teachers think about the
responsibilities and authority of substitute teachers?
Do they think about these issues differently if they are
relying on a substitute for a long-term versus short-
term absence? (Initial literature review; if little is
found in the literature, interviews with teachers)

How do principals think about the responsibilities
and authority of substitute teachers who work in
their buildings? (Interviews of principals; perhaps
those identified through the analysis of district job
descriptions)

No matter which one of these avenues Annie pursued, she would
at some point have gathered a lot of information. That is the point at
which heavy duty Conceptual Reflection comes into play as Annie asks,

"How can I begin to think about what it means to teach authentically as a substitute teacher?" This is the meaning-making work that moves an inquiry from situational details to a conceptual framework that puts the details into a coherent perspective. This is the most demanding and challenging aspect of Metacognitive Reflection in narrative inquiry— sorting through what one has come to understand and presenting those understandings in a way that can be useful to others. Often it is helpful to consider what audience(s) might be interested in knowing what has been learned. Annie, for example, might want to share the results of her inquiry with one or more of the following groups:

> Other substitute teachers
>
> Regular classroom teachers who must rely on substitute teachers during either short-term or long-term absences
>
> Principals who may want to make the best use of substitute teachers or who want to hire the best available substitute teachers
>
> Faculty in teacher preparation programs who may want to raise students' awareness of issues related to the role of substitute teacher.

Depending on her audience, Annie would then select the most relevant information to present. She may, in fact, sort all of the information she gathered based on what would be of most interest to various audiences. Then she would be able to prepare several different reports of her investigation.

Before looking at several aspects of portraying an inquiry, let's consider a slight twist on Annie's experience.

Example 2. Suppose Annie had been allowed to present the science lesson as she had initially planned it and it had turned out well. Her account of the moment might be stated briefly as:

> While substitute teaching I had an opportunity to try
> out a visual representation of an abstract scientific
> concept. I was pleased with the way in which this
> instructional strategy worked and how it seemed to
> engage students.

If Annie stopped with that statement, it might seem self-congratulatory. However, by considering the issues embedded in the moment, she might identify the following options for further inquiry:

> Issue: Pedagogical strategies for engaging students in
> a secondary science curriculum
>
> Issue: Using visual models as a pedagogical strategy to
> illustrate abstract scientific concepts

Again, she could move from these broadly stated issues to more specific inquiry questions:

> What does selected literature say about the issue of
> engaging secondary students in science education?
>
> What is the pedagogical rationale for using visual
> models to illustrate abstract scientific concepts?

Either of these options could be pursued through reviews of relevant literature. Beyond that, the options could be studied by:

> Analyzing science textbooks for examples of activities
> that engage students or use visual models;
>
> Interviewing other science teachers to understand how
> they think about the issue of student engagement and/
> or using visual models; or
>
> Participating in a regional science collaborative where
> educators meet regularly to study ways to engage
> students in learning about science.

Notice how this last approach would connect Annie with a Community of Practice that could inform her thinking and serve as an audience for the results of her inquiry.

We hope these examples help to show how troubling moments can fuel Metacognitive Reflection and, in turn, practice-based inquiries. We consider these to be narrative inquiries, because the outcomes are incorporated into one's Personal Scholar-Practitioner Narrative and because they can be shared publicly in the form of a narrative. In the next chapter we consider several aspects of constructing a narrative account (portrayal) of Metacognitive Reflection.

Metacognitive Reflection and the Telos of Education

For Scholar-Practitioners, Metacognitive Reflection is a process for moving systematically and critically between doing and understanding. It is a recursive process through which action informs theory and theory informs action.

The concept of "practice" focuses on action—what we do during educational encounters. The questions of practice include:

- What do I do? What action(s) do I take?
- How do I do something?
- How can I do something better?

The concept of "praxis" focuses on theorizing—making meaning of experience. Questions of praxis include:

- What does this experience, action, event mean?
- How can I think about this experience, action, event, experience?
- How can I understand what I am doing in practice?
- What theoretical lenses am I using and can I use to interpret experience, action, events?

Metacognitive Reflection is the capacity to create conceptual bridges between the questions of practice and the questions of praxis. It calls for Scholar-Practitioners to:

- Immerse themselves in experience;
- Recognize of moments of potential significance;
- Discern salient attributes of significant moments and identify issues raised by those attributes;
- Formulate questions for inquiry about issues;
- Tolerate the ambiguity inherent in processes of inquiry;
- Delay premature interpretations, judgments, and conclusions;
- Explore discourses to gain multiple perspectives on issues;
- Generate substantive conceptual insights into significant moments;
- Reconstruct one's Professional Narrative in ways that allow insights to inform future experiences, actions, and events;
- Share formally and publicly the results of the inquiry;
- Generate questions for further study; and
- Continue to cultivate one's processes for making meaning.

As this list illustrates, the quality of Metacognitive Reflection intertwines with Pedagogical Wisdom, Theoretical Understanding, Contextual Literacy, and Ethical Stewardship. It also interplays with the quality of Aesthetic Imagination, which we address later. So important is this quality, we invite readers to consider to what extent they have cultivated their capacity for Metacognitive Reflection:

Non-readiness—reiterates situational details from a single perspective; unable to differentiate significant from insignificant situations; unable to identify or articulate the significance of a situation; unable to see a particular situation as representative of a broader issue

Readiness—understands that situations can encompass significant issues; can posit multiple interpretations of a situation from the perspective of different participants; intuits that a situation is significant and may be able to articulate what is significant about it; uses troubling or problematic situations as a source of curiosity

Threshold Competence—formulates questions about significant situations; identifies, articulates, and frames issues embedded in situations; seeks concepts and theories that help to clarify and interpret the issue; recognizes other situations as instances of the same issue; discerns variations among similar situations and, in turn, reformulates more nuanced questions and issues; identifies one or more substantive issues as personally meaningful for in-depth study.

Skillful Artistry—consistently ponders the meaning of troubling/ problematic situations; draws upon conceptual and theoretic frameworks to analyze and interpret the situation; formulates questions for further study; engages with one or more Communities of Practice that are also studying those questions; generates heuristics to represent insights into the questions; uses one or more professional venues to share one's theorizing with others.

When the *telos* of education is seen as the journey of the self, Metacognitive Reflection is synonymous with learning. By cultivating their capacity for Metacognitive Reflection, Scholar-Practitioners can augment the qualities of Pedagogical Wisdom, Theoretical Understanding, Contextual Literacy, and Ethical Stewardship. In turn, they can more skillfully support the learning of others and advocate for the profession of education.

REFLECTIVE PROMPTS

What thoughts and feelings are evoked by the ideas in this chapter?

In what ways do my responses to the ideas in this chapter contribute to my understanding of being a Scholar-Practitioner?

What questions are evoked by the ideas in this chapter? Where do those questions fit within my plan for continued learning?

What ideas do I want to incorporate into my evolving Scholar-Practitioner Narrative?

When I have experienced a troubling situation, how do I tend to respond—initially and over time?

When I am faced with a problem or trying to understand something that is entirely new or difficult, what types of support are most helpful to me?

When I am trying to sort through ideas, what is helpful to me—reading, writing, drawing, meditating, engaging in an unrelated physical activity, talking with others, etc.?

What situations have troubled me over time; situations that I want to understand more fully so I can put them to rest. How would I frame them as an issue to be studied?

NOTES

1 For a discussion of the role of dreams and memories in a practice-embedded interpretive inquiry, see Marjorie Barrett Logsdon, *A Pedagogy of Authority* (Pittsburgh: Learning Moments Press, 2017).

2 For an example of visual sketches as a form of reflective record, see Wendy M. Milne, "Imagining Reflective Artmaking: Claiming Self as Artist-Teacher-Researcher" in *The Authority to Imagine: The Struggle toward Representation in Dissertation Writing*, eds. Noreen B. Garman & Maria Piantanida (Pittsburgh: Learning Moments Press, 2018), 173-186.

13

Formalizing Metacognitive Reflection as Narrative Inquiry

When Scholar-Practitioners engage informally in Metacognitive Reflection, they may be satisfied when they have achieved a meaningful insight into an issue that has troubled them. They may share their insights with colleagues in the course of conversation. Both are important in terms of broadening and deepening one's reservoir of pedagogical wisdom and theoretical understanding. As stewards of the profession, however, Scholar-Practitioners use the results of their investigations to fulfill their responsibilities as advocates for education and as contributors to the well-being and knowledge-base of the profession. By telling the story of their narrative inquiry, Scholar-Practitioners let others see how they moved from discerning a troubling moment, to framing an issue/question for investigation, to informing their thinking through information-gathering, to conceptualizing their insights into the issue/question.

Crafting a story of one's inquiry entails stepping back not just from the moment that catalyzed the inquiry, but from the inquiry process itself. As mentioned in Chapter 11, one criterion for judging interpretive inquiries is the quality of self-awareness—i.e., the Scholar-Practitioner's ability to articulate their thinking process AND their rationale for that process. As Figure 13.1 illustrates, this is a multi-layered process of Metacognitive Reflection.

FIGURE 13.1. LAYERS OF METACOGNITIVE REFLECTION

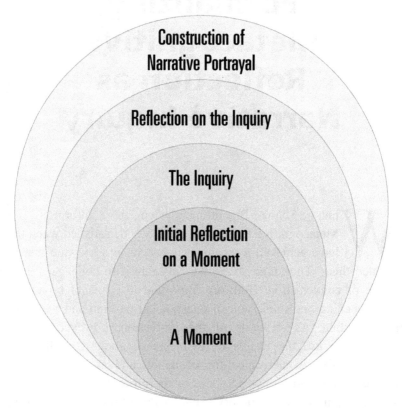

Construction of
Narrative Portrayal

Reflection on the Inquiry

The Inquiry

Initial Reflection
on a Moment

A Moment

What is difficult to convey with Figure 13.1 is the iterative nature of the narrative process in which meaning is constructed <u>through</u> writing. In other words, the struggle to write about the inquiry brings the Scholar-Practitioner to an "aha" moment—a conceptual leap in which the meaning of the investigation comes into focus. Writing the story of the inquiry is as much a part of the inquiry as the activities aimed at gathering information. Once the "aha" moment occurs, it is possible to make a number of "writerly decisions" aimed at portraying the results of the inquiry clearly, coherently, usefully, and persuasively.

The final form of the narrative portrayal will depend to a great extent on the purpose it is meant to serve, the audience for whom it is intended, and the context in which it will be shared. For example, sharing the results of an inquiry with policy makers is different from sharing results with scholars in a field of study. In general, however, the heart of good narrative writing is a conceptual message that the author wants to convey. Successfully conveying this message depends on a number of factors including:

- Ideas are organized to create a coherent message,
- Ideas are warranted (supported by appropriate evidence),
- Ideas are situated within a body of discourse,
- Ideas are relevant and significant to a field of study,
- Language, voice, and stance are appropriate, and
- Writing is grammatically/technically correct.

Regardless of the specific form of a narrative portrayal, it generally encompasses three sub-portrayals. These include:

- Portrayal of the Moment,
- Portrayal of the Investigation, and
- Portrayal of the Conceptual Results.

Although each is discussed separately, keep in mind that these portrayals are interconnected. Crafting one text often leads to revising sections of a previous draft as the Scholar-Practitioner makes "writerly decisions" about how best to tell the story of the inquiry.

Writerly Decisions about Portraying a Moment

The portrayal begins with an account of the moment when trouble arose, thereby letting readers understand why the inquiry was undertaken in the first place. Consider, for example, some of the moments we have shared in the preceding chapters:

- John's teacher during the weeks John hid under her desk
- Marjorie Logsdon in the instant when Gina asked, "Where is all of this going?"
- Sandy in the exchange with the parent who said her efforts to include their special needs daughter in kindergarten weren't good enough

- The teacher whose students were hoarding pencils
- Brianne during her encounter with the angry mother who accused her of cheating her son because all they did in the classroom was play
- Annie when the special education teacher told her she had to read to students because they couldn't understand a science textbook
- The Canny Outlaws as they resisted oppressive forms of accountability.

In recounting these moments, we tried to convey the details of the situation in a way that would allow readers to empathize with what the teacher might have been feeling. This is the quality of verisimilitude we mentioned in Chapter 11. Verisimilitude allows others to enter vicariously into the context of a narrative inquiry. A well-crafted moment does not simply allude to a situation, but rather, recreates the scene. For example, we alluded to a moment when a student threw a chair at a teacher who was pregnant. That situation is sufficiently dramatic that it can evoke an empathetic response, but it lacks the verisimilitude that vicariously immerses others in the scene of the action. If the teacher were to construct a portrayal of the moment, she might include the interactions leading up to the chair being thrown, what the student did next, what the other students did, and what she did. This would offer a more robust understanding of what was at stake in the moment.

Not all moments arise in classrooms. Maria, for example, saw a short blurb about the book *Homo Deus* and was intrigued enough to read it. She really didn't know what to expect, but was surprised (shocked really) to read that artificial intelligence algorithms can customize interactions with students to meet their intellectual and emotional needs as effectively as a human teacher. In fact, since artificial intelligence technology can be deployed throughout the country, it can more efficiently and effectively meet the learning needs of more students. Can this really be true? Can artificial intelligence devices make teachers obsolete? What are the implications of this for teacher education programs? What are the implications for those who feel teaching as a vocational calling? For that matter, if artificial intelligence devices can think better than humans, what is the point of teaching anything to anyone? If these scenarios come to fruition, have human beings themselves become obsolete? This is an example of a moment grounded in the experience of reading. If she simply alluded to the fact that she read a book called *Homo Deus*, readers would shrug and say, "So what?" By adding the line of thinking evoked by the book, she makes an effort to share in her experience of shock and the questions that she now ponders.

Often it is necessary to write several drafts of an educational moment. The aim of the first draft is to get down as much detail as possible. The purpose is to recreate and record the moment for review. The very process of recollecting and retelling the moment may call additional details to mind. These can be inserted into a second draft. Subsequent drafts may entail honing the account of the moment to eliminate extraneous details, to strengthen a point of view, and to foreshadow the issue to be explored.

In crafting a portrayal, it is important to consider when a moment began and ended. Often many different points in time can potentially mark the start of the moment. Generally, however, there is a point at which "the action" of the moment begins. Starting with that point creates a dramatic or narrative tension that can help to draw the reader into the narrative. Sometimes it takes several drafts to decide where it is best to start a portrayal of the moment.

For any moment, there is likely to be background information that provides a context for what happened. Recounting the moment entails deciding how much of the background information is necessary in order for a reader to understand the moment. Imagine reading that Maria had run out of books to read, so when she spotted the blurb about *Homo Deus* she went on-line, requested a copy from the library, and picked it up two days later at the library a mile away from her home. How incredibly boring! None of this adds any significant details to the moment. On the other hand, suppose the chair-throwing student had come to school with bruises on his face and said his father had punched him in a fit of drunken anger. Suppose the pain and anger from that abuse exploded when the teacher asked him to stop bullying another student. Would this background information convey the complexity of the moment—not to excuse the violence but to make the problematic situation more nuanced?

Another decision centers on where in the narrative it is most useful to incorporate the background information. It might seem logical to share the background information before recounting the moment, because that is what occurred chronologically. Sometimes, in fact, this is a good idea. Often, however, providing a great deal of background information diffuses the power of the moment. By the time readers come to the account of the moment, they may already have guessed what happened (which undermines the power of the narrative) or they may simply have lost interest because they see no point to all the details. In a well-crafted portrayal it is often possible to embed key pieces of background information into the account of the moment. In other instances, it is possible to incorporate the background information as the moment is analyzed and interpreted.

When considering "who" was involved in the moment, it is important to consider the nature of one's own involvement. Was I a key actor in an interaction or an observer? If I was directly involved, what was my role; what did I do; what did I say; what did I think? In recounting a moment, the author embodies three distinct, yet interconnected roles:

- The role as a character in the story,
- The role as the narrator of the story, and
- The role as an inquirer into the meaning of the story.

Communicating the differences among these roles is done by assuming different stances, voices, and perspectives. As a character, I may have no more insight into the action of the moment than other characters (a stance of naiveté, befuddlement, confusion, anger, etc.). As the narrator of the story, I am constructing the events to create a specific effect (a stance of witness). As the inquirer into the story, I am probing the moment to understand and explain its significance (a stance of inquirer).

In reconstructing educational moments, it is also important to be cautious about making claims about what others may be thinking or feeling. It is one thing to say, "The students were bored." It is another thing to say, "It seemed to me that the students were bored." Still it is another thing to say, "As I saw Johnny and Timmy passing notes and Mary and Susie yawning, I couldn't help but worry that they were bored." Giving the descriptive detail helps the reader understand why I as the narrator think the students might be bored. Similarly, it is one thing to say, "Bob was a dangerous student." It is another to say, "I was afraid of Bob." It is still another to say, "When Bob, the 6'6" center on the school's basketball team, loomed over my desk and shouted, 'You can't make me do this crappy assignment,' I felt afraid." The first statement makes a claim about Bob. The second statement makes a statement about me, but the reader has no idea whether my feelings about Bob are justified. In the third statement, the reader can imagine what it was like to be in my place and can understand why I am claiming to be fearful.

A few cautionary words about portraying a moment are in order. Sometimes, the concepts of "feelings" and "introspection" conjure up images of "touchy-feely," highly emotive, self-confessional writing. Inexperienced writers may try self-consciously for a "feeling" effect. This can backfire, resulting in a "cringe factor" instead of verisimilitude. Rather than readers resonating empathetically with the narrator's account of the moment, they may become annoyed by exaggerated feelings or repulsed by being privy to intimate, personal details that do not serve the inquiry. While these types of reflection might be part of a private journal or diary, they do not contribute much to a public portrayal of the moment.

That said, initial attempts to "get at" what was going on in a moment may require writing and talking with abandon. If the moment has been especially painful, such venting may be a necessary precursor to more conceptual reflection. This is where membership in a Community of Practice can be extremely valuable. Venting with trusted confidants can alleviate enough emotional pressure to allow for a shift from reaction to reflection. Here, too, a caution is necessary. Providing a sympathetic ear can become dysfunctional if the venting becomes self-sustaining and self-reinforcing. At some point, a nudge beyond venting may be needed.

Another cautionary note concerns the fact that recollections are notoriously unreliable. Readers, especially those with a scientific world view, may ask, "How do we know the writer isn't just making the whole thing up? How can we know what really happened? Maybe the writer is just trying to make herself look good. Maybe he is trying to make others look bad. How can we trust such subjective accounts?" One response to such concerns is acknowledging that Recollective Reflection is inevitably incomplete and always narrated from a particular perspective. One never gets to a singular Truth of a moment. Indeed, that is not the point. The narrative researcher working in an interpretive inquiry tradition is not trying to prove what really happened. The moment is being described to let others know what has catalyzed the inquiry. It is, in essence, saying, "This happened to me and as a result I now want to understand what was going on in that moment. I want to be better prepared for such moments if they arise again. I want to understand this issue better or understand what is at stake." This represents a turn from Introspective and Recollective Reflection to Conceptual Reflection. It represents a turning point in the narrative account of the inquiry.

Writerly Decisions about Portraying the Investigation

Having identified an issue of personal concern for investigation, it is important to establish in what ways it might also be of concern to the profession. This requires some investigation into discourses related to the issue under study. Who is writing about the issue? What have they said and does this help me understand my situation more clearly? Are others concerned about the same issue? With what questions are they struggling? Will I look naïve or foolish if I claim to be the first person or only person to have noticed this issue? How extensive is the issue/problem? As mentioned in Chapter 12, such questions can be explored by tapping multiple sources including:

- Scholarly books and journal articles
- Professional association journals, newsletters, conferences, and websites
- Government and institutional documents
- Various print and on-line media sources
- Formal and informal conversations (face-to-face or via email) with other professionals

Immersion in discourses helps to clarify whether or not additional information will need to be gathered from primary sources via interviews, questionnaires, observations, etc. In portraying the investigation, the Scholar-Practitioner recounts the following types of information:

- What sources of information did I use to further my understanding of the issue?
- Why did I choose those sources?
- How did I make sure that I was conducting my inquiry in an ethical manner?
- How did I keep track of the information I gathered?
- How did I go about analyzing and interpreting it?

Portraying how the investigation was conducted will either undermine or enhance the credibility of the inquiry results. If few sources of information have been used; if little thought has been given to why certain sources would be relevant or irrelevant; if information gathering was done haphazardly; if information was dealt with superficially—readers will look skeptically at the results of the inquiry. On the other hand, when the Scholar-Practitioner has diligently pursued information that illuminates the complexities of an issue and is able to put those complexities into an understandable conceptual framework, the results are more persuasive.

Writerly Decisions About Portraying Conceptual Results

Above, we mentioned that writing itself is inherent in a narrative inquiry process. Writing immerses the author in the jumble of information and ideas generated throughout the investigation. Struggling to make this jumble understandable to others pushes the author to clarify and organize his or her own thoughts. Determining what message is most appropriate to convey, the author can then make decisions about the final format of the narrative story. Deciding which format is most appropriate includes considerations of purpose, audience and context. Here are a few examples:

- An annotated bibliography. When a wealth of information is discovered during immersion in the literature and when it has taken quite a bit of time and effort to identify and compile the sources of that information, an annotated bibliography can be a valuable resource and contribution to the profession. (Also, an annotated compilation of useful websites might be created.) Contexts for sharing these results might include classmates, colleagues, or committees working on a related issue.
- Book reviews. When one or more books offer particularly cogent insights into an issue, a reflective book review can make a useful contribution to the profession. Often professional association journals, newsletters, and websites will publish timely book reviews.
- A review of literature. When a wealth of existing information has been unearthed but is fragmented, a conceptual review of literature can be tremendously useful. Such a review organizes the literature into themes and sub-themes revealing various schools of thought on an issue and identifying who is giving attention to it. These may be published in professional association journals or presented at professional conferences.
- An instructional module. The results of the inquiry may be used to create a structured learning experience that walks others through the issue and helps them apply it to their context. Contexts for sharing results in this form include academic classes, in-service workshops, or on-line self-study programs.
- Institutional Documents. The results of an inquiry might be used to formulate action plans or institutional policies or procedures.
- Advocacy Action. One dimension of ethical stewardship is advocacy in which Scholar-Practitioners may serve as public intellectuals who promote greater understanding of educational issues. Contexts for sharing inquiry results include submitting letters to the editor or opinion pieces to local newspapers, contacting legislators, and speaking at community events, preparing white papers or concept papers for discussion at professional meetings or conferences.
- Heuristic Representation. Heuristics put complex ideas into a coherent conceptual framework and make them more accessible for deliberation and discussion. Heuristics are theoretical, not

in the sense of ideal theory, but in the sense of cogent insights formed through Metacognitive Reflection. Common contexts for sharing such results are conference presentations, journal articles, or even books. Some Scholar-Practitioners maintain blogs where such inquiry results can be posted. Through the course of an investigation, the Scholar-Practitioner may have discovered an existing Community of Practice where the results can become part of the group's on-going deliberations.

Having a format in mind helps a Scholar-Practitioner decide how best to portray the catalyzing moment and the process of investigation. For example, when the final format is a policy or procedure, a letter to the editor, or an email to a legislator, it may not be necessary to include an extensive portrayal of the moment or investigation. Distilling all of one's thinking into a well-reasoned position, persuasively expressed in one or two pages requires highly skillful Conceptual Reflection.

By the same token, highly skillful Conceptual Reflection is necessary to craft an extensive account of a formal narrative inquiry. The account must simultaneously be detailed, engaging, and persuasive. Our colleague Noreen Garman recounts the following comment of a dissertation committee member, "I loved it [the dissertation]. It read like a compelling novel in places."[1] Art teacher Pamela Krakowski expressed a similar surprise at the readability of a dissertation:

> Until the second night of a qualitative research course, I had never read a dissertation. I imagined those foreboding black-bound books were boring, full of hard-to-decipher statistics, with little relevance to classroom practice. I picked up one of the dissertations at the end of class and read the title: "Pictures in Our Minds: A Narrative Study of Creative Dramatics as Pedagogy in Elementary Classroom Content Areas" (Richards 1996). It intrigued me, and so I borrowed it.
>
> That night, instead of watching television, I sat down to read the dissertation. I found that I could not put it down. It read like a story and was full of accounts I

could relate to as a teacher. I kept asking, "Are you really allowed to do this?" I couldn't believe that a teacher was allowed to write about her own teaching, in her own context, much less in a narrative form.[2]

To Pamela's question we respond with a resounding "Yes. You can do such a study—inspired by moments in your practice and carried out within your teaching context." In fact, we contend that this is a major way in which Scholar-Practitioners can contribute to the knowledge-base of the profession.[3]

Narrative Portrayals and the *Telos* of Education

In calling for a new paradigm of educational reform, Anthony Bryk contrasts the model of field trials with that of a practice-embedded model:

> Unlike field trials that tend to focus on testing some new program or policy, these [collaborative problem solving] inquiries tend to zero in on very concrete day-to-day problems in the work of teaching and schooling. Educators are now cast as active agents of improvement rather than as passive receivers of knowledge developed by others. These communities [of learning and practice] seek to break down walls of solo practice and create safe spaces where faculty share and learn from one another.[4]

Interestingly, Bryk goes on to say:

> Compared to clinical trials [in medicine], the actual warrant for the exchanges that occur in these conversations remains less clear. Change ideas may not be well specified, with their success depending heavily on individual educators' tacit knowledge. Especially problematic for closing the quality chasm, there is no formal mechanism for accumulating, further detailing, and testing this individual clinical knowledge [of

teaching] so that it might be transformed over time into
a collectively held professional knowledge-base...[5]

We contend that narrative inquiries conducted and shared by Scholar-Practitioners represent a formal process ("mechanism") for sharing the type of knowledge Bryk is seeking in support of reform efforts. When the results of such intimate inquiries are portrayed through conceptual heuristics, they contribute to the professional knowledge-base.

That said, we question whether narratively generated wisdom can be "accumulated and tested" in the same way that scientifically generated knowledge can be. As Jerome Bruner contended, quantitative (science-based) and qualitative (humanities-based) modes of knowing are not reducible one into the other.[6] Perhaps a new paradigm of educational reform will encompass dual processes for sharing both wisdom and knowledge. Until such a new paradigm gains primacy, however, it is incumbent upon Scholar-Practitioners to continue as stewards of the profession through their commitment to inquiry.

Professor Robert Nash, in discussing the power of scholarly personal narrative, eloquently expresses the way that narrative imbues scholarship into one's life as a learner, a teacher, and a steward of the profession:

> You are a scholar if you are willing to play with ideas. You are a scholar if you can build on the ideas of others. You are a scholar to the extent that you can tell a good, instructive story. You are a scholar if you can capture the narrative quality of your human experience in language that inspires others. You are a scholar if you can present your story in such a way that, in some important senses, it rings true to human life. You are a scholar if you can help your reader to reexamine their own truth stories in light of the truths that you are struggling to discern in your own complicated life story.
>
> You are a scholar if you have a passion for language and writing. You are a scholar if you are driven to

understand what makes yourself and others tick. You are a scholar if you can feel and think at the same time. You are a scholar if you are willing to allow your students, and your readers to enter your heart as well as your head. You are a scholar if you can help your readers and students to realize that their lives signify, that they matter more than they will ever know.[7]

REFLECTIVE PROMPTS

What thoughts and feelings are evoked by the ideas in this chapter?

In what ways do my responses to the ideas in this chapter contribute to my understanding of being a Scholar-Practitioner?

What questions are evoked by the ideas in this chapter? Where do those questions fit within my plan for continued learning?

What ideas do I want to incorporate into my evolving Scholar-Practitioner Narrative?

NOTES

1 Noreen B. Garman, "Imagining an Interpretive Dissertation: Voice, Text and Representation" in *The Authority to Imagine: The Struggle toward Representation in Dissertation Writing,* eds. Noreen B. Garman and Maria Piantanida (Pittsburgh: Learning Moments Press, 2018), 31.

2 Pamela Krakowski, "A Search for Balance: Representing a Narrative Pedagogy," in *The Authority to Imagine: The Struggle toward Representation in Dissertation Writing,* eds. Noreen B. Garman and Maria Piantanida (Pittsburgh: Learning Moments Press, 2018), 105.

3 We recognize that all Scholar-Practitioners may not engage in dissertation research. However, those who are interested in an expanded explication of interpretive inquiry may find it helpful to read *The Qualitative Dissertation: A Guide for Students and Faculty.* See the bibliography for full citation.

4 Anthony S. Bryk, "2014 AERA Distinguished Lecture. Accelerating How We Learn to Improve," *Educational Researcher* 44, no 9 (2015): 469.

5 Bryk, 469.

6 Jerome Bruner, *Actual Minds, Possible Worlds* (Cambridge, MA: Harvard University Press, 1986).

7 Robert J. Nash, *Liberating Scholarly Writing: The Power of Personal Narrative* (New York: Teachers College Press, 2004), 45-46.

SECTION VII

The Quality of Aesthetic Imagination

Aesthetic Imagination entails a capacity to draw upon the arts and humanities to make meaning of one's life and the world.

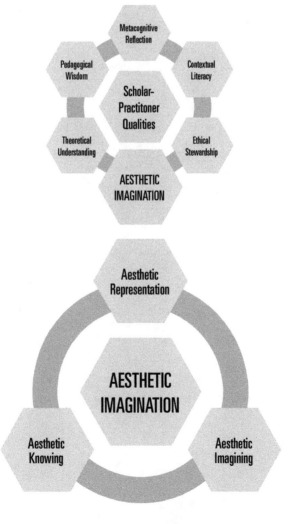

14

Aesthetic Imagination

Often, when we introduce the Scholar-Practitioner quality of Aesthetic Imagination, students translate that into "artistic" and then lament, "I'm not artistic." To counteract this narrow conception of aesthetic, we introduce a continuum of aesthetic expression (Figure 14.1).

FIGURE 14.1 - CONTINUUM OF AESTHETIC EXPRESSION

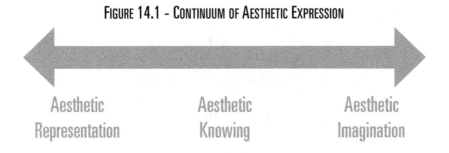

Aesthetic Representation

Aesthetic Knowing

Aesthetic Imagination

In this chapter, we briefly consider how each of these modalities may be incorporated into the work of Scholar-Practitioners.

Aesthetic Representation

In the preceding chapter we discussed the Scholar-Practitioner's responsibility to share their private understandings with a broader, public audience. A well-crafted narrative is one form of aesthetic representation. However, depending on the purpose, audience, and context for sharing one's understanding, aesthetic representations might take any number of forms. Take, for example, the ubiquitous use of bulletin boards in elementary schools. Generally, they are meant to call young students' attention to some idea—e.g., a season, a holiday, an historically significant event, social norms, school spirit. Deliberately or intuitively, teachers incorporate a number of artistic design elements to create an engaging bulletin board: pictures, variety of letter size and shape, balancing elements throughout the space and in relation to each other, variations in colors and textures, moveable pieces. Perhaps this does not seem like a very important use of one's scholarly understandings, but given the purpose, audience, and context, aesthetically pleasing bulletin boards can enrich the learning environment. So, too, can an aesthetic appreciation of the classroom setting.

Art teacher Pamela Krakowski offers an example of how she takes her knowledge of child development and art into account as she arranged her K-2 classroom to welcome students on the first day of school. After reflecting on a pedagogical moment that had not gone well the previous year, Pamela recounts:

> Taking to heart my need to be attuned to the child's emotional concerns, I planned with "heightened awareness" a first-day-of-school art lesson with the theme of feeling safe and welcomed. I decided to use two puppets, a Talking Art Box and a komodo dragon named Felix, to help ease the transition and create an atmosphere of play and imagination.
>
> ~~~
>
> The kindergarten children arrived at the art studio— many for the first time—and I invited them in. They walked in quietly, tiptoeing as if the floor were made of glass. They looked, without touching, and spoke in whispers. It was the kind of quietness that only a first visit could inspire. I found myself also speaking softly, mirroring their inquisitive and shy mood.
>
> Ben broke the quietness. He asked excitedly, "You have a dinosaur in here?" He pointed to the stegosaurus on the ledge next to the Stegovolkasaurus art print. His question seemed to combine, "Why is there a dinosaur in an art room?" and "How did you know that I liked

dinosaurs?" Little did Ben know that I was thinking about children just like him when I placed the dinosaur on the entrance-way ledge.[1]

Pamela, just like thousands of teachers across the country, draws upon an aesthetic sensibility to create a physical environment conducive to learning. In secondary school, college and beyond, this aesthetic sensibility becomes manifest in the presentation of ideas. In Chapter 6, we offered a defense of the often maligned lecture. Those that are dry and boring lack the aesthetic qualities of those that are engaging. In a sense, a lecture is a story that draws the listener into the "action" of an idea. Maria is reminded of a lecture presented by a nationally renowned cancer researcher. Without slides or jokes (the *de rigueur* trappings for an "entertaining" lecture), the researcher told the story of his search for genetic markers to pinpoint specific forms of malignancy. As he finished, one audience member exclaimed, "I wish I could have been a scientist!" The researcher—understanding his purpose, audience, and context—crafted a compelling narrative to share his highly technical knowledge.

Anyone who has struggled to read microscopic print on an overly crowded PowerPoint slide has an intuitive sense of what is NOT an aesthetic representation. Indeed, workshops and on-line resources are now available to teach key principles of designing effective PowerPoint presentations including font size, background color, amount of text, overlaying images, animation, etc. All of these principles are meant to enhance the aesthetic sharing of information and ideas.

Before turning to the concept of aesthetic knowing, a word of caution is in order. In each of the preceding examples, aesthetic considerations are meant to serve a conceptual purpose. The aesthetic qualities of the representational form are integral to the message. This is quite different from adding superficial "decorative touches" that contribute nothing to the substance of the ideas being conveyed. On too many occasions we have worked with students who have spent a great deal of time and effort to decorate the cover on a learning portfolio—time and effort that might have been better spent on the portfolio contents.

Aesthetic Knowing

Throughout the book, we have contrasted scientific knowing with interpretive knowing. In particular, we highlighted narrative as a fundamental modality through which human beings make sense of their experiences. Narrative, however, is only one aesthetic modality for coming to know.

As Clandinin and Connelly (1996)[2] remind us, teachers know more than they can say. They carry within them an implicit, intuitive knowledge, often difficult to access, given the hectic pace of their day-to-day classroom interactions. This knowledge, personal and practical, becomes part of each teacher's *professional knowledge landscape*. Aesthetic ways of knowing invite us to tap into the realm of the intuitive and bring it into the foreground.

Earlier we mentioned our colleague Doug Conlan who doodles as he listens to discourses. For him, these sketches embody a nugget of understanding; they give him a way to clarify and hold on to insights. So central are they to his way of knowing that he wanted to include them in his dissertation, an idea scathingly denounced by his dissertation advisor as unscientific. Recognizing this as a world view issue, Doug took two courses of action. First he found a discourse community that better understood what his doodling represented. Second, he developed a rationale for doodling as a form of knowing. This is important scholarly work for it addresses the dilemma articulated by Anthony Bryk as he struggles to conceptualize a new paradigm of educational reform:

> Change ideas may not be well specified, with their success *depending heavily on individual educator's tacit knowledge*. Especially problematic for closing the quality chasm, there is no formal mechanism for accumulating, further detailing, and testing this individual clinical knowledge so that it might be transformed over time into a collectively held professional knowledge base.[3] (Italics added)

A crucial first step in addressing this dilemma is respecting, supporting, and attending to the modes of knowing that bring tacit, intuitive knowledge into the realm of conscious deliberation. Once accessible for deliberation, this practice-embedded knowledge can be shared and accumulated into a collective knowledge base. Consider the following example.

Wendy Milne, the elementary art teacher we introduced in Chapter 7, came to the final class in an introductory course on qualitative research carrying a 3 x 4 foot, accordion-folded display. On each panel, she had affixed swirls of yellow, layers of orange and red, patches of other bright colors. As she turned from panel to panel, she narrated how each kaleidoscope of colors represented a twist and turn in her path to understanding qualitative research. When she finished, she turned the panels around and revealed the writing on the back. We asked if she had written the explanations first and then created the color representations as an artistic, decorative touch. "No," she declared, "the colors came first. That's how I began to see what qualitative research is." From this experience, Wendy went on to conceptualize and complete an award-winning dissertation on the topic of reflective-artmaking.[4] Since then, she has been active in the state association of art teachers, has given presentations, has mentored pre-service art education students, and been an advocate for art education in her district. This exemplifies a process of inquiry and a mode of knowing that allows Scholar-Practitioners to explore the meaning of experience, surface tacit *[Implied]* understandings, and move them into the public domain.

Aesthetic Imagination

While Aesthetic Knowing can be manifest in the visual, tactile, and performing arts, Aesthetic Imagination brings another dimension to the thinking of Scholar-Practitioners. As curriculum scholar Maxine Greene asserts, the aesthetic realm has the potential to "release the imagination," to see beyond *what is* to *what might be*.[5] The ability to imagine is where hope finds form—in the educational projects we create. Scholar-Practitioners value habits of mind and heart that enable us to look upon the ordinary with new eyes and imagine possible worlds and possible selves. Aesthetic Imagination encourages us to explore meaning, share insights with others, re-evaluate our thinking, express ideas in multiple aesthetic modalities, and critically examine the world in which we live.

A variety of approaches can be taken to cultivate Aesthetic Imagination. For our purposes, however, we focus on the idea of metaphor and metaphorical thinking. Just as personal, cultural, and collective narratives shape the way we see the world, so, too, do metaphors. Discoveries about the nature of metaphor suggest that metaphor is anything but peripheral to the life of the mind. It is central to our understanding of our selves, our culture, and the world at large.[6] As professors George Lakoff and Mark Johnson explain, "The essence of metaphor is understanding and experiencing one kind of thing in terms of another."[7] They go on to say:

> ...metaphor is not just a matter of language, that is, of mere words. We shall argue that, on the contrary, human *thought processes* are largely metaphorical. This is what we mean when we say that the human conceptual system is metaphorically structured and defined. Metaphors as linguistic expressions are possible precisely because there are metaphors in a person's conceptual system. (Italics in original.)[8]

Consider, for instance, the different conceptions of teaching conveyed in the following metaphors:

- Teaching is a finely-tuned machine.
- Teaching is a jazz band.
- Teaching is a scripted performance.
- Teaching is improvisational theater.

Similarly, alternative conceptions of learning and school are evoked by metaphors such as:

- Learning is an obstacle course.
- Learning is an adventure.
- School is a prison.
- School is a playground.

- School is a zoo.
- School is a three-ring circus.

Metaphors (as well as similes, and analogies) create imaginative pairings of phenomenon in which emotional and conceptual qualities of one are ascribed to the other. I.A. Richards' distinction between the *tenor* and the *vehicle* of a metaphor has been widely accepted and is very useful. The *tenor* is the idea being expressed or the subject of the comparison; the *vehicle* is the image by which the idea is conveyed or the subject communicated. Consider the following passage from Shakespeare's 73rd sonnet:

> *That time of year thou mayst in me behold*
> *When yellow leaves, or none, or few, do hang*
> *Upon those boughs which shake against the cold,*
> *Bare ruined choirs, where late the sweet birds sang.*

The *tenor* is old age. The *vehicle* is the season of late fall or early winter, conveyed through a group of images unusually complex in their implications. In the final two lines of the sonnet, Shakespeare gives his metaphor a final twist by using the images of decay and death to express the power of love. That's Shakespeare's genius, but we need not have his aesthetic brilliance to use metaphors to release our own imaginations.

To illustrate Lakoff and Johnson's point that metaphors embody complex systems of thought, let's consider the metaphor "schools are factories."

School-as-Factory Metaphor

In the early 1900s, as our society shifted from an agrarian to an industrial economy, the factory mentality began to seep into society's acceptance of how schools should be run. Newly emerging theories of learning supported the factory metaphor by suggesting that the right set of rewards and punishments would result in the desired learning outcomes—defined as objectively observable changes in behavior.

Children were the raw materials to be shaped into a final product—graduates prepared to enter an industrialized work force. Teachers were the line workers who processed the raw materials. Grouping children in age-segregated classrooms and processing them through in large grade-level "batches" were considered efficient, even if common sense, personal experience, quality assurance measures, and research raised alarms about decreased efficacy.

The factory metaphor also extended to the design of curriculum and instruction. By neatly sequencing content and using technically proficient teachers to deliver that content, the production line could move smoothly, churning out finished products on a reliable and predictable schedule. Standardized measures of standardized content could be used to evaluate the adequacy of student *qua* product in relation to pre-specified criteria of quality. If outcomes are flawed, something within the production system must be broken.

Even in its heyday, the "schools are factories" metaphor did not hold up very well. Neither teachers nor students were as passive and malleable as the raw materials being processed by our nation's massive industrial complex. Yet, vestiges of this metaphor still reverberate as schools purchase "teacher-proof" curriculum materials, expect uniform delivery of content on a highly regulated schedule, and measure the quality of the process and outcomes against one-size-fits-all learning outcomes. Perhaps the most pervasive grip of the metaphor echoes through the constant stream of warnings that schools are not adequately preparing students for the workplace which, in turn, threatens our country's economic power in a globalizing world.

As Anthony Bryk works to conceptualize a new paradigm for school reform, it is important, we think, to consider the underlying metaphor which drives reform efforts. If the "schools are factories" metaphor still drives our thinking, then are reform efforts aimed at making the "factory" work better? Or, in essence, is a new metaphor for schooling needed before meaningful reform can take place?

Marjorie Kelly in writing about our economy begins with a vignette that applies just as well to education:

> We lost a couple of old trees in our yard a few years
> back, big ornamental pears brought down not by

lightning or wind but by their own structural weakness. These trees have a Y structure where two central branches push against one another, and over time the trees undermined themselves, eventually splitting apart. We mourned those trees and wondered what to replace them with. But within a few months, the little magnolia that had seemed so small beneath one of them shot up. It's filled out that space magnificently now. Where the other tree once stood, we can grow flowers in places we couldn't before. Sometimes when you lose something you think you need, life surprises you. What comes next turns out to be unexpectedly good. That may be the case with our economy. There's a lot that's breaking down now, a lot of financial and ecological upheaval—not because crises are coming out of nowhere and hitting us but because the structure of industrial-age capitalism is causing them. It's a good time to open our minds to new things sprouting up.[9]

The interconnection between economics and education remains part of a persistent metaphor of school as factory with its associated values of consistency and efficiency. Standardization and standardized testing are the twin branches casting a shadow over our educational landscape. What new ideas might sprout and flourish if this shadow were removed?

Let us be clear. We are not opposed to standards—what we aim to achieve. Nor are we opposed to assessments that give insights into how well our efforts to achieve those aims are succeeding. We are, however, against fixation on narrowly conceived outcomes that subvert the very purpose of teaching and learning. Unquestionably, standards focusing on reading and math skills are necessary, but they are not sufficient for educators to fulfill the *telos* of the profession. Imagine reading and math skills subsumed under a broader standard in which everyone in schools—teachers and students, superintendents and maintenance personnel, instructional support staff and cafeteria workers—are excited about and committed to the learning of every other person in the building and their own learning. What assessments might let us know how well this standard is being achieved?

Cynics might scoff that this is the stuff (fluff) of fairy tales. Yet such cynicism reveals a meagerness of spirit and imagination when teachers (and other school personnel) have literally laid down their lives to protect students. The heroes and heroines at Columbine, Sandy Hook, Parkland, and so many other schools have demonstrated an ethic of caring far and above technical job descriptions. In the face of their sacrifices, how dare the cynics deny the possibility of standards where the safety, dignity, worth, aspirations, and talents of each person are respected, nurtured, and celebrated?

Imagine the possibilities that might arise if the metaphor "schools are factories" were replaced with "schools are flourishing communities of learning." Scholar-Practitioners live within the constraints of the metaphors society uses to conceptualize the nature of teaching, learning, and schooling. By cultivating their Aesthetic Imagination, Scholar-Practitioners may be able to see beyond what is and express more powerfully what might be.

Aesthetic Imagination and the *Telos* of Education

Scholar Elliot Eisner was among the first advocates for the importance of aesthetic modalities for both the practice of teaching and the practice of educational evaluation and inquiry. Part of the artistry of teaching and inquiry is bringing together different elements into a whole. As Eisner argued, "we have to develop the ability to name and appreciate the different dimensions of situations and experiences, and the way they relate one to another."[10] Eisner encourages aesthetic ways of knowing to do just this kind of critical thinking. He tells us that in shifting to a form of representation that privileges an aesthetic way of knowing, we are able to inquire into an experience as a result of "produc[ing] a structure...that gives rise to feeling."[11]

As stewards of the profession, Scholar-Practitioners have a responsibility to preserve the heart and essence of education. But they are also responsible for training a critical eye toward the future. Being a good steward does not imply stasis or protecting the status quo. As a caretaker of the profession, stewards must be willing to take risks and move the discipline forward. The Scholar-Practitioner quality of Aesthetic Imagination is crucial to fulfilling this forward movement.

REFLECTIVE PROMPTS

What thoughts and feelings are evoked by the ideas in this chapter?

In what ways do my responses to the ideas in this chapter contribute to my understanding of being a Scholar-Practitioner?

What questions are evoked by the ideas in this chapter? Where do those questions fit within my plan for continued learning?

What ideas do I want to incorporate into my evolving Scholar-Practitioner Narrative?

What metaphors shape my thinking?

- Teaching is...

- Learning is...

- Schooling is...

NOTES

1   Pamela Krakowski, "A Search for Balance: Representing a Narrative Pedagogy," in *The Authority to Imagine: The Struggle toward Representation in Dissertation Writing*, eds. Noreen B. Garman and Maria Piantanida (Pittsburgh: Learning Moments Press, 2018), 122-113.

2   D. Jean Clandinin and F. Michael Connelly, "Teachers' Professional Knowledge Landscapes: Teacher Stories—Stories of Teachers—School Stories—Stories of School," Educational Researcher 25, no 3 (1996) 24-30.

3   Anthony S. Bryk, "2014 AERA Distinguished Lecture. Accelerating How We Learn to Improve," *Educational Researcher* 44, no 9 (2015): 469.

4   Wendy A. Milne, *Reflective Artmaking: Implications for Art Education*, University of Pittsburgh, 2000. UMI ProQuest Digital Dissertation, AAT9974457. See also, Wendy A. Milne, "Imagining Reflective Artmaking: Claiming Self as Artist-Teacher-Researcher," in *The Authority to Imagine: The Struggle toward Representation in Dissertation Writing*, eds. Noreen B. Garman and Maria Piantanida (Pittsburgh: Learning Moments Press, 2018), 173-185.

5   Maxine Greene, *Releasing the Imagination: Essays on Education, the Arts, and Social Change.* (San Francisco: Jossey-Bass, 1995).

6   George Lakoff and Mark Turner, *More than Cool Reason: A Field Guide to Poetic Metaphor,* Chicago: The University of Chicago Press 1989, 64, 214.

7   George Lakoff and Mark Johnson, *Metaphors We Live By*, Chicago: The University of Chicago Press, 1980, 5.

8   Lakoff and Johnson, 6.

9   Marjorie Kelly, *Owning Our Future: The Emerging Ownership Revolution, Journeys to a Generative Economy* (San Francisco: Berrett-Koehler, 2012), 1.

10 Mark K. Smith, "Elliot W. Eisner. Connoisseurship, Criticism and The Art of Education," *The Encyclopedia of Informal Education*, 2005. Retrieved September 30, 2018 from www.infed.org/thinkers/eisner.htm.

11 Elliot W. Eisner, *The Art of Educational Evaluation: A Personal View*. Philadelphia: Falmer Press, 1985, 27.

Releasing Imagination

In concluding the preceding chapter, we suggested that Aesthetic Imagination can support Scholar-Practitioners' stewardship responsibilities as advocates of the profession—preserving the best of the past and imagining new possibilities for fulfilling its purpose "to educate." This calls for re-imagining education within micro, mezzo, and macro contexts. This is no easy task; the images of education, schooling, teaching, and learning are deeply embedded in the fabric of our society.

In tracing the history of standardized testing in the United States, journalist Nicholas Lemann offers an interesting insight into the entrenched mindset about education as a social institution. In the early decades of the 20th century, "Four distinct ideas about the future of education, each implicitly leading to a different kind of new social order, were competing with each other."[1]

> One was progressive education, whose adherents believed that schools should promote the individual blossoming of each student as a creative thinker and an active, skeptical citizen, rather than treating young people as drones whose empty heads should be filled with prescribed material in a disciplined environment...

> Just about exactly the opposite was the idea that tough, uniform standards should be imposed on American schools...

> A third idea about the future of education had IQ tests, those shiny new miracles of psychology, playing

the key role. True believers in IQ tests thought they should be given to all American children, so that the high scorers could be plucked out and given the best schooling and the average and low scorers consigned to a briefer, more limited education...

Curiously, all three camps—the progressives, the standards imposers, and the IQ testers—had, for all their differences, one thing in common: at a time when dramatically fewer Americans than now were being educated in high school or college, none of them championed the expansion of education [the fourth ideological camp].[2]

Lemann concluded his discussion of the four different views of education with the following comment:

The reason the competition among the four camps mattered so much was that in the coming years American education, which had been overwhelmingly local, was going to become more national; otherwise there could be no national labor market and the economy couldn't modernize. There had to be an overall governing principle. So whoever won would score a highly consequential victory—would get to configure the basic form that life took for most Americans for the rest of the twentieth century. As out-of-public-view as the competition was, the stakes were very high, including the stakes for the public. *It was like a slow-motion, invisible Constitutional Convention whose result would determine the American social structure.*[3](Italics added)

Several points emerge from these abbreviated excerpts from Lemann's thoughtful work. First, the debates about these various conceptions of education were occurring as the industrial revolution was gaining momentum, which probably strengthened the case for standardization. Second, the progressive view of school never gained sufficient traction to become institutionalized across an expanding educational enterprise. Third, over time, the remaining three camps began to merge as locally controlled districts were pressured to meet national standards and a testing industry evolved to make standardized assessment feasible. Thus, the twin branches of standardization and standardized assessment became firmly rooted and continue to overshadow the educational landscape.

Advocates of any of the four ideological camps would probably be astonished by the scope of education in today's society. Waves of immigration prior to War World II and the G.I. Bill for returning veterans essentially carried the day for those who espoused expansion of access to education. According to the National Center for Education Statistics, as of the 2015-2016 school year, there were 13,584 public school districts in the United States comprising 98,277 public schools. Enrollment during this time was roughly 50½ million students in grades Pre-K through 12th grade. The number of teachers employed was 3,827,000.[4] In addition to public schools, there are roughly 34,600 private schools and approximately 7,000 colleges and universities.[5] Had those early advocates imagined such numbers, would they also have imagined a different system of education? Can we, as heirs to their ideological legacy, imagine uprooting any of the assumptions that underpin today's educational enterprise? This is the question challenging those who are working to improve education. As stewards of the profession, Scholar-Practitioners are challenged to release their Aesthetic Imagination and see beyond what is to what might be.

Invitations to Imagine

In Chapter 1, we cited Anthony Bryk's disheartening assessment of school improvement initiatives. In the face of repeated failures, it is not unreasonable to ask, "What can individual Scholar-Practitioners accomplish? How can we effect change when so many others have failed?" We do not have an answer to these questions. We do, however, have a starting point for imagining how change might happen.

In his book, *The Tipping Point: How Little Things Can Make a Big Difference*, Malcolm Gladwell compares the spread of social change to epidemics:

> Epidemics are a function of the people who transmit infectious agents, the infectious agent itself, and the environment in which the infectious agent is operating. And when an epidemic tips, when it is jolted out of equilibrium, it tips because something has happened, some change has occurred in one …[of] three agents of change I call the Law of the Few, the Stickiness Factor, and the Power of Context.[6]

For our purposes, we focus on his Law of the Few, which holds that epidemics of ideas start with relatively few individuals who play one or more roles—Connectors, Mavens, and Salesmen [sic].

> Connectors know lots of people. They are the kinds of people who know everyone. All of us know someone like this. But I don't think that we spend a lot of time thinking about the importance of these kinds of people.[7]
>
> To be a Maven is to be a teacher. But it is even more emphatically, to be a student. Mavens are really information brokers, sharing and trading what they know…Mavens are data banks. They provide the message. Connectors are social glue; they spread it. But there is also a select group of people—Salesmen— with the skills to persuade us when we are unconvinced of what we are hearing, and they are as critical to the tipping of word-of-mouth epidemics as the other two groups.[8]

Imagine an "epidemic" spreading the concept of Scholar-Practitioner throughout 13,854 school districts. How many connectors, mavens, and salespersons would be needed to tip a district? How many districts would be needed to tip the society's conception of teachers with easy jobs who work only nine months a year? To those who say, "impossible," we respond, "who would have imagined that a small group of outraged teenagers could spawn an epidemic that forced Dick's Sporting Goods and other retailers to stop selling guns and other businesses to withdraw financial support from the National Rifle Association?" Perhaps the Parkland students' social epidemic will be extinguished by greater forces; perhaps not. Only time will tell, but these students remind us that change can come from unexpected places, from previously unheard voices, from moments that jar us from complacency to action.

In July 2018, more than 3,000 educators from around the country attended the biennial conference of the American Federation of Teachers (AFT). As reported in the *Pittsburgh Post-Gazette*, AFT President Randi Weingarten "spoke at length about the wave of teacher strikes for better wages and more investment in education in states including West Virginia, Colorado, Kentucky and Arizona." Weingarten reported that "more than 700,000 AFT members recommitted to the organization" as the Supreme Court released its ruling that public sector unions can no longer charge mandatory dues. Nationwide, the AFT has more than 1.7 million members and many of these members are taking a more active role in resisting changes that will undermine the quality of education.[9] Similarly, "The National Education Association (NEA), the nation's largest professional employee organization, is committed to advancing the cause of public education. NEA's 3 million members work at every level of education—from pre-school to university graduate programs. NEA has affiliate organizations in every state and in more than 14,000 communities across the United States."[10] In short, individual practitioners are not alone. As part of national, state, and local Communities of Practice, they might well precipitate an epidemic for re-imaging education.

> *Imagine that*: Among the millions of teachers, administrators, and paraprofessionals are Connectors, Mavens, and Salespersons who can tip an epidemic.

> *Imagine that:* Educators—serving as Connectors, Mavens and Salespersons—embrace and spread the Scholar-Practitioner stance and mindset.

> *Imagine that:* Scholar-Practitioners raise their voices and share their practical wisdom when school improvement initiatives are proposed.

> *Imagine that:* Communities of practice throughout the country construct narratives of education that advocate learning in support of each learner's life journey.

> *Imagine that:* New metaphors ignite passionate commitment to authentic, engaged learning at all levels of schooling.

Cynics might dismiss such imaginings as pie-in-the-sky rhetoric. Indeed, just as Bryk is now advocating for practitioner involvement in Networked Improvement Communities, his rhetoric harkens back to a long line of teacher-involvement and teacher-empowerment movements that have come to naught. Lest we sound naïve, let us share the wisdom our colleague Kathleen Ceroni came to when she studied the Pennsylvania Lead Teacher Initiative. According to Kathleen:

> The national political context spawning this specific state initiative was thick with the rhetoric of teacher empowerment, reflecting policymakers' reconceptualized belief that top-down reform management strategies failed because they didn't include the voices of teachers.[11]

By the end of her dissertation research, Kathleen had revealed a number of problematic aspects with the initiative, not the least of which was the realization that teacher "involvement" still masked a top-down agenda and "empowerment" was meant to serve an imposed agenda. Drawing from theories of literary criticism, feminist scholarship, and the power of writing to reveal one's own vulnerabilities to the rhetoric of empowerment, Kathleen wrote:

> By engaging in the hermeneutic text of talk, I unmasked myself and came to an understanding not only of how the dominant ideology functions to oppress my class and gender, but also of how I had acted in complicity with the very forces I had been struggling to combat. "Self-reflexivity," as Richardson (2003) points out, "brings to consciousness some of the complex political/ ideological agendas hidden in our writing" (520). For me, this coming to consciousness was painful and the wisdom, bitter.[12]

We resonate with Kathleen's notion of bitter wisdom, because we, too, have participated in programmatic reform efforts that were summarily dismissed when they did not meet the needs or interests of those with greater institutional power. Understandably, such experiences can lead to frustration, demoralization, and cynicism.

Yet, as professor Martha Nussbaum points out in her book, *The Monarchy of Fear*, each of us has a choice when contemplating difficulties and obstacles. We can choose fear and despair. Or we can choose hope. Nussbaum makes a distinction between "idle hope" and "practical hope." The former is impotent, leading to wishful thinking, vaguely hoping that someone, somewhere will make things better. The latter, however, is a hope

> ...that is firmly linked to, and that energizes a commitment to action. But while idle hope surely exists, hope can often be truly practical: the beautiful imaginings and fantasies involved in hoping can energize action toward the valuable goal. It's hard to

sustain commitment to a difficult struggle without such energizing thoughts and feelings. The difference between fearing and hoping is slender. It's like flipping a switch: now the glass looks half full. And these mental images, often at least, do important practical work, preparing me to take action toward the valuable goal and convincing me that it's within reach.[13]

Nussbaum exemplifies her meaning of hope by drawing on the examples of Martin Luther King, Jr. and Nelson Mandela. We might add to these iconic images of courageous hope, holocaust survivor Elie Weisel, educator Helen Keller, and her teacher Anne Sullivan. Fortunately, few of us endure the hardships that these larger-than-life figures overcame. Even so, thousands upon thousands of individuals work tirelessly, with courage and determination, to fulfill their life's purpose.

Parker Palmer, in *The Courage to Teach*, compares teachers like the canny outlaws described by Schwartz and Sharpe, to civil rights activist Rosa Parks. Because few advocates for the vocation of teaching are as eloquent as Palmer, we take the liberty of quoting him at length:

> These teachers remember the passions that led them to become academics, and they do not want to lose the primal energy of their vocation. They affirm their deep caring for the lives of students, and they do not want to disconnect from the young. They understand the identity and integrity that they have invested in teaching, and they want to reinvest, even if it pays no institutional interest or dividends.
>
> What drives the decision to live divided no more, with the risks it entails? How do people find the courage to bring inner conviction into harmony with outer act, knowing that when they do, the force of the institution may come down on their heads, risking the loss of image or status or security or money or power? The

difference between the person who goes to the back of the bus and one who decides to sit up front is probably lost in the mystery of the human heart. But in Rosa Parks and others like her, I see a clue to the answer: when you realize that you can no longer collaborate in something that violates your own integrity, your understanding of punishment is suddenly transformed...

The courage to live divided no more, and to face the punishment that may follow, comes from this simple insight: *no punishment anyone lays on you could possibly be worse than the punishment you lay on yourself by conspiring in your own diminishment.* With that insight comes the ability to open cell doors that were never locked in the first place and to walk into new possibilities that honor the claims of one's heart.[14] (Italics in original)

Let's pause for a moment to reflect on Palmer's contention that the cell doors were never locked in the first place. Certainly Rosa Parks, Martin Luther King, Jr., Nelson Mandela, and Elie Weisel were locked in the harshest of physical cells and the most brutal of social constrictions. They could not simply wish those away any more than teachers can simply wish away counterproductive mandates. Yet, here is the thing. Because they were able to imagine a better world, they never ceded their personal power to others. They held true to a vision and to their purpose of fighting for that vision. No one gave them that power; they owned it for themselves and because of that they prevailed.

Herein lie some lessons.

Imagine that: Scholar-Practitioners understand no one has to empower them; they have power that they can choose to exercise on behalf of the profession and those the profession is meant to serve.

Imagine that: Scholar-Practitioners push back against manipulative rhetoric of empowerment and call upon stakeholders at all levels to remove ill-conceived mandates, policies, and procedures that undermine the very purpose of education.

Imagine that: Scholar-Practitioners reject the notion that they "must be *given* voice" and claim their right to speak and be heard.

Imagine that: Scholar-Practitioners do not wait to be invited into conversations about school improvement, but initiate those conversations—among themselves AND with stakeholders at the micro-, mezzo-, and macro- levels.

Imagine that: Scholar-Practitioners resist the rules-based mentality of those who think (as one congressman said) that education is too important to be left to educators and assert the practical wisdom gained through commitment to inquiry.

Imagine that: Scholar-Practitioners resist all mandates that result in the unethical treatment of those entrusted to their care.

Perhaps these imaginings seem too daunting, too high flown. Let us imagine, therefore, a more humble endeavor. Each educator—regardless of role, setting or stage of career—embraces the stance of Scholar-Practitioner and commits to cultivating the six qualities we have outlined in this book. Sometimes changing one's own mindset is the most difficult challenge of all. Yet, if we are unable to change ourselves, we will never be able to fulfill the *telos* of the profession: to educate ourselves and those whose life journeys we are privileged to share. Imagine, then, a society that values and celebrates wisdom and assures the right of all citizens to gain the wisdom necessary to pursue their life's purpose.

NOTES

1 Nicholas Lemann, *The Big Test: The Secret History of the American Meritocracy* (New York: Farrar, Straus and Giroux, 1999), 21.

2 Lemann, 21-25.

3 Lemann, 25-26.

4 National Center for Education Statistics (NCES), Digest of Education Statistics, https://nces.ed.gov. Tables 214.10, 203.40, and 209.10 respectively. Retrieved from the website on July 28, 2018.

5 NCES Digest, Table 105.50. Retrieved from the website on July 28, 2018.

6 Malcolm Gladwell, *The Tipping Point: How Little Things Can Make a Big Difference* (New York: Little, Brown and Co., 2002), 15.

7 Gladwell, 24.

8 Gladwell, 38-39.

9 Elizabeth Behrman, "Our Voices Must Be Heard. More than 3,000 Educators Gather Here," *Pittsburgh Post-Gazette*, July 14, 2018, B1, B3.

10 National Education Association Website, https://www.nea.org, Retrieved August 13, 2018.

11 Kathleen M. Ceroni, "Coming to Know through the Text of Talk: From Interviews to Inner Views Storied to Interpretation" in *The Authority to Imagine: The Struggle toward Representation in Dissertation Writing*, eds. Noreen B. Garman and Maria Piantanida (Pittsburgh: Learning Moments Press, 2018), 159. See also, Ceroni, K.M. 1995, *Promises Made, Promises Broken: A Literary Criticism of the Pennsylvania Lead Teacher Experience*. UMI Pro Quest Digital Dissertations #AAT9529124.

12 Ceroni, 170.

13 Martha C. Nussbaum, *The Monarchy of Fear: A Philosopher Looks at Our Political Crisis* (New York: Simon & Schuster, 2018), 206-207.

14 Parker Palmer, *The Courage to Teach: Exploring the Inner Landscape of a Teacher's Life* (San Francisco: Jossey-Bass, 1998), 170-171.

Bibliography

Alda, Alan. *If I Understood You, Would I Have This Look on My Face?* New York: Random House, 2017.

Anders, George. *You Can Do Anything: The Surprising Power of a "Useless" Liberal Arts Education*. New York: Little, Brown and Company, 2017.

Association of American Educators. *Code of Ethics*. Retrieved from www.aaeteachers.org on October 13, 2017.

Bartholomae, David and Anthony Petrosky. "Introduction." *Ways of Reading: An Anthology for Writers*, 5th ed. 1-14. Boston: Bedford/St. Martin's, 1999.

Baxter Magolda, Marcia B. "Post-College Experience and Epistemology." *The Review of Higher Education*, 18, no. 1 (1994): 25-44.

Bednarzik, R.W. and Szalandki, J. , *An Examination of the Work History of Pittsburgh Steelworkers, Who Were Displaced and Received Publicly-Funded Retraining in the Early 1980s*. IZA DP No. 6429 March 2012. Retrieved from https://d-nb.info/1024171671/34 May 10, 2018.

Behrman, Elizabeth. "Our Voices Must Be Heard. More than 3,000 Educators Gather Here." *Pittsburgh Post-Gazette*, July 14, 2018, B1, B3.

Berliner, David C., Gene V. Glass and Associates. *50 Myths and Lies that Threaten America's Public Schools: The Real Crisis in Education*. New York: Teachers College Press, Columbia University, 2014.

Bochner, A. P. "It's about Time: Narrative and the Divided Self." *Qualitative Inquiry* 3, no 4 (1997): 418-438.

Boyer, Ernest L. *Scholarship Reconsidered: Priorities of the Professoriate*. New York: The Carnegie Foundation for the Advancement of Teaching, 1990.

Brill, Steven. *Tailspin: The People and Forces behind America's Fifty-Year Fall and Those Fighting to Reverse It*. New York: Alfred A. Knopf, 2018.

Britzman, Deborah P. *Practice Makes Practice*. Albany: State University of New York Press, 1991.

Bruner, Jerome. *Actual Minds, Possible Worlds*. Cambridge , MA: Harvard University Press, 1986.

Bryk, Anthony S. "2014 AERA Distinguished Lecture. Accelerating How We Learn to Improve." *Educational Researcher* 44, no. 9 (2015): 467-477.

Ceroni, Kathleen M. "Coming to Know through the Text of Talk: From Interviews to Inner Views Storied to Interpretation." In *The Authority to Imagine: The Struggle toward Representation in Dissertation Writing*, edited by Noreen B. Garman and Maria Piantanida, 159-172. Pittsburgh: Learning Moments Press, 2018.

Clandinin, D. Jean and F. Michael Connelly. Teachers' Professional Knowledge Landscapes: Teacher Stories—Stories of Teachers—School Stories—Stories of Schools, *Educational Researcher*, 25, no 3 (1996): 24-30.

Connelly, F. Michael and D. Jean Clandinin. Stories of Experience and Narrative Inquiry. *Educational Researcher*, 19 no. 5 (1990): 2.

Davis, Brent., Dennis Sumara and Rebecca Luce-Kapler. *Engaging Minds: Changing Teaching in Complex Times*. 2nd ed. New York: Routledge, 2008.

Dewey, John. *Experience and Education*. New York: Collier Books, 1938.

Edmundson, Mark. *Why Teach? In Defense of a Real Education*. New York: Bloomsbury, 2013.

Eisner, Elliot W. *The Art of Educational Evaluation: A Personal View*. Philadelphia: Falmer Press, 1985.

Eisner, Elliot W. *The Enlightened Eye: Qualitative Inquiry and the Enhancement of Educational Practice*. New York: Macmillan Publishing, 1991.

Fineberg, Walter and Jonas F. Soltis. *School and Society*. New York: Teachers College Press, 1998.

Flinders, David J. and Stephen J. Thornton. *The Curriculum Studies Reader,* 5th ed. New York: Routledge, 2017.

Flyvbjerg, Bent. *Making Social Science Matter: Why Social Inquiry Fails and How It Can Succeed Again*. Translated by Steven Sampson. New York: Cambridge University Press, 2001.

Freire, Paolo. *Pedagogy of the Oppressed*. 50th Anniversary Edition. Translated by Myra Bergman Ramos. New York: Bloomsbury Academic, 2018.

Frost, Robert. "The Road Not Taken." *The Bedford Introduction to Literature: Reading, Thinking, Writing* 5th ed. Michael Meyer. Boston, MA. Bedford/St. Martin's, 1999, 976.

Garman, Noreen B. "Imagining an Interpretive Dissertation: Voice, Text and Representation." In *The Authority to Imagine: The Struggle toward Representation in Dissertation Writing,* edited by Noreen B. Garman and Maria Piantanida, 29-45. Pittsburgh: Learning Moments Press, 2018.

Gawande, Atul. *Being Mortal: Medicine and What Matters in the End*. New York: Metropolitan Books, 2014.

Gladwell, Malcolm. *The Tipping Point: How Little Things Can Make a Big Difference*. New York: Little, Brown and Co., 2002.

Goodman, JoVictoria. "Confronting Authority and Self: Social Cartography and Curriculum Theorizing for Uncertain Times." In *The Authority to Imagine: The Struggle toward Representation in Dissertation Writing*, edited by Noreen B. Garman and Maria Piantanida, 85-102. Pittsburgh: Learning Moments Press, 2018.

Golde, Chris.M. "Preparing Stewards of the Discipline" In *Envisioning the Future of Doctoral Education: Preparing Stewards for the Discipline. Carnegie Essays on the Doctorate*, edited by Chris M. Golde, George E. Walker and Associates, 3-20. San Francisco: Jossey-Bass, 2006.

Gottschall, Jonathan. *The Storytelling Animal: How Stories Make Us Human.* Boston: Mariner Books, 2013.

Greene, Joshua. *Moral Tribes: Emotion, Reason and the Gap between Us and Them.* New York: Penguin Press, 2013.

Greene, Maxine. *Releasing the Imagination: Essays on Education.*The Arts, and Social Change. San Francisco: Jossey-Bass, 1995.

Harari, Yuval Noah. *Homo Deus: A Brief History of Tomorrow.* New York: HarperCollins, 2015.

Herman, Amy E. *Visual Intelligence: Sharpen Your Perception, Change Your Life.* New York: Houghton Mifflin Harcourt, 2016.

hooks, b. *Teaching to Transgress: Education as a Practice of Freedom.* New York: Routledge, 1994.

Hoerr, J.P. *And the Wolf Finally Came: The Decline of the American Steel Industry.* Pittsburgh: University of Pittsburgh Press, 1988.

Huebner, Dwayne. "Education and Spirituality." *Journal of Curriculum Theorizing* 11, no. 2 (1995): 13-34.

Ingersoll, Richard. interviewed by Owen Phillips for NPR, March 30, 2015, "Revolving Door of Teachers Costs Schools Billions Every Year."

Kelly, Marjorie. *Owning Our Future: The Emerging Ownership Revolution, Journeys to a Generative Economy.* San Francisco: Berrett-Koehler, 2012.

Kirsch, Gesa. E and Jacqueline J. Royster. "Feminist Rhetorical Practices: In Search of Excellence." *College Composition and Communication,* 61, no 4 (2010): 640-672.

Krakowski, Pamela. "A Search for Balance: Representing a Narrative Pedagogy." In *The Authority to Imagine: The Struggle toward Representation in Dissertation Writing,* edited by Noreen B. Garman and Maria Piantanida, 105-120. Pittsburgh: Learning Moments Press, 2018.

Krakowski, Pamela. *Balancing the Narrative and the Normative: Pedagogical Implications for Early Childhood Art Education.* Ed.D dissertation, University of Pittsburgh, 2004. UMI ProQuest Digital Dissertation #AAT3139692.

Labaree, David F. *Someone Has to Fail: The Zero-sum Game of Public Schooling.* Cambridge, MA: Harvard University Press, 2010.

Labaree, David F. "The Peculiar Problems of Preparing Educational Researchers." *Educational Researcher* 32, no 4 (2003): 13-22.

Lakoff. George and Mark Johnson. *Metaphors We Live By.* Chicago: The University of Chicago Press, 1980.

Lakoff, George and Mark Turner, *More than Cool Reason: A Field Guide to Poetic Metaphor.* Chicago: The University of Chicago Press, 1989.

Lemann, Nicholas. *The Big Test: The Secret History of the American Meritocracy.* New York: Farrar, Straus and Giroux, 1999.

Llewellyn, Marilyn. *Spirituality and Pedagogy: Being and Learning in Sacred Spaces.* Pittsburgh: Learning Moments Press, 2017.

Llewellyn, Marilyn. "Reclaiming a Spiritual Language and Embracing a Spirituality of Liberation." *Journal of Curriculum and Pedagogy* 2, no 2 (Winter 2005): 70-77.

Llewellyn, Marilyn, Patricia L. McMahon and Maria Piantanida. "Of Foreopters and Fractals: A Scholarship of Educational Praxis for the 21st Century." In *Spectrum.* 23-31. Pittsburgh: The Carlow University Press, 2010.

Logsdon, Marjorie Barrett. *A Pedagogy of Authority.* Pittsburgh: Learning Moments Press, 2017.

Lukianoff, Greg and Jonathan Haidt. *The Coddling of the American Mind: How Good Intentions and Bad Ideas are Setting up a Generation for Failure.* New York: Penguin Press, 2018.

McMahon, Patricia L. "From Angst to Story to Research Text: The Role of Arts-Based Educational Research in Teacher Inquiry." *Journal of Curriculum Theorizing* 16, no 1 (Spring 2000): 125-146.

McMahon, Patricia L. "Narrative Yearnings: Reflecting in Time through the Art of Fictive Story." In *The Authority to Imagine: The Struggle toward Representation in Dissertation Writing*, edited by Noreen B. Garman and Maria Piantanida, 239-258. Pittsburgh: Learning Moments Press, 2018.

Milne, Wendy A. *Reflective Artmaking: Implications for Art Education.* Ed.D. dissertation, University of Pittsburgh, 2000. UMI ProQuest Digital Dissertation, AAT9974457.

Milne, Wendy A. "Imagining Reflective Artmaking: Claiming Self as Artist-Teacher-Researcher." In *The Authority to Imagine: The Struggle toward Representation in Dissertation Writing*, edited by Noreen B. Garman and Maria Piantanida, 173-185. Pittsburgh: Learning Moments Press, 2018.

Nash, Robert J. *Liberating Scholarly Writing: The Power of Personal Narrative.* New York: Teachers College Press, 2004.

National Association of State Directors of Teacher Education and Certification. *Model Code of Ethics for Educators.* Retrieved from http://www.nasdtec.net on October 13, 2017.

National Center for Education Statistics (NCES), Digest of Education Statistics, https://nces.ed.gov.

National Education Association. *Code of Ethics.* Adopted by the NEA 1975 Representative Assembly. Retrieved from www.nea.org on October 13, 2017.

Nussbaum, Martha C. *The Monarchy of Fear: A Philosopher Looks at Our Political Crisis.* New York: Simon and Schuster, 2018.

Palmer, Parker J. *The Courage to Teach: Exploring the Inner Landscape of a Teacher's Life.* San Francisco: Jossey-Bass, 1998.

Pendlebury, Shirley. "Reason and Study in Wise Practice." In *Narrative in Teaching, Learning and Research.* Edited by Hunter McEwan and Kieran Egan. New York: Teachers College Press, 1995.

Perry, Jill Alexa, ed, *The EdD and the Scholarly Practitioner: The CPED Path.* Charlotte, NC: Information Age Publishing, 2016.

Perry, Jill Alexa and David Lee Carlson, eds. *In Their Own Words: A Journey to the Stewardship of the Practice in Education.* Charlotte, NC: Information Age Publishing, 2013.

Piantanida, Maria and Noreen B. Garman. *The Qualitative Dissertation: A Guide for Students and Faculty*, 2nd ed. Thousand Oaks, CA: Corwin, 2009.

Pinar, William F. *What is Curriculum Theory?*, 2nd ed. New York: Routledge, 2012.

Pinar, William F., William M. Reynolds, Patrick Slattery, and Peter M. Taubman. *Understanding Curriculum: An Introduction to the Study of Historical and Contemporary Curriculum Discourses,* 5th ed. New York: Peter Lang, 2008.

Pinker, Steven. *Enlightenment Now: The Case for Reason, Science, Humanism, and Progress.* New York: Penguin Random House, 2017.

Polanyi, Michael. *The Tacit Dimension.* Garden City, NY: Anchor Books, 1967.

Polkinghorne, Donald E. "Reporting Qualitative Research as Practice." In *Representation and the Text: Re-framing the Narrative Voice.* Edited by William G. Tierney and Yvonna S. Linconln, 3-21. Albany: State University of New York Press, 1997.

Richardson, Laurel. *Writing Strategies: Reaching Diverse Audiences.* Newbury Park: Sage, 1990.

Richardson, Laurel and Elizabeth Adams St. Pierre. "Writing a Method of Inquiry." In *Collecting and Interpreting Qualitative Materials.* 3rd ed. Edited by Norman K. Denzin and Yvonna S. Lincoln. 473-500. Thousand Oaks, CA: Sage, 2003.

Richardson, Virginia. "Stewards of a Field, Stewards of an Enterprise: The Doctorate in Education." In *Envisioning the Future of Doctoral Education: Preparing Stewards for the Discipline. Carnegie Essays on the Doctorate.* Edited by Chris M. Golde, George F. Walker and Associates, 251-267. San Francisco: Jossey-Bass, 2006.

Santoro, D.A. "Is It Burnout? Or Demoralization?" *Educational Leadership,* 75 (Online June 2018): 10-15.

Sawyer, R. Keith. *Structure and Improvisation in Creative Teaching.* Cambridge: Cambridge University Press, 2011.

Sawyer, R. Keith. *Social Emergence: Societies as Complex Systems.* Cambridge: Cambridge University Press, 2005.

Sawyer, R. Keith. *Creating Conversations: Improvisation in Everyday Discourse.* Cambridge: Cambridge University Press, 2001.

Schackner, Bill. "Disruptive in Classroom Or Free Speech Denied." *Pittsburgh Post-Gazette*, March 14, 2018, A1-A2. Matt McKinney. "IUP Student in Free Speech Dispute can Rejoin Class." *Pittsburgh Post-Gazette*, March 20, 2018, C1-C2.

Schon, Donald A. *The Reflective Practitioner: How Professionals Think in Action.* New York: Basic Books, 1983.

Schwandt, Thomas A. *The Sage Dictionary of Qualitative Inquiry*, 3rd ed. Los Angeles: SAGE, 2007.

Schwandt, Thomas A. "Responsiveness and Everyday Life." In *Responsive Evaluation, New Directions for Evaluation*, Edited by Jennifer G. Greene and Tincke A. Abma, 73-88. San Francisco: Jossey Bass, 2001.

Schwartz, Barry and Kenneth Sharpe. *Practical Wisdom: The Right Way to Do the Right Thing*. New York: Riverhead Books, 2010.

Shulman, Lee. "Making differences: A Table of Learning." *Change* 34, no. 6 (November/December 2002): 36-44.

Smith, Mark K. "Elliot W. Eisner. Connoisseurship, Criticism and The Art of Education," *The Encyclopedia of Informal Education*, 2005. Retrieved September 30, 2018 from www.infed.org/thinkers/eisner.htm.

Snow, C.P. *The Two Cultures*. New York: Cambridge University Press, 1998 (First published 1959).

Stabile, Micheline. *A Call to Conscience: Problematizing Educational Inclusion*. Ed.D. dissertation, University of Pittsburgh, 1999. UMI ProQuest Digital Dissertation #AAT9928088.

Stark, Joan S., Malcolm A. Lowther, and Bonnie M.K. Hagerty, *Responsive Professional Education: Balancing Outcomes and Opportunities*, ASHE-ERIC Higher Education Reports, Washington, D.C.: Association for the Study of Higher Education, 1986.

Sternberg, Robert J. and Joseph A. Horvath. "A Prototype View of Expert Teaching." Educational *Researcher 24,* no. 6 (1995): 9-17.

Sumara, Dennis. *Private Readings in Public: Schooling the Literary Imagination*. New York: Peter Lang, 1996.

Sutcher, Lelb, Linda Darling-Hammond and Desiree Carver-Thomas. *A Coming Crisis in Teaching? Teacher Supply, Demand, and Shortages in the U.S.* Paolo Alto, CA: Learning Policy Institute 2016. This report can be found on-line at https://learningpolicyinstitute.org/product/coming-crisis-teaching.

Sweet, Victoria. *Slow Medicine: The Way to Healing*. New York: Riverhead Books, 2017.

Tchudi, Stephen and Diana Mitchell. *Exploring and Teaching the English Language Arts*. 4th ed. New York: Longman, 1999.

St. Pierre, Elizabeth Adams. Working the Ruins: Qualitative Research in the Postmodern. Keynote Address Presented at QUIG, January 4, 2002.

Van Manen, Max. *Phenomenology of Practice: Meaning-giving Methods in Phenomenological Research and Writing*. Walnut Creek, CA: Left Coast Press, 2014.

Van Manen, Max. *Researching Lived Experience: Human Science for an Action Sensitive Pedagogy*. 2nd ed. London, Ontario, Canada: The Althouse Press, 1997.

Van Manen, Max. *The Tact of Teaching: The Meaning of Pedagogical Thoughtfulness*. Albany NY: SUNY Press, 1991.

Vance, J.D. *Hillbilly Elegy: A Memoir of a Family and Culture in Crisis.* New York: HarperCollins, 2016.

Westover, Tara. *Educated: A Memoir.* New York: Random House, 2018.

Name Index

Subject Index

Learning Moments Press is a small, independent publishing company dedicated to sharing the wisdom that comes from thoughtful reflection on experience. The Wisdom of Practice Series showcases the work of individuals who illuminate the complexities of practice as they strive to fulfill the purpose of their profession.

Cooligraphy artist Daniel Nie created the logo for Learning Moments Press by combining two symbol systems. Following the principles of ancient Asian symbolism, Daniel framed the logo with the initials of Learning Moments Press. Within this frame, he has replicated the Adinkra symbol for *Sankofa* as interpreted by graphic artists at the Documents and Designs Company. As explained by Wikipedia, Adinkra is a writing system of the Akan culture of West Africa. *Sankofa* symbolizes taking from the past what is good and bringing it into the present in order to make positive progress through the benevolent use of knowledge. Inherent in this philosophy is the belief that the past illuminates the present and that the search for knowledge is a life-long process.

CPSIA information can be obtained
at www.ICGtesting.com
Printed in the USA
BVHW050205120623
665793BV00014B/374